Twin Peaks and Philosophy

Popular Culture and Philosophy® Series Editor: George A. Reisch

For full details of all Popular Culture and Philosophy® books, visit www.opencourtbooks.com.

Popular Culture and Philosophy®

Twin Peaks and Philosophy

That's Damn Fine Philosophy!

EDITED BY

RICHARD GREENE AND
RACHEL ROBISON-GREENE

OPEN COURT
Chicago

Volume 119 in the series, Popular Culture and Philosophy®, edited by George A. Reisch

To find out more about Open Court books, visit our website at www.opencourtbooks.com.

Open Court Publishing Company is a division of Carus Publishing Company, dba Cricket Media.

Copyright © 2018 by Carus Publishing Company, dba Cricket Media

First printing 2018

Printed and bound in the United States of America.

Twin Peaks and Philosophy: That's Damn Fine Philiosophy!

ISBN: 978-0-8126-9981-4

Library of Congress Control Number: 2018938309

This book is also available as an e-book.

For the Charbs:
Christina, Joe, and Simon

Contents

Contents

Contents

Thanks

Working on this project has been a pleasure, in no small part because of the many fine folks who have assisted us along the way. In particular, a debt of gratitude is owed to David Ramsay Steele and George Reisch at Open Court, the contributors to this volume, and our respective academic departments at UMass Amherst and Weber State University. Finally, we'd like to thank those family members, students, friends, and colleagues with whom we've had fruitful and rewarding conversations on various aspects of all things *Twin Peaks* as it relates to philosophical themes.

Premonitions of a Log Lady

MARGARET LANTERMAN: Agent Cole, my log has something to tell you. Thoughts from now and ideas from then. Interpretations. Theories. Can you hear them?

AGENT COLE: WHAT'S THAT MARGARET?

MARGARET LANTERMAN: The Lodge . . . talpas . . . duality . . . woodsman . . . garmonbozia. Veiled in mystery. I can't . . .

AGENT COLE: WHAT'S THAT ABOUT KANT?! I THOUGHT HE WAS DEAD.

MARGARET LANTERMAN: Evil, Agent Cole. Beyond comprehension. My log has seen things. My log understands. My log has whispered to philosophers, poets, and prophets . . . faintly . . . they've understood only fragments . . .

AGENT COLE: WHISPERS? NO, NOT WHISPERS. YOUR LOG WILL HAVE TO SPEAK UP.

MARGARET LANTERMAN: My log is silent now. There is another way. You must commune with those to whom my log has whispered. Listen. Intuit.

AGENT COLE: HOW WILL I FIND THEM? HOW WILL I KNOW WHEN I HAVE?

MARGARET LANTERMAN: My log understands the challenge and my log provides. The revelations . . . the musings . . . perhaps only shadows of understanding cast on the wall of a cave . . . they have been recorded . . . compiled . . . find the compilation.

AGENT COLE: WHY DIDN'T YOUR LOG JUST GIVE THE MESSAGE TO ME DIRECTLY?

MARGARET LANTERMAN: It is not for us to question the ways of the log. It is a different kind of understanding that you seek . . . aesthetic . . . epistemic . . . moral . . . existential . . .

AGENT COLE: I'M GONNA LEVEL WITH YOU, MARGARET. I DON'T KNOW MUCH ABOUT TALKING LOGS, I'M AFRAID I WOULDN'T KNOW WHERE TO START.

MARGARET LANTERMAN: That's simple. Begin at the beginning. Waterfalls . . . trees of pine . . . apple pie . . .

AGENT COLE: DAMMIT, MARGARET, YOU MUST BE TALKING ABOUT TWIN PEAKS.

MARGARET LANTERMAN: Yes, Agent Cole. You must revisit Twin Peaks. All of it. Past. Present. Future. All at once. Go. Find. *Read.*

I

I am one hundred percent sure that we're not completely sure

1
Dream Investigations of Tree House Operations

JAMES ROCHA AND MONA ROCHA

Whatever else happened in *Twin Peaks*—and some strange stuff happened throughout the show, especially in *The Return*—at the end of the day, a young girl was murdered, wrapped in plastic, and left on the beach. While there's so much more going on in the show, *Twin Peaks* is ultimately about Agent Cooper attempting to find justice for Laura Palmer—and he'll do whatever it takes to work toward that goal.

Whatever it takes might begin with your standard, *Dragnet, Hill Street Blues,* or *Hunter* type methods (all shows that pre-date *Twin Peaks*). Then it will even extend to Albert Rosenfield's more *CSI, CSI: Miami, CSI: New York,* or *CSI: Cyber* type methodology (shows that first aired after *Twin Peaks*). Perhaps the existence of that many *CSI* shows suggests that we should be searching for much more scientific approaches to solving crime.

But Agent Cooper will not stop there when it comes to finding Laura's killer. We're talking about *whatever* it takes: Cooper works the case in his dreams, he travels through time (We're pretty sure), and he skips around through multiple dimensions (Maybe? Look, let's be honest: we didn't really understand everything going on in the show. Who is that new Laura at the end of *The Return*? Why are there so many dead people in the Lodge? But clearly, whatever Cooper's doing to find justice for Laura, he's committed to it). Cooper is looking for Laura's killer, *whatever it takes*, even if that means talking to giant tea kettles, or collecting clues from any and every available source: logs, signals seemingly from outer space, and messages from friendly giants. But not from owls—owls are not what they seem.

Agent Cooper provides the philosophically interesting point of view that fighting crime is multifaceted, complex, and not quite an activity where we can apply scientific rigor. In terms of the last point, investigators—whether they're police, FBI agents, private eyes, mystery writers, or fake psychics—use a variety of techniques that are openly not scientific. To dismiss those various techniques is to misunderstand what it takes to solve crimes in the real world. Crime investigation is simply not a science—it involves intuition, guesswork, and luck. That doesn't have to be a problem, unless we become confused about it. If we, as jurors in particular or citizens in general, act as if the conclusions of the police or prosecutors are as well established as the conclusions of physicists or geologists, then we have made a mistake that can permanently damage innocent people's lives. So, it's important that we get this right, and *Twin Peaks* can remind us of that.

Agent Cooper gives us a perspective that allows us to challenge the scientism of crime fighting. The fallacy of *scientism* applies when someone applies the scientific method to a situation where it is not fitting. For example, a certain scientific approach to sports, such as in sports analytics, is becoming the rage lately. And perhaps this approach can benefit the teams who use it in various ways: statistical analysis, enhanced training methods, and so forth will certainly be useful. Yet, we cannot reduce winning in sports to a scientific endeavor: the team that wins will be the one with the players who are the most talented, motivated, and effective. Much of what makes a team great (talent, motivation, efficiency) cannot be scientifically engineered or even measured in most cases. Scientific knowledge of sports cannot make a team win games, but it may help give them certain benefits.

The charge of scientism does not require a doubting position against science in general. As we saw with sports, sports analytics can help a team win, but they cannot create wins by themselves. Similarly, science has a clear and significant place in criminal investigations: DNA alone proves this point. However, scientism becomes a fallacy when the role of science is elevated to a point that goes beyond what science can accomplish. Albert is a key member of Cooper's team, but you still need Sheriff Harry S. Truman and, of course, Agent Cooper. DNA can prove someone was at a scene, but that alone doesn't always tell you whether they committed the crime—non-scientific investigation is almost always needed to accompany the scientific work.

Cooper's methods are openly intuitive, mystical, and even magical. While Cooper is a fun exaggeration of actual police work, the mixture of scientific methods with guts, instincts, and some creative license are probably more accurate depictions than the scientism that is typical of later shows like *CSI* and even *Law and Order*. Agent Cooper's methods are quirky and mysterious, but they also provide an important, philosophically interesting critique of how popular television misleads us about the soundness of crime solving methodologies.

Limiting the Sultan of Sentiment

When Special Agent Albert Rosenfield first enters the Laura Palmer investigation, he does so as an angry, cynical representation of the typical police or FBI investigator who cannot understand the seeming sloppiness of this Twin Peaks homicide investigation. Albert's first words to Cooper when he meets Sheriff Truman (having already insulted Lucy Moran) are, "What kind of two-bit operation are they running out of this tree house, Cooper?" Then when he sees the local pathologist report, Albert responds, "Welcome to amateur hour" ("Zen, or the Skill to Catch a Killer").

Albert originally represents the perspective of the standard cop show: a homicide investigation should be done methodologically, scientifically, and with the utmost seriousness. And, of course, homicide investigations are certainly serious. Yet, the seriousness of the matter should not be conflated with the ability to approach it scientifically. As an analogy, running the government is a serious matter, but if we could scientifically determine the best way to run the government, we would surely have better governments by now. Murder, unfortunately, is just as messy. We have a plethora of suspects (Leo Johnson, Bobby Briggs, Dr. Lawrence Jacoby, James Hurley, just about any Renault brother, and so on), and we cannot even eliminate the unknown: such as a serial killer coming through town or an evil spirit inhabiting the body of one of Laura's loved ones. Murder investigations have to be open to the possibility that there is no clear path from the victim to the killer, and that there are always tons of people who could have had the opportunity and means to commit the murder. And it's okay to explore and scrutinize, as opposed to relying on just one method to arrive at a solution. As Deputy Hawk warns us, "You're on the path. You don't need to know where it leads. Just follow" ("Arbitrary Law"). Science alone cannot divine who's the killer in most cases because divining is not what science does.

Even when the police and prosecutors believe they have the right person based on seemingly scientific evidence, the situation is much more complicated. Albert is brought in as a forensic expert. He can test things like fibers, hairs, tire tracks, shoe prints, or DNA. In fact, Albert is dying to test just such things because he feels like the more time he has with the body, the more he can *scientifically* determine who the killer is. That is why when Dr. Will Hayward suggests that he has no compassion, since Albert does not want to release Laura's body to her family, Albert responds:

> I've got compassion running out of my nose, pal. I'm the Sultan of Sentiment. Dr. Hayward, I have traveled hundreds of miles and apparently several centuries to this forgotten sinkhole in order to perform a series of tests. Now, I do not ask you to understand these tests—I'm not a cruel man. I just ask you to get the hell out of my way so that I can finish my work. ("Rest in Pain")

Albert is arguing that he is being compassionate and sentimental—in fact he's the Sultan of Sentiment—through his scientific work because that is the best way, in his view, to bring justice to Laura Palmer. Albert's seeming and casual cruelty is his way of showing that he is dedicated to finding justice for Laura, which he believes he can scientifically discover.

But how much of that kind of testing is actually good science? Would more time with the body ensure Albert could find the killer as it would in an episode of *Bones*? The jury is still out on how well most forensic tests work. The 2016 President's Council of Advisors on Science and Technology (PCAST) provides an even clearer statement of the size of the problem of scientism in criminal investigation techniques. PCAST is an advisory group, appointed by the President of the United States (for this study, Barack Obama), made up of the nation's top scientists and engineers. PCAST was tasked with studying the validity of using forensic evidence in the courts, especially since a previous 2009 report from the National Research Council was very critical. PCAST's conclusions questioned the validity of a wide range of forensic techniques, including matching bite-marks, latent fingerprints, guns, and footwear. In each of those cases, they found that the ability to match the evidence found at the scene with the alleged culprit did not meet rigorous scientific standards ("Report to the President," pp. 7–14). Even with DNA, matches are sufficiently reliable to meet scientific standards only when the DNA at the scene came from one person or at most two people. When the recovered DNA included complex mixtures of three or more individuals, then the ability to match suspects is sufficiently reduced so as to not meet rigorous scientific standards.

Even though we have grown, throughout numerous television shows such as *Castle* or *Rizzoli and Isles*, to appreciate the seemingly scientific approaches of characters like Special Agent Albert Rosenfield, Dr. Lanie Parish, or Dr. Maura Isles, this work is not nearly as "scientific" as we have been led to believe. Reality is much more complex, and, in real life, the authorities cannot simply match a bite-mark to a set of teeth, a print to a finger, a gun to a bullet, or a shoe to a footprint.

Albert, though, is a much more complex person than he at first seems, as he explains that he is more than just a man of forensic science, but also a man of love: "I choose to live my life in the company of Gandhi and King. My concerns are global. I reject absolutely revenge, aggression, and retaliation. The foundation of such a method is love. I love you, Sheriff Truman" ("The Man Behind the Glass"). And it is in fact Albert who eventually tells Cooper, "Go on whatever vision quest you require" ("Arbitrary Law"). Even Albert recognizes that searching for truth is complex and cannot simply be done in the laboratory alone. But what other methods are there? Let's consider that issue over a slice of cherry pie, shall we?

Not Just a Bookhouse Boy

Sheriff Truman represents old-school police techniques, similar to *Eureka*'s Jack Carter, *Longmire*'s Walt Longmire, or *The Andy Griffith Show*'s Andy Taylor. While *Twin Peaks* has available experts (definitely more than Mayberry, though much less than Eureka), such as Dr. Will Hayward and, to a lesser extent, Dr. Lawrence Jacoby, Sheriff Truman tends to rely much more on standard investigatory techniques and on his deputies: Andy Brennan (his own Barney Fife) and Tommy "Hawk" Hill (a precursor to *Longmire*'s Henry Standing Bear).

In this respect, Harry Truman presents us with the image of a solid, but less fully funded, police officer. Harry Truman relies on intelligence, instincts, and, perhaps most important of all, on team work. And donuts, don't forget the donuts. That's why it is so important that Truman has additional team members available to him, such as the Bookhouse Boys. The Bookhouse Boys extend Truman's team (deputies Andy and Hawk are also members) to include Big Ed Hurley and others; this extensive network also allows him to investigate unofficially. Yet, while the Bookhouse Boys' investigations may include slightly illicit methods, they are largely there to assist Harry. Harry serves as a contrast to Albert precisely because he shows, through his official and unofficial teams, that good police work can be done through a team of hard working, inquisitive, and critically thinking friends.

We the audience are much more on Harry's side than on Albert's. Even though Harry is neither as scientific as Albert nor as mystical as Cooper, Harry shows his willingness, throughout almost all of the investigation, to follow Cooper's lead with no cost to his ego. Harry is flexible in his investigative approaches and he is open to cooperation. The investigation starts with Cooper letting Harry know that he expects to be in charge: "When the bureau get called in, the bureau is in charge. Now, you're gonna be working for me" ("Pilot"). Harry is meant to assist, which helps the two of them to develop into a deeply collaborative investigation. This partnership leads Harry to joke about it:

> TRUMAN: You know, I think I'd better start studying medicine.
>
> COOPER: And why is that?
>
> TRUMAN: Because I'm beginning to feel a bit like Dr. Watson ("Traces to Nowhere").

With Harry playing Watson to Coop's Sherlock, the two work together to find the truth. As viewers, we come to appreciate the unique blend of their styles. And we value the goodness and justice-oriented foundation of this sleepy little town and its dedicated police force. So when Harry punches Albert, we are quite happy he does so: by that point, Albert was constantly rude to Harry and the rest of the Twin Peaks group. Harry represents a perspective that the audience can truly understand and appreciate, but in the end, it is Cooper, and not Harry, who truly gets results and catches Laura's killer.

Unleashing the Dream Chaser

Agent Dale Cooper is like no other investigator on television. Coop's thoroughly good, but he also spends some time on the dark side. Cooper loves his coffee, pie, and donuts, but he is also a damn good arm wrestler. He is brilliant, but he is also Dougie.

Coop's own approach to investigating crime is much more all-inclusive. In the appropriately-named episode, "Zen, or the Skill to Catch a Killer," we see Cooper employing a more creative skill set to narrow down his rather large, initial set of suspects in Laura Palmer's murder. In particular, Cooper will throw rocks while the names of suspects are read out loud, with the hope that the rocks will guide him to the true suspect.

Cooper's method derives from a dream he had that simultaneously provided him with a deep desire to help the Tibetan people and yielded novel ideas for investigating crimes. Cooper explains that the dream gave him a method that was "a deductive technique involving mind-body co-operating, operating hand-in-hand with the deepest level of intuition" ("Zen, or the Skill to Catch a Killer"). This very phrasing suggests a critique of forensic methods popularized on other television shows.

On the one hand, Cooper refers to the method as a "deductive technique." Yet, if it's deductive, and not merely inductive, then it's a method that provides a result that cannot err. Deduction refers to the ability to draw a conclusion that must be true if the inputs are themselves true. A deductively sound argument, for example, is one where the logic is valid, which means that they guarantee the truth of the conclusion if the premises are true, and the premises are true. Thus, in a sound deductive argument, the conclusion must be true. Induction, on the other hand, refers to the ability to draw probable conclusions from true premises. An inductively cogent argument is one where the premises are true and the logic is strong in the sense that the truth of the premises makes the conclusion probable.

In this case, the very genesis of the method (it came to him in a dream that just happens to be about a seemingly unrelated matter—though we can guess that it has something to do with the methodology used to select the next Dalai Lama), the secondary operator for the method (the deepest level of intuition), and the method itself (throwing rocks) all suggest a technique that is quite far from deductive. At best, this technique merely connects to some sub-conscious knowledge that Cooper may have inferred from his early investigation results. Perhaps Cooper's technique can consciously clue him in to suspicions that he has sub-consciously gathered, and those suspicions can be openly and physically manifested as his body throws the rocks best when he sub-consciously feels that the person is most likely guilty. But there is no non-mystical reason to think this technique is connecting him to the real killer, and so it certainly is not deduction.

Of course, the results of Cooper's methods do not yield the killer. The stone hit the bottle, but did not break it for Dr. Lawrence Jacoby and it was Leo Johnson's name that broke the bottle. Perhaps the point of the rock throwing was merely to reveal who Laura Palmer was with the night she died (Leo Johnson was there that night). Yet, if that was the only result, the method is surely misleading since it had appeared that the test was meant to pick out Laura Palmer's killer, who wasn't even listed on Coop's board. On the other hand, while forensic science provides information that could be useful, it also does not always tell us who the killer is with great precision.

Cooper's innovative investigatory techniques shed light on the limitations of treating police investigations as if they were entirely scientific. At the same time, Cooper does not represent a critique of criminal investigation in general, but more of an acceptance that real police work is much more a mixture of induction, creativity, intuition, and luck than just simple deduction. To further underscore this point, in "Arbitrary Law," Cooper lists out his investigatory methods:

> As a member of the Bureau, I spend most of my time seeking simple answers to difficult questions. In the pursuit of Laura's killer, I have employed bureau guidelines, deductive technique, Tibetan method, instinct, and luck. But now I find myself in need of something new. Which, for a lack of a better word, we shall call, "magic."

And, of course, in the end, it's magic that pulls through and reveals Laura's killer. Of course, when Cooper tells Harry that Laura revealed the killer to him in a dream, Harry tells him, "We're gonna need a lot stronger evidence than this" ("Arbitrary Law").

Instinct Is Back in Style

In spite of this use of countless cups of black-as-midnight-on-a-moonless-night coffee, magic, luck, and instinct as investigative techniques, almost all of the investigators on the show appear to be good people, fully dedicated to their mission. They're all different, but they are united by a determination to find justice. Their differences yield a powerful mixture as each one's unique approach to solving crimes contributes something to their joint quest for justice. Sheriff Harry Truman is a good cop, and not at all a scientist. His humbleness, commitment to teamwork, and forthright manner give Coop the confidence to explore mystical investigative techniques. Albert Rosenfield relies quite heavily on science, but is a much more complex character: sarcastic and irritating, but also peaceful and loving. And it is that foundation of love and peace that makes up Albert's integrity and which allows Albert to respect Coop's methods, and thus realize that forensics can co-exist with vision quests. As he tells Cooper, "Go on whatever vision quest you require. Stand on the rim of a volcano, stand alone and do your dance. Just find this beast before he takes another bite" ("Arbitrary Law"). Agent Cooper, our main protagonist and hero, is a good guy who makes a point to appreciate and employ all kinds of investigatory efforts.

In the end, it is these different personalities, and Coop's openness to a variety of methods that include scientific approaches, instinctual approaches, and even magical approaches, that yield results. The point here is not to see *Twin Peaks* as a critique of investigatory procedures in general, but as a critique of the fallacy of scientism, as portrayed in the ways in which TV shows, especially now, depict police procedures as overly scientific.

Agent Cooper represents a good investigator, even though he is not thoroughly grounded in seemingly scientific procedures. In truth, many of those forensic methods are not as certain as they seem to be on a show like *Criminal Minds*. Instead, reports like PCAST show that investigations are much messier and more complex, and certainly cannot produce deductive arguments that show someone to be certainly the killer because of their fingerprints or shoeprints.

This result does not mean that the police should chase down killers by throwing rocks. Though maybe we, as citizens and jurors, should remember that the investigation of murders and other crimes involves a bit more instinct and induction than we realize.

And maybe even a bit of magic.

2
Know Thyself, Agent Cooper!

FELIPE NOGUEIRA DE CARVALHO

Self-knowledge, in one form or another, is highly valued in our society today. Just take a look at the increasing number of self-help books and alternative therapies designed to "get us in touch with our inner selves," and the large number of people who see a therapist on a regular basis.

A survey from 2004 sponsored by *Psychology Today* magazine found that over fifty-nine million Americans had benefited from psychotherapy since 2002, which is of course a form of self-knowledge, since it promises to make us more aware of our feelings, desires, and needs.

But self-knowledge is not only present in therapy sessions and self-help books. It is also one of the central pillars of Ancient Greek philosophy, as we can see in Socrates's famous saying that "An unexamined life is not worth living," and in the carving at the entrance of the Oracle of Delphi which reads "Know thyself." Self-knowledge also figures prominently in various eastern religious and philosophical systems, such as Hindu Vedanta and Tibetan Buddhism (of which Agent Cooper confesses to being an avid admirer). In these doctrines, the highest ideal in life is to come to know our true Self, which they say is different from the person of flesh and blood we normally take ourselves to be.

But I wouldn't be writing this chapter if self-knowledge did not figure in *Twin Peaks* as well. Most obviously, we can see it in Laura Palmer's therapy sessions with Dr. Jacoby and in her secret diary, which are both methods of self-knowledge. But there's another aspect of self-knowledge present in the show that is not so obvious, and that we might miss altogether if we do not look at it with the right mindset.

All *Twin Peaks* fans remember very well the final episode of Season Two, when Cooper enters the mysterious place called "The Black Lodge." What comes next is one of the finest examples of pure Lynch-Frost weirdness: dancing dwarfs, supernatural entities, backward voices, cryptic dialogues, and—although this might seem surprising at first—Dale Cooper's personal journey of self-knowledge.

The path to self-knowledge is not without its perils. People who undergo years of therapy know very well how hard it can be to come to grips with our fears and unbury our hidden traumas. It takes a lot of courage to dig deep within ourselves and undo our psychological defense mechanisms, a process that often involves lots of crying and sleepless nights (and a tremendous loss of money to the therapist).

The Greek philosopher Socrates was sentenced to death for "corrupting the Athenian youth," which is a fancy way of saying he was telling people on the streets to examine their own lives and the ideals they live by. And both Tibetan Buddhism and Vedanta highlight the importance of focusing the mind through years of disciplined meditation, precisely so we don't get lost in the process of knowing our true Self. If we identify ourselves with our own thoughts, sensations, and emotions, we become attached to them and suffer. So, although self-knowledge is highly valued and sought for, the road itself can be a dangerous one, and the seeker of knowledge must be prepared for what will come.

Agent Dale Cooper can't say he hasn't been warned. Before he went into the Black Lodge, Deputy Hawk told him that "if you confront the Black Lodge with imperfect courage, it will utterly annihilate your soul." Well, apparently, he must have gone in with imperfect courage, for we all know what happens at the famous ending of Season Two more than a quarter-century ago (How's Annie, by the way?).

To be fair to Cooper, he didn't go to the Black Lodge seeking self-knowledge. In fact, I'm pretty sure he had no clue he would have that coming. All he wanted was catch his archenemy and former partner Windom Earle, and while at it rescue his sweetheart Annie Blackburn from Earle's hands. And if he also managed to stop killer BOB along the way, well, all the better. But self-knowledge? Hey, I'm in the middle of an investigation here, let's talk about this when I'm done, okay?

Fair enough. So, the Black Lodge isn't necessarily the place you would go to if you were looking for some self-knowledge. Nevertheless, this is what it seems to deliver to the brave soul who decides to enter it. Deputy Hawk speaks of it as a place "every soul must pass on its way to perfection," and in both Tibetan Buddhism and Vedanta this means taming the mind, overcoming your fears and attachments, and ultimately coming to know your true Self. Once you're in there, Deputy Hawk continues, you will be faced with your own shadow, which in Jungian psychoanalysis stands for everything in your subconscious that you wish to hide away—your fears, traumas, neuroses, obsessions, unresolved issues from the past, and so on.

This shadow can take the form of many strange things—including, in Cooper's case, a perfect copy of himself with white eyes and an evil grin—and if you cannot keep it together, you will let your fear get the better of you. And instead of your shadow becoming integrated into your personality, as it should, it will get a life of its own, with terrible consequences. That whole final scene in the Black Lodge can be seen as a journey in self-knowledge, with Agent Cooper facing his shadow and ultimately giving in to fear.

Knowing Yourself or Knowing Your Self?

But what's self-knowledge anyway? Everybody talks of getting in touch with our inner selves, of examining ourselves, and so on. But when we come to think of it, knowing ourselves can be a pretty tricky business. On the one hand, it seems that our selves are the things we're most intimately connected to. We have a direct, special rapport with our inner life that's very different from the kind of relation we have with other people's thoughts and feelings. I can tell right away if I am hungry or angry, but in order to know if you're hungry or angry I must rely on your behavior: are you asking for a sandwich or screaming in fury? And even then, I could be wrong: perhaps you are just an actor pretending to be angry, or requesting a sandwich for someone else. But if I feel hungry or angry, I cannot be wrong about being hungry or angry.

But on the other hand, what is this self that we supposedly know when we look at what's going on inside our heads? Is knowing ourselves the same as knowing our thoughts? If it is, are we nothing more than the sum of our thoughts? If we cease to have thoughts—for example, if we slip into a coma—do we also cease to be ourselves? This puzzle was discussed by the great Scottish philosopher David Hume, who said that "for my part, when I enter most intimately into what I call myself, I always stumble on some particular perception or other, of heat or cold, light or shade, love or hatred, pain or pleasure. I never catch myself at any time without a perception, and never can observe anything but the perception" (*Treatise of Human Nature*, "Of Personal Identity").

In other words, I can know upon reflection whether I'm hungry or whether I'm thinking about the chapter in *Twin Peaks and Philosophy* that I'm supposed to write, but in these cases what I come to know is what I'm feeling or thinking. In other words, I don't come across my *self*—and the last time I checked, the carving at the entrance of the Oracle of Delphi read "Know thyself," not "Know thy thoughts." But how can I know my self if I don't even know what this 'self' might be? What should I look for?

Well, here we can perhaps make a distinction between 'knowing myself' and 'knowing my *Self* with a capital 'S.' The former just means knowing my thoughts, feelings, desires, motivations, and so on. This is the kind of self-knowledge most people are after when they buy self-help books or seek a therapist. Does my job really makes me happy or am I doing it just to for the money and the social status? Do I really love my partner of did I marry her or him just to please my family? Do I really need this new sports car or am I going through a midlife crisis?

We ask ourselves these kinds of questions all the time, and what we want to know, really, is whether we're happy, that's to say, whether our life choices are delivering us a rich, meaningful existence or not. Very few people, except perhaps philosophers, would care if there is really a *self* or not behind these feelings, and what this self might be. "To know myself" in this case just means "to know my feelings, desires, and motivations," not knowing my *Self* with a capital 'S' (whatever that may be). Sorry, Hume, but it looks as if your book is not going to be very popular among this crowd!

When Laura Palmer sought Dr. Jacoby for therapy sessions, this is exactly the kind of self-knowledge she was after. As we can gather from the tapes she used to record him, she often talked about the men in her life, coming to various conclusions about what she really felt for each one of them. This is self-knowledge in the sense of "knowing yourself." It is also, however, a painful example of how difficult self-knowledge might be. Although Laura was going to therapy—and so, presumably, after some sort of self-knowledge—she had so many psychological defense mechanisms that made it hard for her therapist to get to the bottom of her issues.

"Laura had secrets," Dr. Jacoby tells us, "and around those secrets she built a fortress that, well, in my six months with her, I was not able to penetrate." So, on the one hand Laura wanted to get help, but on the other hand, her dark side was so strong that it kept away anyone who tried to help her. This duality is often seen in people seeking self-knowledge: I have a friend who's always saying she wants a happy and meaningful relationship, but in practice she only dates chauvinistic men. My friend, like so many others, is engaging in unconscious self-sabotaging behavior and thus preventing herself from achieving true happiness.

A Scottish Philosopher and a Hindu Swami Walk into a Bar . . .

But besides knowing ourselves, we might also want to know our *Selves,* that is, to do exactly what Hume said he could not do: go past our thoughts, feelings and emotions and experience our true Self, which, at least according to Vedanta and Buddhism, exists beyond all thoughts. If David Hume and a Hindu Swami walked into a bar and Hume started talking about how he couldn't seem to find his Self and all that, I am sure the Swami would just shake his head in disapproval and say: "Hume, my friend, you're doing it wrong. Do not become attached to your perceptions but move beyond them."

The Swami would naturally disagree with Hume and claim that there is a Self—an immutable, eternal, boundless Self, which Vedanta calls Brahman, and Tibetan Buddhism calls Mind. And, further on, that we can know this Self through years of disciplined meditation, whereby we become able to catch a glimpse of ourselves without a perception, contrary to what Hume had supposed. This is exactly the kind of Self-knowledge the Black Lodge is able to deliver, as long we are able to walk in with perfect courage.

Think of the true Self like an ocean: an infinite, timeless ocean. From this ocean there are sometimes waves that come out, briefly exist for a short period of time, and dissolve back in the ocean. The ocean is the Self, and the waves are thoughts and feelings. The reason Hume could not "catch a glimpse of himself without a perception" is that he was looking at the waves, not at the ocean; a classic case of not seeing the forest for the trees. The waves are of course part of the ocean, but it would be wrong to say that the ocean is nothing but the waves. Whenever we are able to experience a quiet space between two thoughts, no matter how short, that is the ocean we are observing. And what these spiritual traditions maintain is that through meditation the spaces between waves gradually start to grow, and we start to focus less and less upon the waves and more upon the ocean, and thus realize our true Self.

So according to Hindu Vedanta and Tibetan Buddhism, we are not what we think we are. We take ourselves to be this person of flesh and blood who thinks, feels, who has needs, desires and troubles, but this is nothing but our *ego*, or lower self, which is an illusion. Identifying ourselves with our egos makes us think we are separate from the rest of the universe, when in reality we are infinite, timeless, and at one with everything else that exists. And it generates the kind of attachment that leads to fear and aversion, as Cooper's experience in the Black Lodge can attest.

But although this is a different kind of self-knowledge from that found in psychotherapy and self-help books, these two kinds of self-knowledge are surprisingly related. Both Vedanta and Tibetan Buddhism emphasize that if we are to go beyond our thoughts and know our true Self, we first need to abandon our fears and attachments, and cease to identify ourselves with our thoughts and emotions. And of course, if we are going to abandon our fears, we first need to know what these are! Why is Laura Palmer screaming at me with white eyes? Why is there a perfect copy of myself with an evil grin?

These are the kind of questions Cooper might have asked at the Black Lodge. And that's where the common, psychological type of self-knowledge can be most useful. "Allow all your monsters to come out and haunt your mind," the Swami might say, "but do not attribute reality to them. They are illusory and cannot harm your true Self." If only Agent Cooper had a Hindu Swami by his side when he entered the Black Lodge . . .

Cooper's Book of the Dead

Many *Twin Peaks* fans look at the Black Lodge mainly as the home of the strange entities that appear in the show: killer BOB, Mike the one-armed man, the dancing dwarf and the helpful giant. Sheriff Truman refers to it as "something very strange in these woods," which the Bookhouse Boys have been fighting against for generations. It is also the place with the red drapes and chevron floor that became a well-known symbol of the strange atmosphere surrounding

Twin Peaks, and which Agent Cooper often visited in his dreams.

But it's also much more than that. Windom Earle speaks highly of the Black Lodge as a place of great power, a power that can be harnessed and explored for one's own purposes. And I like to think of it as a journey in self-knowledge, in the deep spiritual sense of knowing your *Self*, but that will present you with your worst fears and strongest attachments in order to test your will (so it will also make you know *yourself*). If you, like Deputy Hawk says, go in with "perfect courage," you will withstand its turbulent trials and come out knowing your true Self. This is the great power Windom Earle was talking about: none other than the power to become one with the universe! If, on the contrary, you surrender to your fears, they will overcome you and your shadow will take on a life of its own, which stands for everything you fear and wish to keep away. This is exactly what happened to Cooper at the Black Lodge.

Windom Earle talks of evil sorcerers, or "dugpas," as creatures who pursue evil for the sake of evil, and who gained access to the Black Lodge in order to use its power for evil purposes. This makes sense. If the Black Lodge can make you know your true Self, it can unleash the full power of your mind hidden within you, which, according to Buddhism and Vendata, is infinite. In the ancient Vedanta texts known as the Upanishads, we see Prajâpati, the first-born Lord of the Universe, saying that "whoever realizes the Self obtains whatever he wishes, his desires are fulfilled, all powers come to him, and he becomes master of all worlds and of all the realms that exist on this earth as well as in the heavens."

A place of great power indeed! Windom Earle was no fool, and it's no wonder he lost his mind trying to discover the secrets of the Black Lodge. But his ultimate fate there—being forced to surrender his soul to BOB—suggests that this is a place that will not tolerate selfish motives. The final aim of the Black Lodge experience seems to be overcoming and integrating our shadow, and we can't do this on the basis of selfish motives alone.

This reminds me of another story from the Upanishads. In this story, Virochana, the leader of the demons, and Indra, the leader of the gods, both seek Prajâpati in order to gain the power of self-knowledge. Virochana, however, had materialistic and selfish reasons in mind, and so misunderstood the Master's teachings and did not attain self-knowledge. Indra, however, was pure at heart, which led him to be the Master's most cherished pupil, acquiring knowledge of the Self and becoming master of all worlds.

Agent Cooper did have the humility and purity of heart to acquire self-knowledge, but made a fatal error: he overestimated his control over his own fears, and when they all got loose and came after him he couldn't hold it together, and failed to integrate his shadow into his personality. As a result, he was split in two, the good Dale being trapped in the Black Lodge for twenty-five years, and his shadow-self wreaking havoc in the real world.

The Black Lodge scene from the episode "Beyond Life and Death" is terrifying even to us who are viewing it from outside, imagine what it would be like to actually be there and face your fears in the form of creepy white-eyed people speaking backwards! But things don't start out so badly. After Cooper sits in the Black Lodge's waiting room and hears "Under the Sycamore Trees" sung beautifully by Jimmy Scott, we hear the dwarf announcing: "Some of your friends are here."

First, we see the nice old waiter from the Great Northern, who appeared in Cooper's room while he was lying bleeding on the floor, and the giant who gave him so many important clues during his investigations. "One and the same," they tell him. Even the deceased Laura Palmer seems to be quite friendly at this point. She winks at Agent Cooper, and tells him she would see him again in twenty-five years (which of course she did). "This is going to be a stroll in the park," he must have thought.

But things take a rough turn for poor Cooper. As he goes back and forth between the identical looking rooms in the Black Lodge, already a bit disoriented, he meets Laura

Palmer again, and this time there seems to be something odd about her; perhaps it's the white eyes? Or the fact that she runs disconcertingly towards him screaming her lungs out? It is at this point that Cooper starts to freak out, running away from her as fast as he can. But where is he going to run to, when all the rooms look the same? You make a turn, and Jesus Christ, there is screaming Laura again!

We can tell right away that Cooper is disoriented and terrified. He starts bleeding from his stomach as if he'd been shot, just like the time when he tried to protect his lover Caroline and both ended up being shot. And speaking of Caroline, there she is in the next room, lying dead next to Cooper's body, reminding him of his past trauma and failure that got his lover killed. But wait a minute . . . is it Caroline or Annie Blackburn? The vision flickers between the two women, as if the fear he felt with Caroline is now coming back in the form of Annie Blackburn. It's the same pattern being repeated all over again.

This scene has many curious parallels with the *Tibetan Book of the Dead*, a sacred Buddhist text that was written as a sort of "map" of the afterlife, designed to guide the deceased after death of the physical body. The book tells us that in the afterlife we will meet many entities, some of them peaceful and kind (like the giant and the old waiter), and others wrathful and hideous looking, wearing human skulls around their necks and blood dripping from their mouths (or, in Cooper's case, screaming, white-eyed Laura Palmer).

We must, however, never be afraid. For these entities are merely projections of our own mind, and do not have any independent reality. They are aspects and archetypes of the mind that represents our fears and our shadow, and therefore can cause us no real harm. The instructions of the Book of the Dead are clear: do not be afraid, and do not flee, for this might cause you to lose yourself in the afterlife and only drift further down this path, meeting more and more wrathful entities until you can no longer stand the torment and will be reborn in another body (rebirth is an integral part of the Buddhist belief system). The point of this journey, however, is to escape the endless wheel of birth and rebirth called *Samsara,* and realize that you are pure, timeless, infinite Mind that cannot be harmed in any way. This is, in other words, a journey in self-knowledge (in the deep sense of knowing your *Self*), in much the same way as Cooper's experience in the Black Lodge.

Facing the so-called wrathful entities with imperfect courage, Cooper becomes terrified and tries to flee. But just as the *Book of the Dead* has warned, at this point he completely loses his mind. He starts to bleed, to run disoriented towards nowhere until he sees his own shadow-self running after him. Had he faced his shadow instead of running away from it, perhaps he would have a better chance at the Black Lodge, and we wouldn't have evil Dale's killing spree in season three of the show.

If we can imagine Cooper being advised by the *Tibetan Book of the Dead* in the Black Lodge, it would be more or less like this: "Know thyself, Agent Cooper! Realize that screaming Laura is nothing more than the sum of your fears concerning this case and all the bizarre events you experienced since the beginning of this investigation. During this whole time, you never allowed yourself to feel fear, but it was always there, hidden inside you. Accept it. Realize that your vision of Caroline and Annie represents your pain from Caroline's death, and your current fear of allowing your loved one to die once again. Realize this, and you will see that these visions cannot harm you, for they are just projections of your mind. The shadow-self you see running after you is nothing more than the sum of your fears and pains. Face it, recognize it as part of yourself, and it will cease to scare you. Withstand your trials with perfect courage, and self-knowledge will be yours."

Although unfortunately Cooper did not get this piece of advice in time, there is an important lesson to be gained here. We should never fear our shadow, for it is a part of us. We all have things within us that we wish would simply go away—pains, traumas, fears, embarrassments, and so on— but the more we look away and try to escape it, the more power we give it, until we no longer recognize it as part of us, and lose the means to deal with it. But if we realize it is all in our minds, then we'll see there is no reason to fear it.

This doesn't mean we are merely imagining or hallucinating things. What it means is that if something is in our minds, then we can do what we want with it—including letting it go, just as we watch a wave dissolve back into the ocean. This, to me, is the most important lesson to be drawn from the Black Lodge scene, in the light of these ancient eastern texts.

Right, Agent Cooper?

3
Laura Palmer—Madonna and Whore

TIM JONES

Just who exactly is Laura Palmer? The more we search for a certain answer to this question, the more it looks like there's at least two of her.

There's the Laura who's a model citizen and honor student, smiling and happy in her class photo, who tutors the mentally disabled Johnny Horne and helps set up a Meals on Wheels charity service to provide food and companionship to Twin Peaks's most vulnerable residents. So far, so clear.

But then there's also the Laura who manipulates her boyfriend Bobby into drug running to fetch her coke fix (while cheating on him with James!) and who sneaks out of her bedroom window after dark to revel in orgies in the woods.

Can these seemingly contradictory characteristics really belong to the same person? Laura's *Secret Diary* tells us that she spent much of her teen years struggling with this question herself, pulled from one extreme to the other and ultimately driven to cast off what she regards as the "good" side of her identity, just to give that identity the sense of coherence she needs to maintain a grip on her sanity.

Her struggle could easily be explained by the emotional trauma of her long-term abuse at the hands of BOB, who not only torments her sexually but continually tells her how her darker desires mean that all she can be is "dirty and sleazy."

Much of her angst comes from how successfully he manipulates her into believing him on this. But if we look closer at life outside *Twin Peaks*, then we can see that all BOB is doing is intensifying an experience faced by women both inside the show and outside. He doesn't only serve the Black Lodge, but a pernicious trend within popular culture itself.

Other young girls might not have BOB creeping in through their window most nights, but this isn't to say that there aren't cultural signals all around them saying pretty much the same things to *them* as he says to Laura.

Laura Palmer is both a Madonna and a whore—a woman of unimpeachable virtue and a debased hooker. Psychologists from Freud onwards have identified that a large portion of men struggle to see individual women as complete, rounded people, and will instead assign each one they meet one of these two positions. A woman might be good for a cheap fuck, *or* good for keeping the house clean, putting dinner on the table on time and faithfully raising a man's child, but never both—and for the second set of actions in particular, good only just as long as she doesn't act in any way that complicates or suggests a life beyond this singular position.

The Madonna position is fragile enough that the slightest contradictory act can lead to an irrevocable fall from grace, often with physical violence as the result of a woman daring to supersede her shallow template. More recently, feminists such as Naomi Woolf have argued that these perceptions of women as well as the resultant male-driven representations of women within popular culture force growing women to choose between these two positions and develop behaviors (and survival strategies) accordingly.

It's the characterization of women via the Madonna-whore complex that's wrong, rather than Laura Palmer. She's a lovely, charitable woman who cares more than most about the people around her, but who also dreams of being taken by the men in her life in ways that would leave her friend Donna blushing. And so what? In a society without the complex, we'd see there's absolutely nothing that's inevitably odd about this—that she just is who she is and what she desires to do with her body is her own business. Any contradiction in her personality is only a contradiction from the point of view of a mindset that insists women must be one or the other. But the fact that her personality sets her up against such a pernicious societal trend gives BOB the hook he needs to leave her feeling like trash and vulnerable to his manipulations. Imagine how things might have turned out for her if, instead, the cultural signals all around her had told her that it's the message BOB tries to impress upon her that's wrong, rather than Laura herself.

On Madonnas and Whores

The Madonna-whore complex was first envisaged by the founder of psychoanalysis, Sigmund Freud (1856–1939). On observing a peculiar trait amongst many of the men he was seeing as his patients, Freud wrote that "where such men love, they have no desire, and where they desire, they cannot love."

Most men historically grew up being told that they need to marry a pure, virginal woman, whose first sexual experience will be with her husband in the marital bed. The same pressure evidently wasn't placed on men themselves, who'd therefore often have *their* first time with a hooker, or with another woman who, because of the proviso I've just mentioned, would necessarily be barred from becoming that man's wife. The women he knows would increasingly be split into two pools: the woman he sleeps with becomes a whore, while that nice lady who he has coffee and pie with at the Double R Diner every Saturday and whom he's courting as his future wife becomes idolized as a Madonna.

Until, that is, he discovers that she already put out with her last boyfriend. And because you can't take back an action like sex, the move from Madonna to whore can only go one way. That woman would then either become part of the group that the guy in question would be happy to sleep around with but never marry, or she'd experience physical violence as a result of the man feeling "deceived" about what sort of woman he was really spending time with. Maybe even both.

Perhaps predictably for the time, Freud's thoughts on the subject come from the point of view of the men he was treating, who were finding it inexplicably impossible to experience sexual desire for their wives. A man's categorization of his wife as a Madonna would persist into the marriage, so that even when that marriage meant that hot sex was now culturally permissible, for him to indulge any fantasy that wasn't of the straightforward missionary variety would still require a woman outside the home who could be "safely" categorized as a whore. Otherwise he'd have *married* a whore, which isn't how things are supposed to work, thank you.

The advent of the contraceptive pill and the lessening of a woman's need to worry about unwanted pregnancy might have made it much less likely for any man to reasonably expect that a woman he meets would still be "pure." But this doesn't seem to be the case. Men are still reasonably likely to experience a loss of desire for a female partner who is pregnant or has recently given birth. It's like a switch goes off and since this partner is now viewed as a nurturer and a caregiver, she can't any longer also be someone her partner enjoys canoodling with, since these roles are associated with opposing poles of the Madonna-whore complex. These old stereotypes and prejudices have a way of enduring, no matter how progressive it's tempting to think we've got.

What's Wrong with a Whore?

But what exactly does a man who's been influenced by the Madonna-whore complex into categorizing women in this way think of a woman like Laura Palmer who's happy to have sex outside of marriage? What's so wrong with being a whore?

Your answer might depend on why you reckon the Madonna-whore complex historically became a thing in the first place, which I guess relies on us thinking through which psychological need the complex fulfils for the men who consciously or unconsciously subscribe to it. Freud's own reasoning links the complex back to the fear of committing incest, because of course it would. A man is said to feel scarily similar feelings for a partner he's forming a family unit with as he does towards his mother, which, thanks to the incest taboo that's existed across all cultures from our early history as a species, is a bit yuck. The only safe solution is to segregate romantic relationships from sex—and so the married partner becomes idolized as frankly beyond all that dirty stuff, the man's desire for which therefore being channeled towards the women outside the marriage contract.

You might find this entirely convincing, but I sometimes think Freud was a bit too keen to see incest fears wherever he looked. So, what other explanations for the Madonna-whore complex might there be? Another psychological need met by the complex is the need for a man to be sure that a new-born baby he's about to support for the rest of his life (financially and emotionally) is actually his. Sylvia Horne and Sarah Palmer can be reasonably sure that Audrey and Laura are biologically their respective daughters, for reasons I probably don't have to spell out. But the only sure-fire way that Sylvia's husband Ben, or Sarah's husband ~~BOB~~ Leland, can enjoy the same certainty, is if they're convinced that neither Sylvia nor Sarah slept with another man. And if a woman was willing to sleep with one particular guy before being married, she's clearly out to ensnare *all* men using her crafty sexual wiles, so why wouldn't she be willing to continue sleeping around after the wedding? Hence the need for a guy to find the sort of woman who'll save herself until marriage and then cast aside any of the other women who'd been keeping his manly urges sated in the meantime. (I think the men who sign up to this sort of logic have pretty major trust issues, amongst other problems . . .)

So, splitting women into Madonnas and whores and restricting marriage to the former has historically enabled men to feel more secure about the paternity of their partner's children. Further reasons for this complex developing might result from various male fears about female sexuality. If you look at literary depictions of male versus female sexuality from a few centuries back, you'll find no small evidence of anxiety about men's capability to appease a woman's ability to, well, *keep going.*

While all but the most prolific of men are going to need a bit of a rest before getting it on a second or a third (or a fourth) time, the same biological restriction isn't there for women. So how is your partner going to keep herself happy while you're stuck looking downwards and waiting for something to happen? Find another man, so the more anxiety-ridden accounts would suggest, leaving the guy who's just been abandoned alone with his insecurity. The only way to avoid this—short of learning how to go down on a girl, which takes a certain finesse—is to subscribe to a complex that depicts sexually active women as objects to avoid, while those that refrain from sex outside of marriage with a single life-long partner are the ones that are safe to go for. They'll never know what they're missing.

I think these reasons are enough to explain why there's so much value-judgement attached to female "promiscuity"— why a woman openly choosing to explore her sexuality can't be left alone, but is cast as an object of fear, or even revulsion. A woman having sex on her own terms can never remain a neutral act as long as there's reason for insecure men to fear it—and reason therefore, too, for women remaining celibate, or committed to just the one man, to be valorized. But a further and still more pernicious reason for the complex arises from men continually being told that they *need* to be having lots of sex, not only because they (of course) have innate biological urges that need sorting, but because being successful with a string of women is usually depicted as a central feature of successful alpha maleness.

Look at James Bond. Or James Hurley. Okay, perhaps not the second one. But becoming awesome at being a man generally goes together with effortlessly accessing as many women as possible, by fair means or foul. And so, the sense Leo Johnson and Jacques Renault will have of themselves as alpha-males is boosted by the control they acquire over women like Laura and Ronette Pulaski. Committing to a single woman conversely seems a sort of neutering—like this particular woman has ensnared this man into a feminine domesticity and robbed him of his masculine prowess. This is one explanation for why Leo isn't much nicer to Shelly than to the women he meets at the cabin . . .

The reliance men place on seducing lots of women if they're to be seen as alpha-males means that men need to be able to identify the women willing to put out. Whores need to be recognizably distinct from the women who are not whores. But at the same time, these women are given a whole lot of power over the men looking for them—without these women, a man cannot fulfill his role as all-conquering stud. *This* is why I've called this explanation for the Madonna-whore complex more dangerous than the others. It's not only another reason that causes men to fear the women who remain on the wrong side of the binary. It's a reason, too, for an eternal reliance upon the very object of the fear. As long as waiting for marriage—for men—just isn't as cool as getting laid as early and as often as possible, men will be pushed towards a reliance on the very women they've simultaneously been led to fear. So, the fear will increase and the revulsion of the source of that fear increases with it.

I don't want to pathologize any sexual act that's anything less than completely vanilla, but I wonder why Renault ties Laura's hands together in *Fire Walk with Me*, despite her pleading for him not to. Maybe because his subconscious knows that his alpha-maleness is threatened by that part of his identity being *reliant* on the very gender that he's supposed, as an alpha-male, to have power over, driving him to symbolically restrict her by any means possible. He's exerting any form of control he can over her, to deny that women like her really have control over him, since without them he couldn't be the sort of man he wants to be.

The fear of female infidelity leading to illegitimate children; the fear of women's rapacious sexual appetite putting men to shame; and the fear that a vital part of a masculine identity is dependent on the people over whom true men are supposed to have power—all historical reasons for the development of a complex that regulates women's sexual behavior into that of either Madonnas or whores. And reasons, too, for the women who fall onto the wrong side of the complex to be loathed as well as feared, however much—and even *because*—these women are needed by the men who want to consider themselves at the top of the pack.

(It was while writing the above paragraph that I noticed that Laura's two "purer" female acquaintances are named Maddie and Donna. Maddie and Donna. Madonna. Mind blown. Wasn't this book totally worth the money?)

Nice Guys and Firemen

Laura's journey across the *Twin Peaks* franchise speaks to the journey all women go through growing up in a system that conceives of all women as either Madonnas or whores and forces them to choose accordingly which pole they're going to occupy. None of the cultural signals a young woman sees around her would tell her that she can comfortably or safely be both—which seems like it'd present a particularly stressful problem for a person like Laura, whose personality traits are almost a perfect blend of the idolized Madonna and the reviled whore.

And so, the cultural trends that insist she be one over the other are going to make her increasingly susceptible to BOB's insistence that the traits she shares with the whore position mean that she's *only*, as she ends up writing in her diary, "a little bitch, dirty and sleazy." Not the lovely, kind-hearted, charitable girl who just happens to sleep around too, as we can clearly see that she is. Without the prevalence of the Madonna-whore complex, she might be able to see herself in this light too, and avoid the depression that leads her towards seeking a dubious stability by clinging increasingly to the most dangerous stereotypes of the whore position.

I've so far laid much of the blame for Laura's increasing angst on BOB himself, as a demonic representation of the wider societal trends that women *out*side the show face on an almost daily basis. Judging from some revelations in

2017's series, though, I'm not going to let all the other supernatural characters entirely off the hook. The Fireman bears some responsibility too.

But he's a good guy, right? Assuming he's the same character as the Giant (who's only ever given this particular name by other people), he offers Agent Cooper clues to solve the mystery of Laura's death and even tries to warn him that "it's happening again" as Maddie is being murdered. Better late than never I guess. So how can he be singled out for any responsibility for Laura's breakdown and death?

He's not just a good guy, he's a *nice guy*, if you're familiar with that phrase from the feminist blogosphere. A guy who claims to *love* women and would certainly never dream of hurting or abusing one (which isn't a particularly rigorous criterion of niceness, if you think about it), yet beneath the surface acts in ways that show he doesn't really respect women as complete, nuanced and self-determining human beings any more than Leo or Jacques. A nice guy might claim to be totally behind women's sexual freedom, but then react less than nicely when that freedom isn't extended to him. Or his love of women might turn out to extend only to the women that stick to the roles he ultimately considers to be those belonging to women—not because he's trying to control them, honest, but because that's just what women were biologically intended for! Or he might love women because, unlike men, they're pure and virtuous, nurturing, peace-loving, and so on—an entirely reductive set of characteristics that's no less limiting than the whore position and that itself leaves women open to punishment for failing to live up to a supposedly noble calling that no real woman ever actually asked for. It's not actual women that this specific sort of nice guy loves. It's Madonnas.

If you're not sure what I mean by calling the Fireman a *nice guy*, think about the long flashback sequence in the second half of 2017's episode 8. What I get from it is basically this. The weird entity thing that we first see in the glass case in New York, which is probably named Judy, observes the detonation of the world's first atomic bomb at White Sands, New Mexico, in 1944. She/it responds by regurgitating several eggs, one of which includes BOB. It's as though White Sands' manifestation of humanity's proclivity for destruction directly inspires his birth. And after watching this unfold from his observatory, the Fireman produces a golden haze that his friend then beams down to Earth—a haze that includes the face of Laura Palmer.

What's going on here? Given the sequence of events and the angelic associations of the color gold, it looks to me like the Fireman creates Laura and sends her to our realm as a kind of antidote to the evil he's seen created in BOB. Like the Laura we see smiling in her homecoming photo, the Laura in the Fireman's mind is a beacon of purity and virtue produced to counter the vice brought into being by our coveting of nuclear power. No wonder BOB was so keen to possess *her* body in particular and no wonder it was so vital that MIKE gives her the ring that would make this impossible. I wonder whether BOB always knew that claiming Leland would eventually give him the chance to corrupt the girl designed as his antithesis and so who's really the ultimate threat to his existence . . .

How exactly Laura might be able to fulfill the role that it seems the Fireman intended for her isn't entirely clear, but her story arc is strongly reminiscent of one other with which we'll all be familiar. Created by a supernatural force to save the world from its sins. Died. Apparently resurrected and possibly even allowed into Heaven? The big difference between Laura and the guy I'm alluding to here is that she's obviously a woman, which means that the Fireman casting her in this role and placing this responsibility on her shoulders brings a whole new set of problematic associations. Even though this role *seems* on the surface to be so much more positive than the whore role through which BOB continually attempts to degrade her, it's still tangled up with the same complex and so it represents just as much of a trap for her as the whore position, just like it does too for women outside the show.

Virtue Can Be a Burden

By sticking to the Madonna role—by remaining pure, by cultivating her skills as nurturer and homemaker, by repressing her sexuality—a girl is supposed to be doing everything patriarchy is demanding of her. And she might just be rewarded with a nice home and a loving husband, unless, like with Leo, that husband finds different reasons to abuse her.

But being a Madonna isn't easy. Just *one* slip up and you're forever fallen; forever a whore. Avoiding this mistake requires an exhausting amount of self-policing. It's almost as though the system is designed to make maintaining this role such a burden that a woman can't possibly succeed at it. It's almost as though it's a role that she's *supposed* to fail at, so that patriarchy can point to her new status as fallen woman as proof that women need to be ever more tightly controlled if they're to be kept from their inevitably sinful nature. The ultimate importance to patriarchy of the Madonna role, then, might not be that it's the opposite to the whore role, but that it's a transitional stage that women can only ever occupy for a limited amount of time before falling out of it. The Madonna-whore complex ultimately intends for the vast majority of women to end up as whores—it's just that some will spend longer than others as Madonnas on the way.

I'm not saying that the Fireman—or guys like him in the real world, who *love* women and idolize their virtues—is necessarily clued in to all of this underlying logic. What's important is the fact that the role he assigns Laura is fundamentally entangled with the same patriarchal motivations for controlling women's behavior as the role of the whore. And the Fireman hasn't just assigned her the role of any common-or-garden-variety Madonna, but the most important Madonna of all, whose inherent goodness is supposed to redeem mankind itself from its destructive ways. That's a hell of a burden to live up to, even for a woman who isn't being serially abused. And to support my point above, it's this role that makes the show's representation of man's destructive ways—BOB—so keen to debase her. Laura's fate isn't directly the Fireman's fault to the same extent that it's BOB's, but everything that befalls her, the Fireman sets up and makes both possible and desirable. If she weren't originally cast by the Fireman as the ultimate Madonna, then there'd be nothing like the same incentive for BOB to recast her as the ultimate whore.

If we're really getting into the symbolism of Laura's birth, we could note that the *gold* that surrounds her tends to be associated with masculine power, as the color of the sun, while silver, as the color of the moon, is its feminine counterpart. This association further underlines that the idea that it's the responsibility of a virtuous, pure woman to redeem the sins of man, is itself a construct of male power. An individual man like the Fireman (or any other *nice guy*; or David Lynch!) can only cast a woman into this role because patriarchy is on his side and invests him with the authority to do so.

Laura Palmer is a woman pulled by two different male figures between the two opposing poles of the Madonna-whore complex. Weighed down since her birth by the Fireman's envisaging of her as a beacon of purity and virtue, then dragged into a life of prostitution and drug-use by BOB, who not only abuses her sexually but impresses upon her how her interest in sex with other men means that she's inevitably a bad girl, no matter how much energy she invests into tutoring disabled students or taking food to the needy.

Without the Madonna-whore complex and the reductive lens that both poles place over women's identities, she could've been saved from all of this. She could've been able to see her abuse at the hands of BOB and her consensual experimentation with guys her own age as totally different, rather than as equal signs that she's irrevocably debased. And she could've been free to grow up secure in her self-belief that she's a good person who can enjoy both the exploration of her sexuality and helping people in need, without any sense of contradiction between the two and any of the resultant vulnerability to BOB's insistence that what she gets up to at night means that she's ultimately only a "messed up bitch, dirty and sleazy."

That's a freedom that should be enjoyed by all women.

4
Special Epistemic Agent Dale Cooper

Elizabeth Rard

Diane, I've just had a cup of gas-station coffee that was, sadly, weaker than a can of rain water. I'll need to find a diner on my drive up to Twin Peaks where I can track down a cup of the good stuff. As I drive these twisty mountain roads my mind returns again and again to two thoughts. First, that I am surrounded on all sides by breathtaking displays of the beauty of nature. Second, that I can't shake the feeling that the murder I am heading out to investigate is somehow related to the death of Teresa Banks.

As I looked over the files sent to the bureau from the local sheriff's station in Twin Peaks, I can't help but notice similarities. Two young girls, both beautiful, both blonde, both taken too soon. I will need more evidence than my hunch though, if I am to uncover the mysteries that I am sure await me, and I wonder, given the events of last year, if my training as an agent, and my by-the-book investigation techniques, will really be able to lead me to the answers I seek.

My concerns stem mainly from my experience in Philadelphia last year. As you will recall, I had a dream that suggested to me that something of great importance would happen at precisely 10:10 in the morning that day. Shortly after I arrived at Cole's office, the long missing Agent Phillip Jeffries arrived in Gordon's office and began telling us about a meeting he attended above a convenience store. Jeffries disappeared right out of the office, and the front desk claimed he had never been there, but the security footage proved that he was there. At almost the moment of Jeffries's disappearance we received word that Agent Chester Desmond had disappeared while investigating the death of Teresa Banks in Deer Meadow.

Diane, at the bureau we are taught to trust in science, and to seek our explanations in the natural, rather than the super natural. But I fear that science and our traditional methods will not be enough to uncover these mysteries. If there are indeed parts of this world that are not controlled by the laws of nature we cling to for explanation, if there are forces that we do not understand, then the path I will need to walk may well be a strange and shadowy one. I will need to root my approach in a methodology capable of lighting the way in this weird world.

Diane, I want you to get me information on a branch of philosophy known as epistemology. As I understand it epistemology is the study of knowledge and belief formation, a rigorous investigation of the merits of various methods of belief formation, and a look at the sorts of evidence that we should consider in order to aim at true beliefs. Diane, I don't know what's out there, but I think the world is stranger than the scientists at the Bureau have ever considered. If I'm to uncover the truth at the heart of these many mysteries I will need a guidebook to help me proceed in what threatens to become an increasingly unconventional investigation.

An Epistemic Agent

Diane, I have just had the most wonderful cup of coffee, black as a lump of coal in a deep, dark pit, at the Great Northern, where I will be staying for the duration of this investigation. I find the people of Twin Peaks to be refreshingly friendly and hopeful, none of the big town cynicism I have come to expect on my travels.

I received the information you sent me on epistemology. Fascinating. Apparently, this branch of philosophy is mainly devoted to the study of what is called propositional knowledge. This is the type of knowledge that can be expressed by declarative statements. So "This is a damn fine cup of coffee" or "The trees around here are Douglas Fir trees" could be the content of someone's propositional knowledge, if a few conditions are met. These conditions traditionally are that a person, sometimes referred to as an epistemic agent, has knowledge of some statement if and only if they believe the statement, they are justified in believing the statement, and the statement is true.

So, when I asked Sheriff Truman what kind of fantastic trees they have growing around here and he told me that they were Douglas Fir trees I formed the belief "The trees around here are Douglas Fir trees." My justification was the testimony of the Sheriff. While he is probably not an arborist, he has lived in this area for many years, and as a representative of local law enforcement I can take him to be a trustworthy source of information. At the very least I would expect him speak truthfully and to refrain from giving information of which he is unsure. I therefore am fairly well justified in my belief that the trees here are in fact Douglas Firs. If it turns out that I have not been misled, and the trees here actually are Douglas Firs, then my belief might be counted as knowledge.

Whether or not we want to go ahead and count that belief as knowledge though rests on what we make of the justification requirement. Consider that my evidence is the testimony of one person whom I have just met. Perhaps Harry has lied to me, for reasons unknown to me. Perhaps he believes the trees are Douglas Firs but has himself been mistaken about the name of the trees all of these years (they could, for example, actually be called Dougie Firs). It could also be the case that when I asked about the trees he thought I was asking about different trees. There are other sorts of trees in this area, Sequoias to name one. Perhaps the trees I have become enamored with are actually Sequoias, but Harry mistook my inquiry to be directed to the Douglas Firs, and so unwittingly gave me false information.

Diane, my point is that the justification I have is not sufficient to guarantee that the belief I hold is true. The methods I have employed in this rather informal investigation could have easily led me to a false belief, even if they actually led me to a true one. If I wanted to increase my justification I could do many things, ask others around town what sorts of trees are here, purchase a handy pocket guide to the great trees of the majestic Northwest, become an arborist myself and devote my life to the study of trees. However, given that not much hinges on the truth of this particular belief, and given that my investigative energies are needed elsewhere, I will leave off this particular project for the moment.

The question I turn my attention to is this: given that the world I am in may contain mystical forces which operate outside the laws of nature, which would guarantee that the traditional sources of evidence will be insufficient to lead me to true beliefs in this case, what methods should I employ to ensure I arrive at justified beliefs which are at least likely to be true? As I pored over the pages you sent me one particular distinction jumped out as being of particular relevance to my investigation. This is the distinction between an internalist approach to justification and an externalist approach.

Let's imagine that on the popular television show *Invitation to Love*, Jade is found murdered and Chet suspects Emerald of the murder. Chet consults a Ouija board, which tells him that Emerald did not commit the murder, but rather it was Montana who committed the crime. We can rightly ask whether Chet would be justified in forming a new belief about the murder based on this information. Let's assume that Chet has no previous experience with the supernatural that would lead him to believe that the Ouija board is a reliable source of information, such as having previously met a ghost. What Chet does not realize though is that in the universe of *Invitation to Love* ghosts do exist, and they quite frequently use Ouija boards to communicate with the living. In addition, when Chet used the Ouija board Jade was actually there with him, guiding the planchette (that little triangle shaped piece with the hole in it) to spell out M-O-N-T-A-N-A.

Now whether or not we think Chet is justified in forming a new belief that Montana, not Emerald, killed Jade, based on the message from the Ouija board, depends on whether we take an internal or external approach to justification. If we take an internal approach to justification then Chet himself must have good reason to believe that his source of evidence is a good one. In other words, Chet must be justified in his belief that there are spirits in his world that use Ouija boards to communicate with the living. Since Chet does not have good evidence that Ouija boards are a reliable source of information he cannot be said to be internally justified in his belief that Montana is the murderer.

But we as the audience of this television show have access to additional information that Chet is not aware of. We're aware that within the fiction of the universe there are spirits who use Ouija boards to communicate information to the living, and we're also in possession of the information that it was Jade herself who sent the message that Montana was the murderer. Since we know that the Ouija board is a reliable (at least in this instance) source of information for Chet, if we adopt an externalist view of justification we can say that Chet is justified in forming the belief based on the pronouncements of the board. This is because the belief has been formed in a way that is likely to produce a true belief, even if Chet does not realize that his source of evidence is a good source.

Diane, it may become necessary over the course of my investigations to employ non-traditional methods in order to arrive at the truth. I am a lot like Chet was in my example, I do not know what the world is actually like. Do all events obey the laws of nature or are there forces operating outside the realm of the ordinary? Should I stick to the Bureau-approved investigation techniques, or should I listen to my gut and follow leads arrived at through dreams? There's this technique that I seem to have subconsciously learned of while dreaming, which involves co-ordinating my mind and body in such a way that I access my deepest intuitions. Could I ever be justified in using such a technique to identify suspects? What sort of epistemic agent must I be to uncover the dark truths buried in this once peaceful slice of the American dream?

A Damn Fine Plan

Diane, let me tell you about the dream I had last night. I dreamt I was in a room with a chevron pattern floor, and red curtains covering all the walls, floor to ceiling. In my dream Laura's mom had a vision of the killer, and his name was BOB. I also saw BOB in my dream, and he said that I might think he's gone insane but that he promises he will kill again. There was a dwarf who told me that the gum I like will come back into style. I was old, and Laura was there. She said that sometimes her arms bend back. She whispered her killer's name in my ear, but I can't remember what she said. I feel as if my dream is a code. If I can crack the code I will catch the killer. But can I trust my dream? Can I take the messages in my dream as evidence, or are they merely random pictures my mind has created to process the events of recent days? I think I might have an idea of how I should proceed.

Let's consider Chet's predicament once more. He is unsure whether he can trust the information that he gets from the Ouija board. We as the audience know that the board is reliable, but how does Chet, from his point of limited information, justify his reliance on such methods? It's simple! Use the board to make predictions and then test those predictions. The larger number of accurate predictions he can get from the board, the more reliable he can take it to be as a source of information. In science, when we want to verify a hypothesis we use it to make testable predictions. If I have a hypothesis that the best pie is made from fresh ingredients rather than frozen or canned ingredients, I can predict that a slice of the Double R Diner's delicious huckleberry pie, which is made with particularly fresh huckleberries, will beat a pie made with frozen berries in blind taste test. I can then arrange such a test and if my prediction is correct, that will lend support to my claim that fresh ingredients make better pie.

Likewise, Chet could flip a coin and, keeping the result hidden from even himself, ask the Ouija board whether the coin is heads or tails. If there really are invisible spirits directing the planchette he would expect the board to give the correct answer every time (assuming the spirits are willing to go along with this experiment), if there are not then he would expect about a fifty-percent hit rate, assuming the answer given was always either H for heads, or T for tails. We as the audience already have the information we need to judge the Ouija board as a reliable source of information. By using this experimental method Chet can come to have his own good reasons for considering the Ouija board as a source of justified beliefs.

Testable predictions, Diane! That's what we're in need of now. If we were on a television show then there would be an audience watching at home, and that audience might already have good reason to believe that the world we are in is one in which dreams can be believed. But like Chet, I need to find my own internal justification for my reliance on non-traditional sources of information. In my dream Laura Palmer said that sometimes her arms bend back. I think this might be a reference to the circumstances of her death somehow. I'm meeting with Albert later today to get the results of his autopsy report, and I have a suspicion that he's going to have information about Laura's arms. In the interest of a true experiment I will not tell Albert about my suspicions, lest I influence his report in any way.

Her Arms Bent Back

Diane, I had my meeting with Albert. We were right. Laura was tied up on the night of her murder, once around her wrists, and once with her upper arms behind her back. "Sometimes my arms bend back." Based on the information from my dream I predicted that Albert would find something out about Laura's arms, and he did. But this is far from a conclusive test of the reliability of my dreams. It's possible that when I examined her body I noticed some marks on her arms that I did not focus on at the time, but that my subconscious brought to my attention during my dream. In addition, many murder victims are tied up during their attack. It would be reasonable to assume in this case there was a good chance that Laura's arms had been tied up in some way.

But I have a second bit of confirming evidence. Laura's mom did have a vision of a man she believes is Laura's killer. Since I also saw this man in my dreams I sent Andy over without me so that he could draw a picture of the man Laura's mom saw. As you know I'm a very strong sender and I didn't want to influence her account. Diane, remind me sometime to tell you about Andy and Lucy. The people in this town really must be seen to be believed, but I'll do my best to paint you a word picture.

The drawing that Andy brought back was of the same man I saw in my vision. Again, I made a prediction based on my hypothesis that my visions are giving me reliable information about the case, and again the outcome was the one you would expect if my hypothesis about my dreams is true. So, should we start to take my dreams seriously? Can the beliefs formed from my dreams ever have a high level of justification? I think we should consider that there may be forces in this world beyond our comprehension, but I think we must proceed with caution and not rush to embrace my dreams without a thorough test of their reliability as a source of information. The problem is that, unlike Chet and his Ouija board, I cannot manufacture predictions on demand. I must wait for a dream or vision to offer up testable predictions before I can make any headway on this project.

I Will Tell You Three Things

Diane, by now you will have heard that I was shot in my hotel room last night. I assure you I am fine, but the concern I anticipate you will have is still very much appreciated. It was all on account of a darn wood tick. The little bugger had crawled up underneath my bullet proof vest and I had lifted the vest to get at it, hence the wound in what would normally be a protected part of my torso. As you know I am a firm believer in the power of the spirit to control the body. As such I intend to return to work immediately, using my unshakable will power to drive my wounded flesh. Now if I can just figure out how to use my unshakable will to get my shirt buttoned.

I need to tell you about the vision I had while I lay bleeding on the hotel floor. While I do not recommend such extreme measures as getting oneself shot for the purpose of verifying a hypothesis, the vision that followed my injury has given us a wealth of testable predictions.

A giant appeared to me in my room, he said that he would tell me three things. He asked me if, once he has told me these things and they have come true if I will then believe him. Diane, it's almost as if this giant was aware of our experiments and has given me the means to verify that my dreams and visions are indeed a credible source of information in this investigation. Of course, it's entirely possible that this experience was a hallucination brought on by shock and loss of blood, and more than a little wishful thinking on my part.

The first thing the giant told me was that there is a man in a smiling bag. The second was that the owls are not what they seem. The third and final prediction was that without chemicals he points. Diane, we must proceed with caution. While we now have three testable predictions, they are not the precise predictions that science would prefer. These are vague prophecies and we must be careful that we do not try so hard to find their confirmation that we bend our interpretations of evidence to ensure that we find the confirmation we seek. We must wait until we have truly convincing evidence that the giant's predictions were correct before we conclude we can rely on my visions.

Diane, one more thought, this one of currently pressing relevance. The world is vast and mysterious, and the people as varied and beautiful as the trees in the woods up here. But for all of our differences, for all of our disagreements, there is one thing that is common to all places and all walks of life: hospital food everywhere is a poisonous muck not fit for consumption by those who value their health.

A Vision Confirmed

Diane, I have much to tell you. The three things the giant told me have all come true. The first thing the giant told me was that there is a man in a smiling bag. I saw Jacques Renault in a body bag at the morgue. Later I saw the bag hung up to dry. It was hanging in such a way that it really did look to be smiling. This seems to confirm the giant's first prediction.

However, I must be careful. This sort of prediction would be easy to confirm because it is vague and open to interpretation. Imagine I made a prediction that you would see a cloud shaped like a bunny rabbit. If you wanted me to be right (wanted to believe that I had the power of prediction) you would probably convince yourself that every cloud you saw looked suspiciously bunny shaped. It was the same with this prediction. Did the giant rightly predict that I would see a smiling bag, or did I see a smiling bag because I wanted the giant to be right? It would have been considerate of him to offer up at least one nicely specific prediction, such as today's lottery numbers.

I believe, however, that I have found the confirming evidence in his second prediction that I failed to find in his first prediction. "The owls are not what they seem". I was recently visited by Major Garland Briggs, a man of singular poise and the highest character. He revealed to me a transmission that was recorded on deep space monitors which he oversees as part of his work for the government. Diane, the evidence is unmistakable this time. Strings and strings of gibberish and then "The owls are not what they seem." Then a little later on a second message of "COOPER/COOPER/ COOPER." Diane, these transmissions were received around the time I was shot, around the time I was having my vision.

There is no way that I could have accidently been made aware of this transmission prior to my vision and hence incorporated it into my experience. Likewise, the proximity of the times eliminates the possibility that someone learned of my vision later and faked the transmission in order to mislead me. This evidence is consistent with the giant's predictions, and hence is consistent with the truth of my hypothesis that these visions are a dependable source of information. In addition, there is no plausible alternative explanation for the evidence.

One last piece of the puzzle, the giant's third prediction. "Without chemicals, he points". We have located one Philip Michael Gerard, also known as Mike. He has been taking a drug combination that includes haloperidol, a drug used to treat schizophrenia and multiple personalities. Diane, we have been denying him access to this drug, not an ideal course of action, I agree, but without the drug a second personality has emerged, one calling himself Mike. Diane, I now believe that Mike is a spirit who knows BOB, and can lead us to capture Laura's killer. But almost as importantly, this is confirming evidence of the giant's third prediction. A man who takes chemicals and, without them, claims he can track the killer. While not quite as clear cut as the second prediction, I think that when taking all the evidence together we are finally justified in trusting my visions to guide us to the answers we seek.

A Truly Special Epistemic Agent

Diane, we began this journey from a place of ignorance, unsure whether we were justified in taking dreams and visions, traditionally not considered to be legitimate sources of evidence, to be a reliable guide to this investigation. Through careful attention to the clues and a diligent commitment to faithfully investigate the testable predictions suggested by our hypothesis, we have become justified in our use of evidence found in my dreams and visions to form our beliefs about this case.

We're closing in on Laura's killer, and I am confident we will have our man, or whatever he be, in custody soon. But we have already achieved an epistemic victory. If there were an audience watching our world the way we watch *Invitation to Love*, they will have known early on that the information contained in my visions and dreams was a reliable source of evidence. Therefore, I might always have been justified from an external perspective in forming beliefs based on my dreams.

But by using my hypothesis to make predictions, and then verifying that those predictions were accurate, I have given myself the internal justification that was needed for me to truly become not just Special Agent Dale Cooper, but Special Epistemic Agent Dale Cooper.

5
Albert Among the Chowder-Head Yokels and Blithering Hayseeds

JEFFREY G. PHILLIPS

AND KRISTOPHER G. PHILLIPS

In the original run of *Twin Peaks* including the feature movie, Albert Rosenfeld spends comparatively little time onscreen, considering he's one of eighty-two characters—he commands his presence for roughly fifty minutes in twenty-three scenes. Yet few characters make such an immediate impression.

Contrasting the serene, easy-going demeanor of most inhabitants of the seemingly sleepy town of Twin Peaks, Albert is abrasive, confrontational and almost totally devoid of social graces. He seems to revel in narcissistic superiority.

As his character develops, we see Albert step up in our estimation, insisting that despite his "certain cynicism," his concerns are global, and he chooses to live his life according to the principles of nonviolence and, curiously, love. This surprising admission seems at first to contradict his daily behavior as he deals with "chowder-head yokels."

No doubt Albert is smart, and there is virtually no room to question his commitment to a strict moral code. But what is this code? We argue that Albert embodies Kant's categorical imperative. His refusal to censor his opinions seems strikingly in line with Kant's perfect obligation to fidelity. Albert will not lie to Sheriff Truman to spare his feelings, for to do so would violate the universalizability test. An unflinching commitment to the letter of Kant's moral theory would also explain Albert's insistence that Sheriff Truman be charged and brought to justice for Truman's (understandable) assault against Albert, and Albert's shocking reply, "I love you, Sheriff Truman."

Albert's Path Is a Strange and Difficult One

Our introduction to forensic specialist Albert Rosenfield comes forty-four minutes into the pilot of *Twin Peaks*, though it is only through a passing comment. Sensing the gravity of the death of Laura Palmer and the letter "R" extracted from underneath her fingernail, Special Agent Dale Cooper recommends Albert and his team investigate, not Agent Sam Stanley, as "Albert seems to have a little bit more on the ball." Having worked with Albert on the Teresa Banks murder (detailed in the feature-length prequel, *Fire Walk with Me*), Cooper is well aware of Albert's track record as well as his off-putting interpersonal skills.

We first meet Albert in the flesh as he arrives in Twin Peaks at Cooper's behest in "Zen, or The Skill to Catch a Killer." Within the span of two minutes, Albert browbeats the innocent Lucy (referring to her as "Curly"), opines "What the hell kind of a two-bit operation are they running out of this treehouse, Cooper? I have seen some slipshod backwater burgs, but this place takes the cake," demeans the pathology report as "Amateur Hour," and evokes a heated threat from Sheriff Truman to go "looking for his teeth two blocks up on Queer Street." Not bad for a Twin Peaks howdy-do.

Still, it's interesting to note that in the face of Harry's invitation to employ dentures Albert demurs, simply glancing downward and backing away, evidently preferring to deliver his acidic salvos at a distance or from behind dark glasses. This is our first real indication of Albert's duality—his uncompromising disdain for life not measuring up to his exacting standards and his cautious attenuation when those bombastic proclamations are physically confronted.

The Only One of Us with the Co-ordinates for this Destination and Its Hardware Is You

Perhaps a key influence on Albert's personal credo, Immanuel Kant (1724–1804) has contributed significantly to the history of moral thought. Displeased by the trends in moral philosophy that prevailed at the time he was writing, Kant introduced a sophisticated account of morality based on integrity, fairness, respect for persons, and abstract reason. Let's consider what Kant believed made actions morally right, what kinds of obligations we have to ourselves and others, and what that might mean for how we behave in difficult situations. Through this lens of Kant's views on morally right action, Albert's behavior might seem a bit less divisive.

There can be little doubt that many of the characters in *Twin Peaks* fail to be good people. But how do we determine that? Competing views argue exactly what determines right actions. Some think it's a matter of seeking pleasure—that is, the right action is the one that maximizes pleasure (for oneself, for all living things, or for some specific group of individuals). Others think that it's a matter of our emotional response to a situation. When we cringe at the thought of Ben Horne spending an evening at One-Eyed Jack's with his daughter Audrey, that cringe is not a carefully reasoned moral claim; it's an emotive, perhaps instinctual response: "Yuck!"

According to Kant, both of these views are problematic. Our emotions have nothing to do with right action, and neither does pleasure. Kant says that the use of abstract reason sets us apart from other animals. Acting on instinct is not to act morally, but animalistically. To be sure, we don't hold animals *morally* accountable for killing or stealing, or owls for not being what they seem. We might get irritated if our dog has an accident, but we don't think it's a moral failing on her part.

When Leo Johnson shot Waldo, the talking bird, it was likely not because Waldo was about to violate some high-minded principle concerning whether one should rat out one's associates, but because the bird was mindlessly repeating information that could have incriminated Jacques or Leo. The bird isn't a moral agent, but Leo is. The difference, it seems, is the role one's capacity for reason plays in determining action. By placing reason at the outset of his moral theory, Kant thought we should recognize that what makes an action right is not pleasure or happiness (for animals seek those out of instinct), but having a good will.

How exactly do you have a good will? According to Kant, your will is good when you act intentionally, and out of your rational recognition of your duties or obligations. It's not good enough to perform a kind, generous, or even seemingly right action, YOU must perform the right action *for the right reason*.

This is all well and good, but working out just what the right reasons are isn't at all obvious. Thankfully, Kant offered us a few ways to think about our duties, and to test whether what we think we are obliged to do *really is* what we're obliged to do. The vague principles of "respect" and "fairness" are only useful up to a certain point.

When Albert is asked to throw his principles to the wind—as he is blocked from performing an autopsy on Laura Palmer ("Rest in Pain")—he lashes out at Ben Horne: "I realize that your position in this community pretty well guarantees venality, insincerity, and a rather irritating method of expressing yourself. Stupidity, however, is not an inherent trait." Clearly, Albert sees himself as being "fair" to Laura (and his moral duty) even as he appears to be disrespectful to Ben. Reasonable people can disagree about how you show respect, and the notion of fairness is notoriously vague. So if we want a guide to which actions are right, we'll need some help. Kant gives us a couple of tests for right action.

Kant's formula of universal law (sometimes called "the principle of universalizability") helps us determine just what our duties are by focusing on our intentions. Since morality is, according to Kant, a matter of reason, and reason is within our control, it's important that we ground the moral evaluation of our actions in what we can control.

We have control over *what* actions we take, and more importantly *why* we choose to act. Each action has two parts: the *why* Kant calls a "maxim," and the *what* is the act itself. Every intentional action is open to moral evaluation, and what makes an action intentional is that it is based on a maxim. A maxim is the *real* reason we have for doing something. Often we don't formally spell out, either in thought or speech, what the maxim is, but we *do* have reasons for acting.

In his autopsy confrontation Albert not only articulates his maxim but also his logical underpinning of it. "You can have a funeral any old time. You dig a hole, you plant a coffin. I, however, cannot perform these tests next year, next month, next week or tomorrow—I must perform them now" ("Rest in Pain"). In other instances, we must *infer* whether acts are subject to moral evaluation.

Sheriff Truman's act of punching Albert would have looked very different if, instead of an expression of frustration it had been a result of Truman's arm flailing and striking Albert by accident caused by a slip-and-fall. Instead, we have Truman acting on some sort of principle. What maxim it was on which Truman acted we are not sure, but we could hazard a few guesses. Any number of principles might justify assaulting Albert: Some of us may have our favorite already lined up, but this highlights an important point. Two or more people may perform the *same* action but on the basis of *different* maxims. As a result, the same action could be performed morally by one person and immorally for another. Again, this is because for Kant, doing the right thing means doing something out of a sense of duty. We don't know Truman's *real* maxim, but he *did* act for *some* reason. The question Kant would have Truman ask himself is whether his maxim was universalizable.

To say that a maxim is universalizable is to check it against a world where literally everyone, at all times, performs the same action for that same reason. Can we imagine successfully performing this act, for this reason, while everyone else did too? If so, we have ourselves a moral act. If our intentions would be thwarted, then the act is impermissible. Gordon Cole is a peculiar figure. He seems to have some trouble hearing, and as a result, wears a seemingly quite sensitive, but oddly ineffective hearing device. As a result of his seeming ocular difficulties, he shouts a lot, answers questions that were not asked (but are close to what someone asked), and has some tense interactions.

But does Gordon really have trouble hearing, or is it a ploy? Is he manipulating people? There is some reason to think that maybe he is. He has no trouble at all hearing Shelly ("On the Wings of Love"). Similarly, twenty-six years later, Gordon and Albert share a tense moment in Cole's office as Cole tells Albert that he must accompany him to meet Diane; Albert insists that Cole say, "please" to which Cole responds with a characteristic, *"What?!"* But what follows is telling. Albert responds, "You heard me," and Cole acquiesces ("There's a Body All Right"). Finally, it doesn't seem out of line for the Deputy Director of the FBI to lie from time to time, something Albert obviously understands.

But what could Cole's maxim be? Why would he lie? We could imagine that it's an attempt at manipulating others into doing or saying something they otherwise would not. So the act is to lie, and the maxim on which he bases the act is to convince them to divulge information they otherwise would not. Is such a maxim universalizable? Put another way, if *everyone, at all times* were to intentionally mislead others to get them to divulge information they otherwise would not, would the ruse still work? Clearly not! After all, we're imagining a world where everyone has the same intention, and all communication is known to be intentionally misleading. Why would anybody respond genuinely in such a world? Nobody would trust anyone else enough to get the lie up and running in the first place.

I Do Not Suffer Fools Gladly and Fools with Badges Never

We can see that lying will fail the test. Indeed, Kant himself thought that lying was *never* permissible; that there would never be a circumstance where intentionally misleading someone would pass the universalizability test. To act on a maxim that fails this test is not only to act immorally, but to act *irrationally*, as the two are inextricably linked. To act on such a maxim is to contradict yourself. After all, in the case of lying above, we see Cole applying a special exemption to the rule to himself—he gets to lie successfully, only because everyone else accepts that lying is inappropriate. And while Cole is special in that he is the Deputy Director of the FBI, that does not entitle him to a singular exemption from categorical rules. He's not acting out of a sense of obligation, we might say, but out of a sense of self-importance.

In "The Past Dictates the Future" Cole seems to have recognized this breach as he says to Albert, "For twenty-five years I've kept something from you, Albert. . . . This plan, Albert, all I could tell you about, and I'm sorry." Though Albert responds, "I understand," Cole persists: "I know you understand, Albert, yet I'm still sorry." In this fragile moment of connection, we see the bond and respect these men hold for one another.

In this way, we can also think of the formula of universalizability as a principle of fairness. We cannot perform any sort of action if our intention implies that an entire universe of people performing the same action, for the same reason wouldn't make sense. This rules out Catherine Martell's insurance fraud (insurance wouldn't work if everybody always filed false claims), most of Ben Horne's behavior, and Norma and Big Ed's affair (breaking promises is a no-go for Kant too) as well as Josie and Harry's intimacies (is their relationship spontaneous and loving or calculated and dishonest?).

But what about actions that are not obviously moral, but are still things we desire? For instance, Cooper seems to be just delighted by Norma's cherry pie. Having a slice of pie doesn't seem either morally required, nor does it seem to be prohibited. (In Coop's case we also see the agent's sharp adherence to this principle, as evidenced by his sweet rebuff of Audrey Horne's temptations, "What we want and need are two different things, Audrey" in "Realization Time")

To address this kind of situation, Kant distinguishes between two kinds of rational imperatives (or commands): hypothetical and categorical. Hypothetical imperatives are what reason dictates when the object that we are pursuing is in our self-interest or is something we care about. Of course, these kinds of imperatives can change. Cooper presumably doesn't *always* want a slice of pie, presumably there are times when he's not hungry. And engaging the affections of an eighteen-year-old vixen might create all manner of unintentionally undesirable complications. So reason will tell him not to pursue the course of action that results in his fulfilling that need.

But if hypothetical imperatives are malleable and shifting, what about morality? Wouldn't morality depend on individual wants? Not quite. Morality is governed by the *categorical* imperative, according to Kant. Reason dictates that some acts are simply inconsistent, regardless of what we want. Consider the difference between lying and eating a slice of pie. There is nothing *incoherent* about everybody wanting pie. There is a practical challenge to such a world; presumably Norma cannot bake enough pies to feed the entire universe. But that's not a conceptual problem, it's a practical problem. There is, however, a conceptual problem with lying. If everybody lies all the time, then nobody can get away with it, so the very purpose of the lie is defeated. Universalizability seems to get us to Kant's Categorical Imperative. That is, the rules that apply regardless of what we want. In short, the rules of morality always trump an individual's desires.

Indeed, for Albert, distinguishing between the hypothetical and the categorical initially is daunting if not flat-out frustrating. Agent Cooper waxes poetical over Buddhist tradition, Albert deadpans, "Agent Cooper, I am thrilled to pieces that the Dharma came to King Ho-Ho-Ho, I really am, but now I'm trying hard to focus on the more immediate problems of our own century right here in Twin Peaks" ("Coma"). When Cooper asserts the connection between Buddhism and Laura's murder may be surprising, we are introduced to the powerful dichotomy between romantic and classical reasoning.

There's Only One Problem with You— You're Perfect

In the apparent schism between the intuitive, emotional response and the coldly rational lies the key to recognizing the dynamics of *Twin Peaks* law enforcement. For in this corner of the jelly-donut wielding Twin Peaks Police Department is Sheriff Harry Truman, a man of emotional integrity, loyalty, pride, and at times sentimental deportment. And in this corner, direct from the FBI offices in Philadelphia, the right-hand man of FBI Deputy Director Gordon Cole, is Albert Rosenfield, a man of blunt logic, rationality, extensional insight and often caustic comportment. Refereeing this match tonight will be Agent Dale Cooper, a consummate professional whose personal philosophy fuses the intuitive with empirical perspicacity.

Employing abductive reasoning (or reasoning to the best explanation—a form of reasoning like that employed by Sherlock Holmes), Cooper negotiates the treacherous terrain, the deep forestation that rests between Harry Truman and Albert; his presence at the frequent head-butting serves as the calm voice of empathetic reason and proves to be a leavening agent in Albert's acclimation to life in the sedate wilderness.

So how are we to interpret Sheriff Truman's assaulting Albert? Can we craft a maxim that would pass the universalizability test? It's difficult to say. Kant did believe that we should punish people who commit crimes (but specifically *because* they committed a crime, and for no other reason), and that the punishment should be proportionate to the crime. Does Albert's off-putting lack of self-censorship constitute a crime, and if so, is violence the proportionate response? Perhaps if we turn to Kant's second principle, the formula of humanity, we can get a clearer picture of how this might look.

Kant believed that what he called the formula of humanity prescribed the same set of moral rules as the formula of universalizability, but that it might be helpful to consider morality from another perspective. Contemporary philosophers don't necessarily agree with Kant about this, but let's look at what he had to say.

Kant's second formula states that we should respect all other persons as rational, autonomous beings who are ends in themselves. As such, the other person should *never* be treated as a *mere means* to an end. We often utilize means-ends talk when we discuss our hypothetical imperatives. If I want a damn fine cup of coffee, there are *means* by which I can achieve that goal (or "end"). I might go to the RR Diner and ask for a cup, knowing that they brew coffee and serve it. In this way, I am using the diner, and the diner's employees as a means to my end—they help me achieve my goal of getting coffee. But the employees at the RR are *people*, and as such, according to Kant, deserve respect simply because they are people. He says that people are ends in themselves. Since people are rational beings, they are both creators of, and essential grounds to morality (since reason is what creates and grounds morality).

If the formula of humanity states that it is never acceptable to treat another as a mere means, did I do something wrong in ordering my cup of coffee? No! This is where Kant draws a distinction between treating another as a means to an end, and treating another as a *mere* means to an end. As long as I treat the RR employee with respect, I'm honoring her humanity. To treat someone as a *mere means* would be to treat them as an object rather than as a person who has dignity.

The guests at One-Eyed Jack's were likely not particularly interested in the humanity and autonomy of the young women Blackie O'Reilly provided. Ben and Jerry (Horne) had one thing on their minds, and it was clearly not a deep respect for women. As such, we can say for sure that they were using the young women as *mere means* to their own selfish ends.

It's because we recognize the humanity of others that Kant believes that we have an obligation to punish those who do wrong. Because each person is a rational being who is autonomous (literally: self-legislating), the proper response to a wrongdoing is to respond in kind.

This is the result of both formulas above, combined. When we act, according to the formula of universal law, we are willing that our maxim be universal—that it be law. Similarly, when we punish someone who has acted immorally, we are respecting that individual's ability to act on a maxim, and treating him as he believes all ought to be treated; in other words, we show respect by abiding by *his* maxim in our treatment of him.

We strive to make sense of Albert's choice of actions in terms of the letter of Kant's theory. Sheriff Truman is not obviously acting on a maxim that can be coherently universalized when he assaults Albert, and it's not obvious that Truman's response is one of respect for Albert's humanity. If anything, Truman seems to be acting out of emotion rather than reason, but he clearly does have a maxim in mind; his action is not unintentional. So what do we make of Truman's assault? And what should we make of Albert's response?

I've Got Compassion Running Out of My Nose, Pal

It's not immediately obvious that Albert's behaviors cleanly map onto Kant's moral prescriptions, but we think that they do. In our discussion of Kant's views, we appealed to some admittedly artificial scenarios to spell out what it is that Kant is committed to. But in the world of David Lynch, "artificial scenarios" takes on a new meaning. To be sure, weird things happen in *Twin Peaks*, but part of what makes the show compelling is that despite all the unlikely occurrences, there are moments that feel quite real.

In the real world, not everyone is an ideally rational Kantian who understands the categorical imperative, respects the autonomy of others and acts as if his own maxims are universal law. That much is obvious. So what does a true Kantian look like in a world of deeply flawed individuals? We believe that the short answer is: Albert Rosenfield. And it's no coincidence that the motto of his employer, the FBI, is "Fidelity, Bravery, Integrity."

Albert's attitude toward Sheriff Truman, suggesting he might "practice walking without dragging his knuckles on the ground," is just what we'd expect from him. So doesn't this seem like the perfect counter-example to our claim? Doesn't this seem to suggest that Albert is neither fair, nor respectful of the humanity of the townsfolk?

It doesn't. In fact, it may be just what Kant himself would have prescribed! Many philosophical thought experiments are artificial in their specificity—we carefully control *every* possible variable in order to be precise. But the world around us rarely works out that way. It's a complicated mess of people with conflicting maxims, differing moral codes and unexpected variables. Navigating a world like this is not at all like navigating a world in which everyone is ideally rational and in fact a Kantian about morality. So let's look again at the circumstances that result in Albert's derision for Sheriff Truman's investigative team.

In a sense Albert holds Harry accountable for supervising a less than professional investigation, in his estimation, largely due to the FBI's agent's unmitigated contempt for Twin Peaks's slow, full measured approach to life. Albert hails from a world with sharply defined perimeters: scientific accuracy, hard concrete (evidential and environmental), and diamond sharpness. Albert also does not lie. Both of these demonstrate respect for Harry's autonomy. Since he is a person, Harry is deserving of praise or blame accordingly. Since Albert respects the sheriff's autonomy, he is not going to appeal to emotion or paternalistic notions of politeness simply to spare feelings. That kind of subhuman sympathy is fine for "morons, dolts, dullards and dumbbells"—but not for a serious lawman, even if he does live in a land of square dances and hayrides.

We could suggest Albert's initial general unpleasantness stems in part from his sense of moral duty and in part from his being a fish out of water (thrust into a percolator). He still acts by his own maxims applied universally and is frustrated when those codes go unfollowed. He strikes out as a method of holding others accountable for his own moral vision. If they're part of that great fraternity of arbiters of social justice, they must be held to a certain standard, able to stand boldly in the face of judgment.

Deputy Andy Brennan is a particularly easy target of sarcasm, starting early ("Rest in Pain") as he remarks of Andy, "Aww look, it's trying to think," refers to him as a "hulking boob," and persists into "May the Giant Be with You" as Albert asks, "Where do they keep his water dish? and "It's another great moment in law enforcement history," as Andy staggers in a daze upon being smashed in the face with a loose board at Leo's cabin. Admittedly, Andy can be at times passive, regressive, non-confrontational and meek; for the bulk of the series he cannot even speak his mind to Lucy, who holds all the intimidation prowess of a pine weasel. In Albert's estimation, Sheriff Truman's consistently protective eye leveled at his staff demonstrates a serious moral flaw.

And so it is that, nose to nose, Albert goads Harry into physical confrontation, in essence suggesting the sheriff is not up to the standards of a "real" officer of the law. "You've had enough of me?" The answer is swift and decisive, prompting Albert's indignant call for Harry's badge. How can any respecting law officer stoop so low as to pummel an exacting moral agent for simply speaking the truth? Actions hold consequences. Though this memorable scene takes place in the fourth episode of Season One ("Rest in Pain"), Albert vigorously renews his verbal assault on everything and everyone in Twin Peaks until the Great Confrontation ("The Man Behind Glass"):

> Now you listen to me. While I will admit to a certain cynicism, the fact is that I am a naysayer and hatchet man in the fight against violence. I pride myself in taking a punch and I'll gladly take another because I choose to live my life in the company of Gandhi and King. My concerns are global. I reject absolutely revenge, aggression, and retaliation. The foundation of such a method . . . is love. I love you, Sheriff Truman.

Spoken like a true Kantian.

Color Me Amazed

While we have seen shards of Albert's evolution into a more understanding, dare we say *empathetic* agent, the second season of *Twin Peaks* chronicles a much more holistic, less bombastic Albert Rosenfield. The case could probably be made that Agent Cooper is no small influence in those changes, as following Harry's smackdown and Albert's incredulous observation, "He hit me," Coop calmly asserted "Well, I'm sure he meant to do that."

Like Albert, Coop refuses to lie or compromise out of respect for his fellow women and men. His refusal to support Albert's petition to punish Sheriff Truman demonstrates his steadfastness to moral principles and his unwavering ability to understand both classical and romantic tenets.

Under Coop's insistent, quietly assertive guidance throughout the first and second seasons, it is a kinder, gentler Albert Rosenfield we meet in "Lonely Souls," an almost unrecognizable doppelgänger straight from the White Lodge. Seeing a newly suspended Agent Cooper sporting a fashionable plaid-and-khaki ensemble, Albert remarks, "Oh, Coop, uh, about the uniform . . . replacing the quiet elegance of the dark suit and tie with the casual indifference of these muted earth tones is a form of fashion suicide, but, uh, call me crazy—on you it works." A kind word with barely a trace of irony and vitriol? Color us amazed. Could it be that Albert has sensed this is a low point for Cooper due to his suspension, and perhaps begrudgingly admits some empathy for his colleague, if not his friend?

Now for the cynical among us, we hasten to add that Albert still maintains an aloof, occasionally acerbic tone when circumstances dictate. He has not completely morphed into a self-effacing huckleberry pie of a man—a little tart, a little sweet, eminently satisfying. No, he still has his moments of sarcasm; otherwise, how would he still be Albert? Something interesting marks Albert's change. After mocking Andy with "I know, Andy. I know, I know, I know. It's what we call a real three-hanky crime," once again Albert faces someone taking him to task.

In a rare display of self-confidence, Andy blurts out, "Albert Rosenfield, I don't like the way you talk smart about Sheriff Truman or anybody. You just shut your mouth! Laura Palmer is dead. Jacques Renault is dead. Ronette Pulaski and Leo Johnson are in comas. Waldo the bird is dead." And Albert demurs, looking down as Andy leaves in a huff. No smart comebacks this time, just respect for the deputy's finally growing a spine.

Finally, it is rather satisfying to see him hear him discussing Harry with Cooper in earnest honesty:

> **ALBERT:** Coop, as you know, Truman and I have had our differences in the past, but the big lug's got his heart in the right place, if nothing else, and I'm not above feeling a little sympathy for the stalwart and the dull.
>
> **COOPER:** What's your point, Albert?
>
> **ALBERT:** Speaking frankly?
>
> **COOPER:** Feel free.
>
> **ALBERT:** Our sheriff's got a serious problem with his girlfriend.

In the final episodes of the series, and in the last memorable scenes of our fabulous Miguel Ferrer who gave Albert breath and piss and vinegar, we will see a less cantankerous, contemplative Albert Rosenfield. We will see him quietly tolerate the antics of his boss Gordon Cole, accept with little fanfare the two-word expletive directives of Diane Evans, simmer as a French daughter of a turnip farmer languidly puts on her shoes to leave, and dispatch a deadly *tulpa* with unflinching accuracy. He will save his boss from being sucked into a whirling vortex and elicit grateful respect from him, even when Albert stifles any reaction whatsoever from Gordon's fragile attempt at humor, prompting a response many of us have felt since our first meeting of the agent: "Sometimes I worry about you, Albert."

For us, despite our abiding concern for Albert's peace of mind, we would still delight in his labeling us with a well-intentioned pejorative, nudging us to become better versions of ourselves. Albert didn't need to split into two people under the influence of the Black Lodge, for he was always in touch with his classical and romantic selves, resorting to one or the other when circumstances warranted.

The final words of Log Lady Margaret Lanterman come to mind: "What is a reflection? A chance to see two? When there are chances for reflections, there can always be two—or more. Only when we are everywhere will there be just one. It has been a pleasure speaking to you."

II

My log does not judge

6
But What Does It Mean?

S. EVAN KREIDER

For every dedicated fan who will tell you that *Twin Peaks* is the best show ever made, there's another viewer who is left dumbfounded. "What just happened? What does it mean? Is this show anything more than a random collection of strange and disturbing images?"

Philosophy helps us to see that *Twin Peaks* is less about communicating completely explicit and determinate content, and more about presenting the viewers with incomplete information, while connecting them with a content that leaves room for personal interpretation.

Intuition and Purposiveness

Immanuel Kant is one of the first philosophers to say that people are capable of a special kind of aesthetic intuition that is distinct from our other psychological faculties. The use of this aesthetic intuition does not involve specific concepts (the way that objective scientific thinking does, for example), and it is not related to the satisfaction of any practical need or desire (the way the subjective pleasure of eating food does, for example). Instead, our aesthetic intuition involves the "free play of the understanding and the imagination," a kind of psychological pleasure that derives from contemplating beauty.

According to Kant, this comes from an enjoyment of "purposiveness without purpose" that aesthetic objects display: they have the appearance of purpose, function, or design where there is none. For example, the Grand Canyon's shape and sedimentary patterns look as though they were carefully designed, despite the fact that they are the result of random natural processes, and that is what our intuition responds to.

Kant's ideas are demonstrated nicely in David Lynch's *Twin Peaks*, especially the idea of nature's "purposiveness without purpose." Examples can be found in the very opening sequence of the original series. Much of the natural beauty of the town is showcased in a way that suggests the appearance of design, often contrasted against shots of man-made objects with actual design and purpose.

The very first shot of the opening sequence is that of a bird sitting on a branch. Nearby pine needles frame the bird, seeming to reach out to the bird, while also pointing up at the sky, as though purposely placed there, despite occurring naturally. This shot immediately transitions to a shot of the lumber mill, its smokestacks also pointed toward the sky, and quite purposefully so, given their function. Next, we move inside the lumber mill, and see automated machines fulfilling their intended design by sharpening the blades used to cut the lumber. This then transitions to a shot of the road and the town's welcome sign, over which the mountains can be seen, their subtly jagged peaks resembling the jutting pattern of the blades in the previous shot, resembling their purposiveness, but without actual purpose. These few simple shots contrast the appearance of purpose in nature with the intentional purpose in artifacts, drawing attention to nature's "purposiveness without purpose."

The very next scene is that of waterfalls. Lynch repeats this and similar depictions of the falls throughout the series. The lingering shot of the water descending the cliff is beautiful, to be sure, but the repetition and variation of the shot throughout the series calls our attention closer to it. The water doesn't simply fall; it cascades down the face of the cliff, forming patterns that seem orderly despite being random. One could imagine an artist specifically attempting to create that purposeful effect by designing it just so, but nature manages to mimic that purposiveness all on its own.

On some occasions, the waterfall is even shown with the Great Northern Hotel sitting just above it. Once again, Lynch seems to be drawing our attention to the contrast between the natural appearance of design by juxtaposing it with the actual design and purpose of a man-made structure. It also reminds of us the earlier contrast of nature and the lumber mill, which brings the mill and the Hotel together in our minds, suggesting a purposeful connection between the two, which is of course revealed in the plot of the series, primarily through the machinations of Benjamin Horne, owner of the Hotel, and aspiring owner of the mill.

As a final example among many, there are also the trees and forests around the town. Obviously, the woods have great significance in Twin Peaks. The livelihood of the town revolves in large part around the mill. The Great Northern Hotel, center of many events in the series, is built from the same lumber.

Many of the more terrifying and tragic events of the series take place in the woods. As a constant reminder of this, Lynch spends many a scene lingering over the trees. In the recent Season Three, a number of episodes include shots of the dense trees, typically during dusk, with the camera moving overhead. The tops of the trees and the shadows tucked deeply within their trunks create patterns that suggest purposiveness, and in this case, insidious ones, each shot contributing to a sense of growing unease as the season's events unfold. There is almost a sense of meaning to the trees, but not specifically revealed by these shots. In this way, Lynch seems not only to draw upon Kant's aesthetics of purposiveness without purpose, but also on notions of incompleteness and underdetermination found in the philosophies of twentieth-century philosophers of language and logic.

Incompleteness and Underdetermination

Careful viewers notice the many scenes between which Lynch transitions with a lingering shot of a traffic light against a dark sky, the light changing back and forth from red to green. The light sways slightly in the breeze, and soft but unsettling incidental music plays in the background.

Clearly, this shot has significance, given the frequency and occasions of its occurrences. For example, we see it twice in the very first episode ("Northwest Passage"): once after Agent Cooper's press conference to announce Laura Palmer's murder, and once just before Mrs. Palmer's first vision/nightmare. The traffic light is clearly a symbol of some kind, but an unspecified one: it means something, but it is difficult to ascribe any very specific meaning to it. Rather, the audience, having their attention drawn to it by the director, must complete the meaning of the symbol on their own, giving it its own context and content.

Although he may not have had aesthetics in mind, Bertrand Russell's idea of "incomplete symbols" provides a clever way to connect with Lynch's aesthetic approach. According to Russell, some linguistic symbols (such as words or phrases) are incomplete, in the sense that they can be meaningful in the right contexts, but do not necessarily refer to anything clear and specific on their own. The classic example occurs in the sentence "The present king of France is bald." The sentence certainly makes sense on some level, but it also presents some confusion (is it true or false?) because, of course, there is no present king of France.

Russell would say that this confusion arises because the phrase "the present king of France" is an incomplete symbol. Thus, incomplete symbols such as these cannot be said to be completely meaningless, but there is also something missing or confusing about them. In *Twin Peaks*, the traffic light serves as a sort of incomplete aesthetic (rather than linguistic) symbol: it is meaningful, but in a manner that cannot be fully determined in any one, objective way.

Another example of incompleteness can be found in an exchange between Donna Hayward and her younger sister

Harriet, once again in the pilot episode ("Northwest Passage"). Apparently working on a poem, Harriet asks Donna if "the blossom of the evening" or "the full flower of the evening" is better. Donna doesn't answer the question, but Harriet eventually settles on "the full blossom of the evening."

This amusing exchange serves to lighten the mood a bit between more serious scenes, but it also serves nicely to demonstrate the idea of an incomplete symbol. Part of the joke is that, out of context, Donna has no way of deciding between the two original alternatives: they clearly mean something, as they are composed of meaningful terms, but lacking further context, their meanings remain incomplete. Even when settling on "the full blossom of the evening," Harriet seems to be choosing more on the pure aesthetics of the phrase, the way it sounds, rather than what it means, enjoying the "free play of the understanding and the imagination" (as Kant would say) as she lingers on the words. Doing so, she demonstrates the aesthetic value of incompleteness: the phrase ultimately means whatever audience wants it to mean, within the limits of the literal meaning of the phrase itself.

W.V. Quine's notion of the "underdetermination" dovetails nicely with Russell. According to Quine, all scientific theories are underdetermined by the available facts; that is, all the available empirical evidence will always be consistent with more than one scientific theory, without giving us strictly empirical grounds to support one theory or another.

Although Quine was talking about science, there's a clear analogy here with the arts. One could compare an interpretation of a text to a theory explaining evidence, where the interpretation is akin to the theory, and the text is akin to the evidence. Analogously with scientific underdetermination, we might say that a text is compatible with more than one interpretation, with no purely textual reason to prefer one to another. In the arts, though, this is actually a good thing. One of the things we like about the arts is that they can mean different things to different people. Certainly not every interpretation is a valid one (minimally, an interpretation must be based on the text rather than not) but more than one interpretation may cohere equally well with the text. This actually allows the reader to play with the meaning of the text, much like the "free play of the understanding and the imagination" that Kant was talking about.

Almost any scene in the Black Lodge serves as an example of both incompleteness and underdetermination. The very first occurrence takes place during Cooper's dream, in which he is given various clues about Laura Palmer's murder ("Zen, or the Skill to Catch a Killer"). Some of the puzzle-like clues do eventually result in determinate meaning; for example, the phrase "the man in the smiling bag" directs Cooper to a body bag that has a smile-like appearance when hung on the wall in a certain way. Even in this case, we might say that the original phrase is still technically underdetermined, since any number of occurrences might have been consistent with it, and it is only Cooper who gives it determine meaning by attaching it to that specific thing. Nevertheless, there are still many other aspects of the Black Lodge scenes that are never fully determined.

The character of "the Arm" provides several examples, uttering a number of mysterious phrases, some of the meanings of which are eventually revealed, and some of which are not, leaving the audience to fill in the gaps by way of any number of consistent but ultimately unprovable theories. Even the Arm himself is a bit of a mystery, as we are left to wonder what it means when he makes his distinctive "whooping" sound, or whether he is somehow quite literally Mike's missing arm. Viewers can speculate and create any number of plausible explanations, but ultimately, these remain undetermined by the cinematic evidence.

Combining these ideas of incompleteness and underdetermination and applying them to aesthetics (especially *Twin Peaks*), the result is a rather interesting notion of art. Art is a type of incomplete symbol, in which the meaning is not wholly determined; and being underdetermined, it allows for a variety of different but legitimate interpretations that can be derived from the formal features of the art. Of course, it can also function in part on a more literal level (sometimes something just means something in a straightforward way) but what gives it its aesthetic value is more than the surface-level literal content, and more about the "free play" that its incompleteness and underdetermination allow in each individual member of the audience, through their intuitive reactions to it, and not simply by analyzing it in the "right" way. *Twin Peaks* clearly trades very much on these features of cinematic art, while also bringing in a significant emotional content, which some additional notions can elucidate.

Feeling and Form

In *Feeling and Form*, Susanne Langer puts forward a theory of aesthetics that complements the ideas of Kant, Russell, and Quine, and provides the last piece of the puzzle for understanding the effects Lynch is attempting to convey in *Twin Peaks*.

According to Langer, art creates something virtual; it is a kind of illusion. Different artistic media create different kinds of illusions. A painting creates the illusion of a three-dimensional space, despite its merely two-dimensional surface. Architecture creates a virtual environment that is more than just the physical structure. Music creates a virtual sense of the passage of time.

According to Langer, movies creates a virtual present (as in the present moment of experience), and do so in a mode of presentation that is like that of a dream. Just as the dreamer is always in the center of changing places and situations, so too the audience is in the center of changing scenes and events of the movie, creating an illusory present which the dreamer (the audience) inhabits. The immediacy of viewing of a film is the same as the immediacy of a dream, and the experience of watching the movie has the same sense of authenticity as that of the virtual present that is experienced in a dream.

Langer further claims that all art, including movies, act as expressive symbols. They connect us to expression and feeling that cannot be conveyed in straightforward language, but can only be experienced in more direct ways, more as an intuition (as Kant might say). Just as life feels a certain way when you experience it, and as ordinary language is often inadequate to describing it, art reproduces, in virtual form, similar feelings, and allows the artist to communicate feelings to the audience in ways that she could not accomplish explicitly in normal language. Since art is unlike language in its incompleteness (as Russell might say), and because it is underdetermined (as Quine might say), it also allows the audience to interpret it within a certain range and ascribe their own emotional meaning to it as well.

We see a small example of this very early in the very first *Twin Peaks* episode ("Northwest Passage"). Pete is on his way to go fishing, and he hears a foghorn blow in the distance. Apparently appreciating the sound and feeling the need to verbalize it, he says "The lonesome foghorn blows." This phrase serves as an incomplete symbol—not meaningless, but not completely determinately meaningful either—and one that specifically carries emotional connotations. Obviously, the word "lonesome" suggests loneliness, but the appreciative reaction also suggests one taking pleasure in solitude or perhaps connecting with another's isolation. Either way, the phrase invites the listener to fill in the gaps with their own emotional reaction, perhaps nostalgic memories, or even just dream-like imaginings of solitude. The pleasure that Pete seems to take from the sound is like that of Kant's "free-play," but now with the incomplete emotional content of Langer.

This same episode presents another example later when James finds himself in jail, with Bobby and Mike in another cell just across from him. Attempting to intimidate James, they start barking at him, louder and faster. Then Bobby begins to howl, and the sound is suddenly layered with various pitches and volumes overlapping, before the sounds trail off completely. The sounds themselves have no obvious literal meaning or purpose, but the effect is quite terrifying, while also inviting reflection on unusual nature of the sounds themselves. They have emotional content, but still require the listener to reflect on their incomplete meaning, plugging in the gaps with his own interpretation.

Perhaps the best example, and one that ties all of the aforementioned ideas together, is the now famous sequence from "Part 8" of *The Return*, starting with the detonation of an atomic bomb in New Mexico on July 16th 1945. This begins a lengthy sequence filled with a wide variety of imagery, not the least of which is a long shot of the detonation itself. We see the mushroom cloud form, rise, and expand, shockwaves spreading out from the center, as we viewers appear to move ever closer.

As per Langer, we are as in a dream, experiencing a virtual present of that moment, in the center of the event in a way that we could never be in a real present. The patterns of the clouds and shockwaves display patterns that suggest purposiveness. As we move even closer, we find ourselves in a tunnel of flashing lights and overwhelming sounds, and then find a floating figure (identified in the credits only as "The Experiment") that appears to vomit forth the spirit of BOB, as well as an egg that later gives birth to a small creature of both insect-and-amphibian-or reptile-like appearance that eventually crawls into the mouth of a sleeping girl, whose identity we can only speculate.

The entire sequence suggests various meanings and interpretations, but ultimately underdetermines any specific theory. It also raises a variety of emotional responses, especially awe and fear, without ever making it clear to what the fear is a reaction, leaving the viewer to fill in the gaps about the nature of the various entities that are introduced. The entire sequence is so very like a dream (or perhaps nightmare), in which the viewer is present and center, especially near the end, in which the Giant, in a heaven-like realm, looks on as the world enters the Nuclear Age, and then, as though in response, creates the spirit of Laura Palmer, and sends her toward the Earth. Without further information revealed in future seasons, the audience is left to interpret the events, in precisely the same way that we interpret a dream.

S. Evan Kreider

Meaning, Feeling, and Dreaming

"But what does it mean?!" we might still ask of any given scene in *Twin Peaks*. If the preceding ideas are indeed relevant, we seem to have discovered that this is simply the wrong question to ask. In *Twin Peaks*, Lynch is not concerned merely to tell a simple story that can be explained in such explicit, literal ways. Rather, the series is meant to provide the opportunity for us to supply our own meanings, within the range that the text of the show provides.

In this process, it's no accident that Lynch leans so heavily on dream imagery, since, if Langer is correct, that is the very essence of cinema itself. As such, *Twin Peaks* demands that we not only interpret the events of the show, but that we also reflect on the very medium and methods of movie-making.

7
The Art of Playing Along with Dancing Little People

ROB LUZECKY AND CHARLENE ELSBY

Laura Palmer has been murdered. Her body has been discovered wrapped in clear plastic. A stranger shows up in town to uncover the cause of this strange death.

Throughout the series, it's revealed that nothing is as it seems. There are aliens at work. There are giants that visit hotel rooms. There's an owl that may be a killer. A housewife (who is obsessed with inventing silent rollers for the living room blinds—cotton balls, the secret is cotton balls) becomes a lovelorn cheerleader. The local business tycoon becomes a lunatic, obsessed with the Civil War.

There is international drug trafficking. There is a serial killer. There is a cosmic battle between the "Light" and the "Dark" lodges. There is a woman who seems to hold the keys to the mysteries, but she spends altogether too much time talking to her log. To the casual viewer, it might seem that there is too much going on in *Twin Peaks,* and none of it really seems to go toward any satisfying resolution. All of the seemingly inexplicable plot points might lead a viewer to question whether *Twin Peaks* can be considered art at all.

Twin Peaks is a work of art. We base this claim on Aristotle's observation that works of art always have dramatic reversals. This is obvious in patently dramatic works like lyric poems, but holding that this claim applies to visual works of art requires a bit of justification. Think of paintings like Leonardo da Vinci's *Last Supper* (1490). The painting is dramatic, in the sense that it has a diminished meaning unless the viewer is aware of religious or mythological content that informs the images. If you're unfamiliar with Christianity, da Vinci's painting is just a representation of a perhaps too brightly lit figure standing in the midst of various supplicants who are arrayed to both of his sides.

When you're aware of the stories of the Gospels, however, this painting becomes meaningful as a dramatic representation of the last supper of Christ. The claim that visual works of art are dramatic becomes a bit more challenging for paintings that seem to represent no figures, like anything by Mark Rothko. But here, the way that the viewer's eye moves from one color to another, expecting something and either having that expectation met or flouted—the way the viewer's emotions, and expectations are conditioned by the painting—evidence the painting's drama. All in all, nothing is less artistic than a document that contains no surprises.

These dramatic reversals are fundamentally a state of play (an on-going relation of "give and take") between the viewer and the work of art. What's the audience supposed to think when there is a little person dancing in a red suit, while a dead girl stands silent? We suggest that *Twin Peaks* invites the audience to sit back, enjoy the spectacle, and play along with all the weirdness occurring in the Washington town. It is precisely this state of play that reveals the nature of *Twin Peaks* as a work of art.

The Art of Dramatic Reversal

The first real criticism of art and the role of the artist occurs in Plato's *Republic*. In Book Two, after the briefest of analyses, Socrates declares that the storytellers should be subject to supervision by the government. We all know that the bureaucrats, be they in Washington DC or ancient Athens, might not be the best qualified people to determine what constitutes good or bad art, but—this probable ineptitude aside—Plato claimed that bureaucrats, should, in fact, hold the lives of the artists in their hands.

There have always been storytellers, from the caves of Lascaux to the painted booths of the agora, to the streets of a quaint little town in northern Washington, there have always been those who delight in telling us tales of wonder and mystery. But, at least for Plato, those that tell the wrong kind of stories, or those that do a bad job of being artists, should pack up their bindles, because they'll face the judgment of some set of government officials, who (most likely) will kick them out of the city.

Plato's condemnation of the artist relies on a summary judgment about the nature of the work of art. For Plato, art is fundamentally a copy of real life that tends to confuse the audience. Because no one likes a confused audience, the artists should be exiled. For Plato, art is mimetic (which is just a fancy way of saying that it is a copy of reality). Unfortunately most artists do a really shitty job of copying reality. In ancient Athens, back in the time when there weren't TVs—and no wonderfully artistic TV shows—people tended to get their artistic fix by going to watch the performance of dramas in lyric verse.

A lot of art tended to be masked guys and girls standing up on a stage and telling the stories about murdering your dad and eating your children. People got quite confused by the spectacle. And this is when the chorus came in. From the sides of the stage another bunch of masked actors would shout summaries of the story at the audiences. Plato claimed that the whole artistic spectacle—actors in masks telling strange tales in strange ways—was all very confusing, in the sense that it did a really shitty job telling us what reality was really like.

When we get to Book Ten of the *Republic* the proverbial writing is on the wall: the poets and painters (and by extension all the artists) are condemned because they gratify the irrational part of the soul. Because their copies of reality just confuse the audience, artists have no place in the city—perhaps, in their wanderings in the wilds they can find some shelter in a lodge, where they can find the company of like-minded souls in rooms of red drapes.

But maybe the artists shouldn't be sent to the wilds. Aristotle came along after Plato and had a different view of art. Maybe art should transfix us, leave us spellbound, vexed, and bemused. Maybe art should make us wonder what the hell's going on. Maybe art should place the audience at a conceptual crossroads where nothing seems to make much sense. Maybe the purpose of art is to place the audience in a moment of indecision that's like standing in a traffic intersection at the dead of night, staring at a traffic light that flashes red, then green, then red again, as you try to figure out whether you should go or stop, with no idea of where you're going or why you're staring at the traffic light.

Remember when—in *The Return*—Dougie came back all messed up from the other dimension? He walked around stupefied and stumbled into a casino in Vegas where he shouts "hell-ooo" to win all sorts of money from the slot-machines. Dougie's actions were completely absurd, in the sense that the results were completely unexpected. No one, not Dougie, not the casino bosses, and not the old lady at the other slot-machine, could have predicted the pay-off. It was as if the very ordering of reality had come off the rails. Dougie spent most of Season Three walking around stunned because he was experiencing reality that was different from the reality that he had experienced for the previous twenty years. Maybe the function of art is to make the audience members feel like Dougie—stumbling around, seeming lost, communicating with seemingly inanimate objects (and having them seem to communicate with us).

If Aristotle had seen Dougie flummox everyone, he would have loved it. In the *Poetics* Aristotle identifies the capacity to confuse the audience as one of the essential functions of art. Some of the time, life is so boring. Some of the time, when we wake up, there seems to be nothing new in the small town that we live in. Everyone goes to the Double R Diner, for the amazing pie and the damn fine coffee, but nothing seems to change day after day. All of it loses interest, because there is no drama.

Aristotle identifies this drama as the essential aspect of any work of art. The key component of any story is that the hero undergoes dramatic reversals. The identity of a work of art depends on its ability to surprise us.

Now this is not to say that Aristotle's philosophy lacks a conceptual apparatus to criticize art. There were bad lyric poems in Aristotle's day, just like there are poorly executed TV shows now, and Aristotle could identify bad art. A poem was bad when the words were "barbaric" (which is to say, they didn't flow off the tongue and ring nicely in the ears of the audience). Certain sounds just shouldn't be put together, because their combination makes us want to stop listening. When the sounds make us want to stop up our ears—when the sounds are jarring, harsh, and put together in a way that produces a cacophony—then the poem is bad art.

We can find a correlate standard of judgment in contemporary TV shows. When ugly images are put together, in a poor way, then the finished product (the TV show) is not worth watching. A TV show is bad when it leaves us wanting to gouge out our eyes because the images it presented were hideous to behold. For Aristotle, the criterion of the aesthetic judgment does not have to do with whether or not the images correspond to reality (whether or not they are a good copy), but whether or not the things presented engage us, transfix us, and makes us want to continue experiencing work of art.

The Work of Art as Play

The German philosopher Hans-Georg Gadamer read his Aristotle, and probably would have enjoyed the coffee and pie at the *Double R Diner*. Gadamer thought that something is a work of art only if we participate with it. The identification of the work of art as that which keeps its spectators engaged implies that the work of art is not so much a thing as it is a process. The work of art is not merely that which is presented on the TV, it is that which keeps your interest.

It's not enough that David Lynch wrote a brilliant script and brought together a great production team and camera crew. It's not enough that the actors read their lines on a soundstage. It is not even enough that the hours of footage were edited together to produce the spectacle to be broadcast to the world. In order for *Twin Peaks* to be considered as a work of art, it has to be viewed. In order for the attempt to solve the mystery of the death of Laura Palmer the stuff of art, the story has to keep us engaged.

Just as the coded language of the of the beings in the other dimension reveals key clues to the solving the mystery of Laura Palmer's death, Gadamer's analysis of the meaning of the words we use to talk about our experience of art, will allow us to solve the great mystery of its nature. Gadamer points out that German speakers use the German word *"spiel"* to identify both their experiences works of art and the works of art themselves. The word *spiel* translates in English to the verb "play" and to the noun "game." These linguistic clues are highly important, in the sense that they suggest that the action of playing a game is analogous to the action of viewing a work of art.

Gadamer strengthens his analogy between games and works of art by pointing out that both involve symbolic gestures. One of the most interesting aspects of games and art is that they both involve their own set of symbolic meanings. When we're playing a game of soccer with our friends, the physical action of the ball crossing a painted line carries with it a certain specialized meaning (of a goal scored) that applies only in the game.

If our neighbor sees us brandishing a stick and swinging wildly, they'll probably draw the curtains and call the cops, because they think that our gestures imply danger. If, however, they recognize that our actions are just us swinging at a low pitch in a pick-up game of baseball, that is, if they recognize that our physical gestures occur within the context of a game, then they won't dash to the phone to call 911. In the third season of *Twin Peaks*, when we see the furnace produce smoke, we recognize that has a meaning that is quite different from the meaning we would apply to action of an old wood furnace producing smoke that we might see in real life. That we give different meanings to symbols in different contexts is evidenced by the fact that when we see the images we lean closer to TV to see what the smoke will "say" instead of running to get the nearest fire extinguisher. When we're talking about the meaning of symbolic gestures, context matters in the senses that the context gives a unique meaning to the gestures—a meaning that is different from the meaning we give to the gesture in a different circumstance. This implies that the meanings we give to gestures are incredibly fragile, amazingly unique, subject to being destroyed and perhaps never to be recovered, at the very moment we stop participating in the system in which the gestures occur.

The Polish phenomenologist Roman Ingarden elaborated on our participation with works of art with his observation that all works of art are schematized, in the sense that none of the represented images are ever complete, self-sustaining entities. There's a little guy dancing in a room that has red floor-to-ceiling drapes instead of walls. There's some vaguely out of style furniture in the room. The flooring consists of black and white tiles ordered in chessboard fashion. Music seemingly comes from nowhere. Agent Dale Cooper sits there and watches the spectacle.

The scene is incomplete in two senses: 1. none of the aspects of the scene—not the furniture, not the drapes, not the flooring, etc.—are to be taken in isolation (they are all part of a continuum), and; 2. in order to be considered a work of art, this continuum demands our participation with it. The first sense of incompleteness is pretty clear, in the sense that we can recognize that the image of the little guy dancing, means very little if we try to analytically (and artificially) separate it from the room in which it occurs and from the rhythm which provides the beats of his bodily movements. The second sense of incompleteness is also easy to recognize when we note that the figure's movements would have no meaning if it were not for the concerted actions of the artist (in this case the entire film crew, production staff, and actors) and our actions as viewers of the images.

The image on the screen comes to life as a meaningful piece of art as the consequence of the actions of the artist, the continuum of images of which it is a part, and the actions of the viewer who sits there watching the spectacle unfold and thinks that guy dances just like my mildly intoxicated uncle at my cousin's wedding.

But what would a dance be without any rhythm? Both Ingarden and Gadamer note that all works of art (and all games) have a certain type of rhythm to them. Ingarden characterizes the process of an artwork's coming to be as the movement from potentiality to actuality—think of what happens when a seed becomes the plant. We identify this movement as rhythmic, in the sense that it is ordered and repeatable.

Gadamer characterizes the creation and maintenance of the work of art as an ongoing process of "to and fro" that involves the artistic image presenting something incompletely to the viewer, and then the viewer completing (fulfilling) the image. This back and forth between the image and the viewer, between the little guy dancing and the viewer sitting there attempting to make sense of it all, is the on-going rhythmic exchange that allows the creative vision of the artists to come become actualized as a work of art.

So, What's It All About?

There are all sorts of mysteries presented in the three seasons of *Twin Peaks*, but perhaps the greatest mystery concerns the nature of the work of art. Early on in the third season we have Agent Cooper seeming to drift off in space, perhaps inhabiting some other dimension or some other reality, where the rules that govern our existence seem to not apply. Later on, in the episodes which focus on Dougie's misadventures, we have a character who seems to be not quite normal—to say the least.

Throughout, the viewers are left wondering what the hell is going on. What sort of thing is this that we are viewing?

While it certainly seems that *Twin Peaks* shares aspects with other television series. (It has actors, there are characters that are doing things, there are episodes, and so on). It is also the case that *Twin Peaks* has aspects that are more befitting scenes from paintings—such as all the shots of the gas station exterior that looked as though they were taken from Edward Hopper paintings ("Part 8: Gotta Light?"). Also think of the haunting radio broadcast in which the grotesque figure recites "This is the water, this is the well". The broadcast is more akin to a few lines from T.S. Eliot's poem "The Hollow Men" than the dialogue typically found in serialized television.

When we think of all those moments when Dale Cooper was in the other dimension, it seems too reductionist to say that *Twin Peaks* is only representational. This is not to say that there isn't representation going on, it's just to say that there's something more going on when we are transfixed by a gold orb floating through a black and white universe ("Part 8: Gotta Light?"). At these moments, we the viewers are involved with the work of art. We are besotted with it, we are enraptured with it, and we are fundamentally participating with it. *Twin Peaks* fascinates us. This gives us a clue to its nature.

We're fascinated with art because we're part of its production, in the sense that we play a key role in its creation—along with the artists and the context of presented objects. Art doesn't exist separately from our participation with it. The nature of the work of art, in this sense, is interactive. When we see the images on the screen, their meaning is partially dependent on the all the other events we see being portrayed.

Dale Cooper's talking to the giant is quite meaningless without reference to all the events that led up to that fateful encounter in the Light Lodge. This context is partially dependent on the actions of the artists who attempted to bring life to their artistic vision. No matter how detailed this vision is rendered, it is still incomplete, in the sense that what is presented must involve the viewer, who engages in a rhythmic exchange with the images presented to her.

When the little guy dances, we sit there and try to make sense of his movements; we try to conceive of a world in which these actions would make sense. In our making sense of the actions we are participating in the process of the work of art's creation.

8
I Sure Feel Uncomfortable Being in This Situation with You

RICHARD ROSENBAUM

When I first watched *Twin Peaks* (which consisted at the time of the first two television seasons and the movie *Fire Walk with Me*), I discovered it to be stylish and deeply bizarre—which I knew it would be; it is a David Lynch joint, after all.

But what struck me the most was how *uncomfortable* it often made me feel. It's more than just creepy, although it's not quite full-blown horror, either. Instead, it seems to occupy an interstice at the convergence between a few different technical, dramatic, and genre boundaries, and employs a mandate of creating intense audience discomfort to make its point about the limitations on human understanding and the blurriness between areas we prefer to consider distinct.

Twin Peaks tends to point toward a grander existence of which our known universe and our accepted truths are only a tiny, insignificant, and very poorly understood fragment. It does this primarily by evoking feelings of awkwardness or discomfort in its audience, using the techniques of melodrama and cringe comedy; ambiguously diegetic music; and the juxtaposition of the horrific with the banal.

Between Melodrama and Cringe

At its best moments, Twin Peaks dances along that thin line between *cringe comedy* and *melodrama*—sometimes almost literally—through the actors' performance style.

Melodrama is a dramatic form that emphasizes *heightened emotional experiences*, often heightened to a cartoonishly exaggerated degree. Melodrama was popular in the eighteenth and nineteenth centuries, but ever since the Russian theatre practitioner Konstantin Stanislavski devised the system of "method acting" in the 1910s, most contemporary movie and television actors have aimed for more realistic-seeming portrayals of characters, and the melodramatic style has mostly been relegated to the not-too-well-respected hinterlands of the soap opera.

But *Twin Peaks* is concerned with heightened emotions and credulity-stretching occurrences. Not only does it want to portray the extremity of experience that goes along with discovering mysterious tragedies and unravelling tragic mysteries, it wants to make you feel really weird about it at the same time. It wants to make you question the nature of experience, the nature both of emotion and of realism. *Twin Peaks* runs right up against the border between realism and melodrama—and occasionally stumbles over it.

To show us, the audience, that it's doing this deliberately (that they didn't just hire a bunch of terrible actors on the cheap, but rather that the actors are behaving in this over-the-top fashion for a specific aesthetic purpose), *Twin Peaks* includes a show-within-the-show, a patently ridiculous though evidently popular fictional soap opera called *Invitation to Love*, which we see being watched by various citizens of the town of Twin Peaks, often during important plot points throughout the series.

Invitation to Love is classically melodramatic, over-the-top, and seemingly always on, and it frequently mirrors the subject matter and emotional exaggeration of the events in Twin Peaks itself—although its viewers don't appear to notice these parallels.

The other side of that border is *cringe comedy*. This is the genre into which fall shows like *Curb Your Enthusiasm* and *It's Always Sunny in Philadelphia*, where the humor derives from the characters' unknowingly violating social boundaries because of their own self-absorption or general obliviousness to the feelings of others. Cringe comedy is controversial because people with too much empathy can't enjoy it, since it relies on a certain degree of dehumanization of the character whose actions cause us to cringe. It's still supposed to be *funny*, though, and this is where *Twin Peaks* straddles that line so deftly.

Twin Peaks is rife with bizarre people behaving bizarrely, but while characters like Nadine, Andy, and the Log Lady are initially set up for the most part as objects of ridicule, as the show progresses our empathy for them grows, and so behavior that would have been funny early in the series becomes tremendously sad when we feel close enough to the characters to mourn the loss of what must have been their connection to reality at some point in the past.

Similarly, the exaggerated emoting that drives melodrama makes us roll our eyes today because we're accustomed to seeing actors behaving naturalistically. But in *Twin Peaks*, some horrible stuff goes on. In the first episode, we learn of the murder of high-school student Laura Palmer—and so do her parents. So very early on in the series we're forced to watch Laura's mother's complete breakdown and her father's more staccato descent into the madness of despair.

These performances are so over-the-top that they're almost funny, but because we also empathize with the characters and recognize that their feelings come from a place of genuine and unfathomable pain, we can't laugh—yet we also can't take them completely seriously, either. That tension between the absurdity of their overwrought emotional displays and our knowledge of and sympathy with the causes of those feelings is a big part of what creates the intense discomfort we get from watching the show. But it's also what makes it so compelling. We're learning about the frailty of the human psyche even as we're being deliberately distanced by the unrealistically histrionic performances.

Where's That Music Coming From?

Another element the show uses to evoke discomfort by simultaneously inviting us to empathize with the characters while also distancing us from them is *music*. Composer Angelo Badalamenti's very loud and sentimental score is often played during scenes of intense emotion to overemphasize what the audience is meant to be feeling. This calls attention to the exaggerated lyricism of the dialogue at moments when we might otherwise be in danger of empathizing too closely with these characters who are often very, very upset by something. At other times, a jazzy score accompanies many more casual scenes, sometimes underlining a comedic incongruence.

These are typical tropes for a melodrama, but *Twin Peaks* also complicates the use of these leitmotifs by moving back and forth without warning between music that's diegetic (existing within the world of the show, so that the characters in the story can hear it) and non-diegetic (existing outside the world of the show, music that the audience can see or hear but the characters can't)—so that we'll be watching a scene, listening to that familiar tune, and our brain categorizes it as incidental; until someone reaches over and turns off the record player or the radio and the music immediately stops. The show wants to make us aware of the music as one of those conventions that we just accept and then ruptures that acceptance by forcing us to question whether the characters we're watching in the scene can hear it too, or if it's just us.

It's something like the "estrangement effect" employed by the twentieth-century German playwright Bertolt Brecht. Brecht erased the imaginary fourth wall that separates the actors from the audience, so that the characters onstage are aware that they are being observed by the audience, and the audience knows that they know. This destroys the sense of objectivity in audience members and thus makes it difficult or impossible to "lose yourself" in the performance or fully empathize with the characters.

Twin Peaks doesn't break the fourth wall in this way, but its use of ambiguously-diegetic music and its signaling self-awareness of its melodramatic tone have a similar effect to what Brecht was going for—causing the audience discomfort by, in part, calling attention to the constructedness of the narrative; periodically reminding us that we are watching a performance and compelling us to recoil when there's a danger of us coming to empathize too closely with the characters onscreen.

The Banality of Horror

In the theory of aesthetics, the *Uncanny Valley* refers to a point at which the appearance of a figure (typically a robot or computer-generated image) almost-but-not-quite resembles a realistic human. At this point, a person observing the figure doesn't register it as an object, but also doesn't register it as another person—it's some other thing, something in between, that nearly triggers our empathy response but falls just short. So instead of feeling the way we would feel about another human, we feel a sense of unease or even revulsion.

Now, in *Twin Peaks*, mysterious figures, such as the Man from Another Place (a red-suited, dancing dwarf) and the cryptic giant credited in the first two seasons only as "The Giant," are supposed to creep us out with their appearance and their bizarre modes of speech. This is an "uncanny valley" effect like what you'd get from not-quite-convincing robotic or computer-generated humans. But the people of Twin Peaks—the actual human beings—inhabit a kind of *behavioral uncanny valley*, wherein the ways that they act and the things that they say (rather than the way that they look or the sound of their voice) are what signal that they must not be quite as they seem.

The show also likes to highlight absurdity to discomfit the audience by frequently juxtaposing the horrific with the banal. That kind of thing is a literary effect called *bathos,* wherein a serious topic is emotionally defused or deflated by an immediate subsequent irreverence or mundanity. Most of the time bathos is used for comedic purposes or to prevent a scene from getting too intense or pretentious. But while *Twin Peaks* is definitely funny, a lot of the time it uses bathos not to lighten the mood of a scene but rather to make things *even weirder and creepier.*

In one episode Cooper is discussing the gruesome details of a murder and then all of a sudden pauses, produces a stick of gum, and casually shoves it into his mouth. The action is so incongruous, so out of step with the prevailing emotion of the scene, that we, the audience, get a sense that Cooper maybe just doesn't quite fully understand how ordinary human beings actually behave, as if maybe it's *everyone in town* who's doing an unconvincing impersonation of a person.

There are a few different ideas about how and why the uncanny valley effect exists, but a couple of them seem especially apt for describing how *Twin Peaks* achieves it with the characters' performances. Sorites Paradox holds that looking at something containing traits identified with both human and nonhuman entities undermine our intuitions about what "humans" are supposed to be like. It also could be related to the violation of human norms; entities that appear mostly human but with just enough nonhuman characteristics to trigger our empathy response but also our sense of abjection or alienation. When these two opposing perceptual experiences coincide, the paradox generates a sense of creepiness or unease, as if something nonhuman were pretending to be human—if not a human, what is it *really* and what is its motive in performing humanness?

Besides the characters who are deliberately non-human, a lot of the ostensibly human citizens of *Twin Peaks* aren't quite real people either, or at least aren't *always* real people; but we, the audience, don't consistently know who is what or when, and so when we see the characters behaving in such unusual ways we think, *what the hell is wrong with this town?!*

Which is the real mystery at the heart of the series. While it begins with a perfectly conventional premise—the murder of a young girl and the lawman deployed to investigate it— Lynch is interested in something much more enigmatic, something much more cosmic. It's not so much the answers that disturb while at once reassuring us, as in an ordinary murder mystery. In the case of *Twin Peaks* the nature and even the very *existence* of the questions themselves, the clues and suggestions that compel us to ask what could possibly have happened here, the threat of unveiling truths that prove the world is not and never was what it seems—that's what *Twin Peaks* does to make its audience unsure of our knowledge and our place in the world.

That's what unnerves us so. The *uncertainty*.

III

**It's like I'm having the
most beautiful
dream and the most
terrible nightmare
at once**

9
My Dharma Is the Road that Never Ends

MICHAEL K. POTTER AND CAM COBB

David Lynch and Mark Frost took the television world by storm in the spring of 1990. As viewers across America and abroad were seduced by the mystery and charm of a Northwest coastal logging town and its quirky inhabitants, *Twin Peaks* became instant fodder for watercooler talk. Yet something else was happening, something unmistakably strange. Over time, *Twin Peaks* settled into a state of unrelenting mystery—not a story that wouldn't end, but a story that *couldn't* end.

Twin Peaks began as a narrative that revolved—or seemed to revolve—around a central mystery, a single question: *Who killed Laura Palmer?* Consequently, Lynch and Frost faced the problem of satisfying viewers (and television executives) who expected resolution. A large portion of the show's audience wanted the mystery of Laura Palmer's murder solved; that, in their view, was the whole point of *Twin Peaks*—the destination. But solving the mystery was not a priority for Lynch and Frost, who cared more about the mystery itself, emphasizing the process: the ongoing consequences of the murder and the pain of not having answers.

Although Lynch and Frost resisted at first, eventually they were forced to capitulate to audience expectations midway through Season Two by 'solving' the mystery. And of course, the solution was unsatisfactory. As mysteries are romantic in nature, the resolution of a mystery is inherently dissatisfying. Mysteries endure because of the experience of not knowing, the pursuit, the questioning, the wonder—the immersive experience of perpetual becoming.

The romantic ideal is one of constant dissatisfaction; it is restlessness, the sense there's something more to discover, that drives romantics forward. There is a delicious tension in the romance of mystery between the thirst for solution and the necessity of denying that satisfaction. The appeal of romanticism lies in the tension between these poles, which emerges from Romanticism's prime mover: wonder. "To romanticize the world is to make us aware of the magic, mystery, and wonder of the world; it is to educate the senses to see the ordinary as extraordinary, the familiar as strange, the mundane as sacred, the finite as infinite," wrote Novalis in a widely-quoted passage. This is precisely what *Twin Peaks* aims to do.

Clearly uncomfortable with the resolution provided in Season Two, Lynch and Frost turned that 'resolution' on its head in *Fire Walk with Me*, revealing that the 'end' was merely a veneer, not an end at all, but one moment, one step, on a road that had no endpoint—a journey without a destination. Endings, after all, are fictions we impose to foster resolution and closure. As Orson Welles famously said, "If you want a happy ending that depends on where you stop your story." Mysteries that don't resolve, or have a clear resolution, are mysteries people return to again and again. They have an enduring power over our imaginations that solved mysteries cannot approach. Few people would be talking, thinking, and writing today about Jack the Ripper if we knew who he was. Unsolved mysteries are living mysteries. Solved mysteries die upon their resolution. *Fire Walk with Me* made this point subtly. Yet still audiences weren't ready for it.

Twenty-five years later, Lynch and Frost were done with thematic subtlety. *Twin Peaks: The Return* arrived after two decades in which television viewers were gradually trained into new expectations, more refined tastes, and more complex appreciation. Programs like *Mad Men*, *Lost*, and before them *The Sopranos* introduced mass audiences to the idea that series needn't wrap up in tidy endings. Series that *could* have—should have—embraced this notion but opted instead to wrap things up with a bow, like *The X-Files*, seemed to betray themselves. Television audiences, or a larger contingent of them, in 2017 were ready for Lynch and Frost in a way that they clearly weren't in the early 1990s.

Twin Peaks: The Return reinforces the messages Lynch and Frost tried to get audiences to accept in *Fire Walk with Me*—there are no resolutions, the process is the point—by revealing that Cooper is trapped in an existential time loop. What happened *will* happen. Any attempt to stop it results in a new cycle in which the same major beats recur, even if the spaces between them differ superficially. Cooper must learn *amor fati* (Nietzsche, *The Gay Science*). He *must* accept, even love, his fate and every horrific event in his journey, no matter how miserable he feels, no matter how painful the acceptance.

Cooper isn't the only one living a sort of spiral existence. He isn't even the only law enforcement officer locked in this cycle. As FBI Agent Tamara Preston says in Frost's offbeat novel, *Twin Peaks: The Final Dossier*:

> I'd like to believe that's more to life than what we can see or lay our hands on, but the "job" keeps us so focused on the evil that men do that it's a challenge to hold both thoughts at once. My research tells me that people drawn to law enforcement professions, if they're thoughtful at all, perpetually struggle with this conundrum: How do we dig ourselves out of *that* particular shit? I suspect this is part of why you've asked me to take all this on: to investigate the process of confronting that riddle within myself. Is that the secret at the heart of the Blue Rose and the work we do? (p. 86)

And so, *Twin Peaks: The Return* expresses a commitment to the Nietzschean concept of eternal recurrence, drawing from Schopenhauerean, Buddhist, and Hindu thought. Although eternal recurrence is implicit throughout the eighteen episodes of *The Return*, it's perhaps most obvious on two occasions:

1. when Wally introduces the concept of Dharma in Part 4 (entitled ". . . Brings Back Some Memories")

2. when Cooper/Richard begins a sort of reconfigured do-over in the final episode (entitled "What Is Your Name?").

In *The Gay Science*, Nietzsche presented the idea vividly, foreshadowing Cooper's realization:

> What, if some day or night a demon were to steal after you into your loneliest loneliness and say to you: "This life as you now live it and have lived it, you will have to live once more and innumerable times more; and there will be nothing new in it, but every pain and every joy and every thought and sigh and everything unutterably small or great in your life will have to return to you, all in the same succession and sequence—even this spider and this moonlight between the trees, and even this moment and I myself. The eternal hourglass of existence is turned upside down again and again, and you with it, speck of dust!" Would you not throw yourself down and gnash your teeth and curse the demon who spoke thus? . . . Or how well disposed would you have to become to yourself and to life to crave nothing more fervently than this ultimate eternal confirmation and seal? (p. 273)

Over eighteen episodes—or as Lynch and Frost call them, *parts*—the eternal recurrence and the intricately interwoven nature of individual human lives emerge as major themes in *Twin Peaks: The Return*, connected by a starkly Romantic theme regarding authorship that depends upon Lynch and Frost's willingness to break many commonly accepted rules of storytelling.

Storytellers Tell Stories

One of the first rules broken in *Twin Peaks* is that: *a storyteller or author must create and tell a story.*

In Season One, *Twin Peaks* is clearly Lynch and Frost's story: they're creating it, using their cast and crew and set to tell it. Yet from the first episode of *Twin Peaks: The Return*,

Lynch and Frost begin to argue that we're all, as audience members, involved in a meta-story about the relationship between the narrative of *Twin Peaks* and the meanings, demands, expectations, hopes, fears, and attachments we bring to it as viewers.

In many regards, this bond connects to *Lost*, a show where viewer response and fan responsiveness influenced plotlines as well as the paths of various characters—including the longevity of Ben Linus, the multiple returns of Dr. Artz, and the fleeting tale of Paulo and Nikki. Just as the viewers of *Lost* at once experienced, and in a way even *contributed* to the construction of the narrative, *Twin Peaks: The Return* is a story *about* storytelling, and *experiencing* a story. Standard presumptions regarding authorship and storytelling appear broken as Lynch and Frost lead us to see, really see, the intricately interwoven nature of Life, which contains all individual lives within itself.

Protagonists Solve Problems

Thus, we are brought to a second storytelling rule that *Twin Peaks* breaks: *a story should present its protagonist with a problem, with the plot of the story developing as the protagonist attempts to solve the problem.*

At first, the problem to be solved seemed to be the mystery of Laura Palmer's murder. *Twin Peaks*, in Season One, is presented as a story *about* Laura Palmer. The protagonist of this story, by the time Season Two begins, is Dale Cooper. The basic structure—*Lesson 101 in "This is How Plot Works"*—is easy to understand.

Then *Fire Walk with Me* pulled the rug out from under audiences by revealing that the resolution of the mystery was no resolution—and Dale Cooper is barely in it, so maybe he isn't the protagonist at all. Finally, two and a half decades later, came *Twin Peaks: The Return*, which removed the floor entirely, demonstrating that the story wasn't about solving any problems in particular—and that Dale Cooper was never really the protagonist. Cooper, rather than being the subject, is the object. *Twin Peaks* has always been about Cooper, and through him, us. He is our avatar; we learn this as Cooper learns it. Just as Cooper (as Dougie Jones) needs to relearn how to eat and drink and talk and move and make his way through an unfamiliar world, so we must relearn how to navigate a complicated, once-familiar setting where meaning, narrative logic, and even truths are elusive—and sometimes a riddle. When Cooper (who was once Dougie Jones) becomes Cooper/Richard in the final episode, it all begins again. And everything must be relearned. It's both confusing, and troubling—for him *and* for us. As the Log Lady observes:

> We are born into this world, not another one. It's not perfect, but it is what it is. This world presents some simple, certain truths. It helps us grow if we accept them, but many of these truths seem to trouble or frighten us. (*Twin Peaks: The Final Dossier*, p. 94)

Twin Peaks: The Return is a defiant refusal to solve problems. Present problems? Certainly—a host of problems are introduced and puzzled over. But Lynch and Frost refuse to solve any of them, daring viewers first to recognize what's being done to and with them, then daring them further to accept it. Why? Because their vision is Romantic: solutions—fleeting and illusory—are the wrong goals to seek. The engine of life is powered by problems that will never be solved because wrestling with them is an essential characteristic of what it means to be conscious human beings engaged in the continual construction of meaning.

Life, Lynch and Frost argue, is about finding, thinking about, experiencing and accepting the mysteries, puzzles, and problems that we encounter—to find satisfaction in the experience. To embrace and accept the eternal process. Dale Cooper's confrontation with the necessity of *amor fati* is ours as well.

Stories Have Endings

And that leads to a third rule of storytelling that Lynch and Frost violate: *stories should have endings*.

As far back as *Fire Walk with Me*, Lynch and Frost indicated a disinterest in endings. They see endings as a trap, an illusion, a lie. If Life is eternal process, then even when individual lives end insofar as we can perceive them, Life itself does not. The story continues just as it did before any certain strand of any certain life was woven in.

The end of any given life is not the end of the story, for The Story, Life, is larger than individual people. This is so, Lynch and Frost are arguing, even if we elevate certain persons to positions of unnecessary importance—as Cooper did with Laura Palmer, and as we, the audience, did with Dale Cooper. As we do with ourselves.

The story of *Twin Peaks* cannot end because it is about Life, the Story that cannot end. Even at the level of individual stories, the notion of an ending is inauthentic if we think of it as a termination point. Endings are imposed upon narrative from without. We choose moments in endless stories that seem to offer resolution and bestow upon those the term 'ending'. Remember what Orson Welles told us: "If you want a happy ending that depends on where you stop your story."

Yet the stories continue in memory and conversation, the rippling effects each life causes in others. Take one more step backward from the object-narrative in *Twin Peaks* for a fuller perspective and we see that, since every life is interwoven with every other, all stories are strands in a larger rope that contains all human and non-human history, stretching endlessly forward and backward far beyond our view. Life is a process with no objective destination, ending, or beginning.

Echoing the Buddhist idea of *pratityasamutpada*, Bertrand Russell observed: "There is no reason to suppose that the world had a beginning at all. The idea that things must have a beginning is really due to the poverty of our thoughts."

The ~~Play's~~ Audience's the Thing

Understood in this way, the story of *Twin Peaks* became the story of its relationship with its audience. The narrative we call *"Twin Peaks"* became woven into millions of other narratives over the course of twenty-five years, creating a meta-narrative, a larger Story, that is now the story of *Twin Peaks*, which is the story of Life.

The first noticeable step in this direction occurred over the last half of Season One and throughout Season Two, as the story fragments and viewers discover that perhaps *Twin Peaks* is also about the town itself, and its various denizens, rather than merely Cooper's investigation of Laura Palmer's murder. As Caden Cotard—the writer-protagonist in *Synecdoche, New York* (2008)—says, "There are nearly thirteen million people in the world. None of those people is an extra. They're all the leads of their own stories. They have to be given their due."

In *Twin Peaks: The Return*, Lynch and Frost push their argument to an even greater extreme, presenting over two hundred characters with speaking roles and plot strands that appear, superficially, to be utterly disconnected. But through experiencing this dissolution of priority, viewers come to see that the story of *Twin Peaks* is not an object; it is entangled in the subjective experiences of all who view the series, think about it, discuss it, write about it. Not only is every character the protagonist of their own story, actively creating meaning, so are viewers.

Viewing a television series, like everyday perception, is not a passive process: viewers create meaning through their relationship with the stories and characters in the series. We combine and rearrange what we see and hear through the interpretive lenses of our own ideas, experiences, intentions, values, expectations, fears, hopes, and attachments. This complex relationship between narrative and meta-narrative is unavoidable. It was unavoidable when *Twin Peaks* premiered, and it is especially unavoidable in *Twin Peaks: The Return* because Lynch and Frost have deliberately crafted an experience that forces us to acknowledge its inevitability.

So, there is no one single 'story' to be puzzled over or enjoyed in *Twin Peaks*. Stories, always multiple, exist in the space between the narrative-as-object and the viewer-as-subject, creating a meta-narrative about each person's experience with the narrative-as-object. As Lynch and Frost spun a story partially created by chance and locked into a perpetual state of becoming, the characteristics of that narrative seeped into its relationship with the audience.

There's an inherent romanticism to Lynch and Frost's conception of storytelling, with both fate and chance at the forefront. Fate does not imply determinism, which is dependent on the past. Fate is dependent upon the future. Paths to the inevitable are littered with randomness, serendipitous encounters, and accidents of interaction. Fate demands only that whatever happens along the way, its figures are headed in a predetermined direction.

One aspect of chance essential to *Twin Peaks* is the unpredictability of what each member of the audience brings to their interaction with the narrative-as-object, and thus to the meanings and certain experiences that become part of the meta-narrative. Lynch and Frost can neither know nor predict what viewers bring with them beyond the broadest generalizations.

To even speak of the narrative as a perpetual state of becoming is misleading, pushing against the limits of our language, for 'state' implies position and being, rather than becoming. The meta-narratives constructed between *Twin Peaks* and its audience are never static. They are always in process, always becoming. As we continue to become through time, we bring new ideas and experiences, new associations and interpretations, new emotions, and thus new meanings to how we experience *Twin Peaks*. With each of these come changes in the meta-narratives created through our interactions.

The accidental characteristics that define, in fragments, who we are, not only influence the meanings we create as we watch, but also the meanings we create when we remember what we watched, and beyond that, how those meanings affect our interactions with the world beyond *Twin Peaks*. And when each of us dies, the larger meta-narrative continues, and our individual meta-narratives continue to influence the individual narratives of each person with whom we have communicated.

"It's Wally!"—The Beats' Debt to Buddhism by way of Existentialism

By the time we finish watching *Twin Peaks: The Return*, we understand it as a story about unfinishedness and chance, contrasting romantic ideals of perpetual becoming with a qualified refutation of Romanticism's glorification of fatalism—qualified in that it rejects fatalism to the extent that it assumes that 1. fate is knowable, and 2. that it involves an endpoint.

The larger meta-narrative of meta-narratives is also about unfinishedness and chance. Lynch and Frost didn't have the opportunity to realize their initial vision for *Twin Peaks*, as they discovered through the process of creating it two and a half decades ago that their intentions were constrained and modifiable by accidents of viewership, the expectations and demands of audience and corporations. So much was simultaneously foreseeable and unforeseeable.

In *Twin Peaks: The Return*, with the benefit of hindsight, they embraced the perpetual becoming of their own storytelling to make their own unpleasant learning experience part of the grander tale. In their defiant devotion to their own creative vision, which took more than two decades to bear fruit, their Romanticism becomes impossible to ignore. As Isaiah Berlin wrote in *The Roots of Romanticism:*

> The painter, the poet, the composer do not hold up a mirror to nature, however ideal, but invent; they do not imitate (the doctrine of mimesis), but create not merely the means but the goals that they pursue; these goals represent the self-expression of the artist's own unique, inner vision, to set aside which in response to the demands of some 'external' voice—church, state, public opinion, family friends, arbiters of taste—is an act of betrayal of what alone justifies their existence for those who are in any sense creative. (pp. 57–58)

Lynch and Frost's long effort to bring their idiosyncratic vision to life embodies the dogged attitude Nietzsche found necessary for *amor fati*, of embracing the eternal recurrence and committing to love even the most miserable episodes in your life . . .

> To *endure* the idea of the recurrence you need: freedom from morality; new means against the fact of *pain* (pain conceived as a tool, as the father of pleasure . . .); the enjoyment of all kinds of uncertainty, experimentalism, as a counterweight to this extreme fatalism; abolition of the concept of necessity; abolition of the "will"; abolition of "knowledge-in-itself." (*The Will to Power*, pp. 545–46)

How does this affect us? *Twin Peaks* has always presented constant tension between hope and hopelessness, tension that becomes explicit at the end of *Twin Peaks: The Return*. Hope and hopelessness are symbiotic. One cannot exist without the other, as their relationship is one of mutual rejection and antagonism.

Cooper/Richard, in the final episode of *Twin Peaks: The Return*, learns that he faces a Sisyphean task—and he decides to accept it. He is an avatar of hope, of the dream that problems can be solved, that lives can be saved, that the state of things at present is not eternal. His task is ours. We, the audience members, bring our hope to the narrative of *Twin Peaks*—hope which will be continually disappointed. Do we accept that and immerse ourselves in its world nonetheless? Do we have Cooper's integrity and courage?

It doesn't matter. Lynch and Frost set out to haunt us, in waking life and in dreams. As FBI Agent Tamara Preston—who, in a sense, is one of *us* in the audience—says, about one of many mysteries that lies before her, "For my report, let's accept that as a 'known unknown'." (*Twin Peaks: The Final Dossier*, p. 107).

By the time we learn about the burden they have given us, *Twin Peaks* has already seeped into our souls. Even if we decide to reject it, we cannot escape what *Twin Peaks* has done to us. Once a certain epistemic threshold has been crossed, *amor fati* ceases to be a choice.

10
The Miss Twin Peaks Award Goes To . . .

ELIZABETH RARD'S DOPPELGÄNGER

A group of Norwegians sit diligently poring over the details of an investment contract that they're preparing to sign, a contract that will make Benjamin Horne a lot of money. In slinks a beautiful young woman in a pink sweater and a plaid skirt. Here hair is perfectly curled and her lips are a flirtatious shade of pink. She wanders over to the buffet and feigns interest in the spread. No one takes any notice of her. She walks lazily back along the wall, dragging her feet on the ground as she moves, letting out a sad little sigh. Still, no one notices. She leans against the wall, sticks out her perfectly tinted bottom lip, rolls her eyes, and releases a louder sigh. Slowly every head in the room turns to look at her. "Excuse me, is there something wrong, young pretty girl?" "They found my friend Laura, lying face down on a rocky beach, completely naked. She'd been murdered."

Cut to the lobby of the Great Northern. Chaos erupts as the Norwegians all check out at once, without signing the contract. A hotel employee stands behind the counter yelling "the Norwegians are leaving! The Norwegians are leaving!" while ringing a bell. Benjamin Horne can be seen through the window trying in vain to talk the potential investors back into the hotel. The same young woman watches the pandemonium unfold, laughing to herself. This is Audrey Horne. She has just destroyed her father's deal with the investors, and she has done it by getting other people to do what she wants them to do. Audrey Horne has power.

The town of Twin Peaks is at first glance a peaceful and charming small American town. There's a local diner where you can get a cup of coffee and a great piece of pie, a saw mill that employs many of the locals, and a bar where the citizens can unwind to some oddly surreal music at the end of a hard day's work. Everyone seems to know everyone by their first name here in Twin Peaks. But just below the surface there are enough secrets to keep an audience guessing for seasons to come. Many of these secrets involve power struggles between the various characters who call Twin Peaks their home, and many of those involved are women.

Twin Peaks has some truly memorable female characters, and these characters often use whatever means are at their disposal to gain fortunes, safety, and even love. But to a large extent the power they exhibit is the type of power Audrey displayed with the Norwegians, it is *power-over*, or the power to get other people to do the things that you wish. This is different than having the power to do something for yourself, and as some of the women will learn as very dangerous lessons, relying on your ability to manipulate others can leave you powerless when your charm runs out.

Twin Powers in Twin Peaks

When we talk about someone having power we usually mean that they have the power to control outcomes, or to make the things happen that they desire to have happen. But there are two types of power we can consider. *Power-over* is the power that one person has if they can get another person to do what they want. So, when Donna flirts with Harold in order to manipulate him into reading to her from Laura's secret diary, Donna is exerting power over Harold. He is doing something he would not normally do because of the influence Donna has over him. Many of the women in Twin Peaks rely on this type of power in order to get what they want, with varying degrees of success. The problem with this sort of power is that it is completely dependent on the reactions of other people. Donna, Laura, Audrey, and Josie especially use their beauty and charm in order to get men to do what they want, but when they're dealing with people who are immune to their charms they become powerless very quickly.

Another type of power, one that is not so easily lost, is *power-to*. This is power that comes from an individual's ability to directly change outcomes or circumstances for themselves. This power stems from abilities, talents, and resources. Since the individual has the ability, or has access to the resource, it is not dependent on the reactions of other people, and tends to be a more stable sort of power. An extreme example of this sort of power can be found in Nadine after her suicide attempt. In addition to believing she's a teenager ready for cheerleader tryouts, one upshot of Nadine's attempted suicide is that her body begins producing high levels of adrenaline, which makes her extremely strong. She can bench press her wrestling partners and tear doors from their hinges without breaking a sweat (often to the nervous surprise of those around her). This strength gives Nadine the power to do many things for herself, including giving Hank (the local thug and ne'er do well) a good walloping when he tries to attack Nadine's husband, Ed. Her ability is not dependent on the reactions of other people, and so it is power Nadine can count on regardless of who is around.

Poor Josie

The very first person we see in the pilot episode of *Twin Peaks* is Josie Packard, a beautiful and mysterious woman, sitting in front of a mirror slowly applying makeup to a face that looks like a porcelain mask. Josie has gained a small fortune here in Twin Peaks, inheriting a share in the local saw mill from her husband, Andrew Packard, who apparently died in a boating accident several years earlier. Josie uses her beauty and charm in order to get the men in her life to do what she desires, and she uses this influence for fortune, safety, and to undermine her main rival, Andrew's sister Catherine. Josie can't control Catherine directly, but she can control Catherine's husband, Pete Martell, to an extent.

In the first episode, after Laura's body is discovered, and it is learned that a saw mill worker's daughter has also gone missing, Josie calls for a work stoppage over Catherine's strong protests. Josie tells Pete to call the stoppage, which will cost the company money, and it is Pete who carries out the order. It's not immediately apparent why Pete would side with Josie over his own wife, but we soon see the way Josie interacts with Pete at home. When Josie thanks Pete later she is very cute with him, almost flirtatious. She is a young, beautiful woman and he is an old man, and her charms are not lost on him. Over the next few episodes we see Josie making Pete sandwiches, and agreeing to enter a fishing competition with Pete. We get the sense that Josie really does quite like Pete, but also that she needs him as an ally in her battles with Catherine. At one point Josie gets Pete to help her gain access to Catherine's safe, where she has two sets of books for the Mill, one authentic and one fake. This information allows Josie to uncover Catherine's plot to bankrupt the mill.

When Sheriff Harry S. Truman takes Special FBI Agent Dale Cooper to interview Pete about finding Laura's body, he also introduces him to Josie Packard. Harry calls her one of the most beautiful women in the state. Agent Cooper quickly infers that Harry is in love with Josie. Josie clearly has strong feelings for Harry, but she also attempts to use his love for her, and his position in law enforcement, to her advantage. After discovering the second notebook she tells Harry, who promises to keep her safe. When Josie is observed staking out a motel to get pictures of Catherine meeting with her lover and co-conspirator in the mill plot, Benjamin Horne, Harry confronts Josie about her involvement. Josie tells Harry that she hears Catherine talking about a fire at the mill. Josie is misleading Harry, as she herself is now working with Benjamin Horne in a plot to burn down the mill. Josie has even taken out a life insurance policy on Catherine, and plans to lure her to the mill so that Catherine will be killed in the fire.

If Harry had been able to view the information objectively and without emotional attachment, he might have suspected that Josie was not an innocent victim in this power struggle. As it is, when he comes to Agent Cooper with his concerns for Josie's safety, Cooper asks how much he really knows about Josie. Harry says that he knows all he needs to know, that he loves her and she's in trouble. Harry is unwilling to consider Josie's guilt because of the feelings he has for Josie, feelings that Josie is willing to exploit to keep suspicion off of herself, and to gain herself the protection of law enforcement.

When Josie returns to town after the fire, Harry is suspicious that Josie was involved somehow. However, when Harry tries to question her she dances around in her brand new and very expensive black negligee, insisting that he rip it off of her. Poor Harry gives up his line of questioning all too quickly and succumbs to Josie's seductions. Josie is using her beauty, and Harry's attraction to her, to control him. Every time he starts to question her about her involvement in illegal activities she responds with either tears that he could think such a thing, or with seduction meant to distract him from his investigation.

But Josie relies heavily on her charms to acquire her wealth and power, and her charms do not work on everyone. It is uncovered that Josie used her beauty to seduce Andrew Packard in order to steal his money, and that she arranged his supposed death and the cover-up with the help of Andrew's rival, Thomas Eckhardt. Everything begins to fall apart for Josie when she finds herself surrounded by people she cannot manipulate. Catherine returns, having not actually died in the fire. Pete seems so overjoyed with Catherine's resurrection that he sides with her more and more. Andrew Packard then returns as well, and reveals that he went into hiding when he realized that Josie and Thomas wanted to kill him. Knowing what he does about Josie he is completely unresponsive to her charms, and thus Josie no longer has power over him. And Thomas Eckhardt comes to town to claim Josie as his possession. We see that her charms have backfired with Eckhardt. She has seduced him in the past in order to control her situation, but rather than creating a willing servant, she has created a man who is dangerously obsessed with her, and will stop at nothing to own her.

Josie loses her control over Harry, not because he does not love her, but because she loves and cares for him too much to put him in danger. She is warned that if she goes to Harry for help that he will be killed. Unwilling to put his life in danger, she gives up the last ally she has, losing all of her power over the people and the world around her. Poor Josie ends up trapped in the wood in the great Northern Hotel (somehow) because her only source of power is her ability to manipulate the men around her. When that power crumbles she is left helpless and afraid.

Like Ducks at a Shooting Gallery

Audrey Horne is the beautiful, charming, and rather mischievous daughter of one of the richest men in Twin Peaks. She has the power to make men do what she wants, just by batting an eye or sticking out a pouty crimson lip, and she usually uses this power to create chaos for her own amusement. But when Laura is murdered, and dreamy Agent Cooper comes to town, Audrey decides to put her talents towards the task of helping to solve the murder, in part in the hopes that Cooper will realize that she is the perfect woman for him. Audrey flirts with Cooper every chance she gets, getting him to touch her hand and asking if his palms ever sweat the first time they meet. Cooper is clearly taken with her, although her young age (she's eighteen, he checked) and her involvement in the case guarantee that a man of Cooper's principles will not act on his interest. His affection for her does come in handy though. When she is later kidnapped he stops at nothing to rescue her.

But flirting with men is not the only way that Audrey exercises power over other people. When Audrey decides to help in the investigation she takes it upon herself to go undercover at the perfume counter where Laura worked, a perfume counter that is in the local department store owned by her father. Up to this point Audrey and Ben have had a strained relationship. After her stunt with the Norwegians, which Ben tied to her almost immediately, Ben tells her that, while Laura died only a few days ago, Audrey has been dead to him for years. Audrey is not on good enough terms with her father to simply ask to be placed at the perfume counter, rather she must manipulate him into doing what she wants. And she knows she can use the prospect of a loyal daughter to tempt him.

Audrey begins by asking her father if he's ashamed of her. She says that she wants to change and to learn the family business so that she can take over some day. Audrey is telling her father exactly what he wants to hear, and it is apparent that Ben genuinely wants to believe that his daughter is sincere. She goes on to say that she's willing to start at the bottom, perhaps at the department store working in cosmetics (or something). She asks if she can please be his daughter again. Ben agrees to get her started at the department store. Audrey has power over her father, which in turn gives her access to some of his power. He owns the store where she wants to work. She persuades him that she is sincere in her desire to reconcile and she can then use his power to get the desired position.

When she arrives at the department store she must once again rely on her ability to control the people around her, this time she exerts power over the manager. Audrey is set on getting a part-time job at the perfume counter, the place where Laura and another victim, Ronette Pulaski, both worked. But when Audrey arrives for her first day of work the manager informs her that she should start in the gift-wrapping department. A resourceful and (at times) unscrupulous young woman, Audrey quickly maneuvers the manager to give her exactly what she wants. She gets very close to the manager's face and whispers that she has her heart set on working the perfume counter. She tells him that he is going to assign her to perfume, but that he will tell her father that she is going to work in the wrapping department. She then tells him that if he doesn't do what she asks that she'll rip her dress and claim he made a pass at her. While we might not want to praise Audrey's methods in this particular situation, she does get results. She exerts power over the manager and pushes him to give here exactly what she desires, a spot at the perfume counter.

But as we saw with Josie, if your main source of power resides in your ability to get other people to do what you want, then that power can disappear quickly when you're surrounded by people who are not susceptible to your manipulations. Audrey is able to use her new spot at the perfume counter to discover that Laura and Ronette both worked at a Canadian brothel called One-Eyed Jack's, however when she arrives posing as a prospective employee she quickly realizes that she is in over her head.

She initially is able to convince the Madame of the brothel, Blackie, to give her employment as a prostitute. After admitting that she lied about her credentials, Audrey uses a rather suggestive trick with a cherry stem to demonstrate her qualifications. But Audrey loses control of the situation rapidly when Blackie discovers that she is unwilling to actually service the clients at One-Eyed Jack's, especially after she is placed in a room with her father, Ben Horne, who, as co-owner of the brothel, gets first crack at the new girls. Audrey is able to fend off his advances by disguising her identity with a mask and acting shy, but Blackie is furious that she allowed Ben to leave unsatisfied. Blackie then discovers that Audrey is Ben's daughter and decides to hold her captive in order to blackmail Ben for control of the brothel.

Audrey is in a huge amount of danger at this point. Blackie and her accomplices plan to kill her, and they keep her high on heroin while she is captive. Audrey has lived a life where everyone danced to her song, people were easily controlled and so Audrey would usually get exactly what she wanted. But now she is surrounded by people who are immune to her charms and her threats, and she is completely powerless for maybe the first time in her life. Like Josie she has relied mainly on her power over other people (mostly men) to get what she wants, and like Josie, when her control ran out she found herself in rather dire straits.

Luckily for Audrey her charms had a powerful impact on Agent Cooper, who will eventually come to rescue her, but Audrey has also learned an important lesson about the limitations of power over others, and the dangers of relying too heavily on that type of power. Fortunately though, after Audrey is rescued (and detoxed from the heroin she was pumped full of) she has a chance to begin to change her approach. Audrey begins to actually learn how to run the business. She acquires skills and ability that will give her power to do things for herself, rather than merely relying on her ability to help other people. When her father, Ben, suffers a nervous breakdown she helps run the business and enlists aid from people he trusts in returning him to his full health. Ben begins to trust Audrey and gives her more responsibilities, sending her on business trips, and having her run his "save the pine weasel" campaign.

Audrey never loses her charm, and throughout the second season she will flirt with the men around her in order to grease the wheels a bit, but she shifts from relying on her ability to manipulate others as her primary source of power, to acquiring the skills and knowledge needed to gain the power to do things for herself. By the end of the second season Audrey Horne is one of the more powerful characters on the show, and it is a power that is stable and dependable. Of course, by the time we catch up with Audrey in season three she seems to have lost all of her power, but we are not given quite enough clues to determine where her downfall originated, so we will leave off speculation until all of the information is in.

An Honorable Mention

Both Josie and Audrey are beautiful and charming women who exercised great manipulative power over the men they interacted with, and both find themselves powerless and in danger when they are surrounded by people they cannot control. Audrey is able to transition from her precarious reliance on power-over to a more sustainable form of power, the power to do things for oneself. Josie is, unfortunately, unable to make a similar transition, and it leads to her eventual tragic downfall. The upshot here is that typically having the power to do something for yourself is to be preferred to having the power to get other people to do things for you, as the later sort of power can disappear more easily with the changing of your circumstances.

But there is one woman in Twin Peaks who may have so much power over (some) of the people around her that she is safe relying merely on her power over other people to keep her secure in both health and fortune. The cursed widow Lana Budding Milford has such a strong ability to control the men around her that it insulates her from almost all negative outcomes. Lana is introduced as the fiancé of Dougie Milford, another of Twin Peaks's most wealthy individuals. Every man who meets her seems immediately taken by her, charmed to the point of being almost hypnotized by her beauty and sexual energy. The implication is that Lana is using her incredible powers of attraction to marry an old, wealthy gentleman, in order to procure financial security. When Dougie dies the first night of their honeymoon due to, er, overexertion, all of the men in town fall at her feet comforting her and trying to assure her that Dougie's death was not her fault (she believes she is cursed).

The only person who is initially suspicious is Dougie's estranged brother Dwayne, who believes that Lana is an evil temptress who married Dougie for his money and then caused his death. Things escalate until Dwayne shows up at the sheriff's station brandishing a firearm and threatening to shoot Lana. Cooper has noticed Lana's unusual ability to completely control the men around her, and takes a risk by placing Lana and Dwayne in a conference room together to work things out. When, a few moments later, they take a peak in on the two they find them kissing and planning to adopt a child together. Lana's power over men seems to have no bounds, and thus gives her more reliable power over other people than either Josey or Audrey could manage. Her power does have its limitations though, as it does not extend to women—a limitation that she feels when she loses the coveted Miss Twin Peaks competition, due in part to there being a female member on the jury.

A Powerful Lesson

Twin Peaks is a place of both danger and opportunity, and to survive and prosper in this microcosm you need to have power that you can depend upon. Many of the female characters rely heavily on their delightful personalities and their well-groomed appearances in order to control the people around them, giving them power over others. But time and again this power fails them at just the wrong moment. There is Donna, who couldn't quite get control over James, and so loses him again and again to the temptations of other women. There is Shelly, whose happiness and well-being are largely at the whims of the men in her life. And there is of course poor Laura, who could make every man in Twin Peaks dance to her tune, every man except her tormentor Bob. In the end Laura had to die in order to escape from Bob, as she had no power to control him, and she had no other recourse.

But some of the women of Twin Peaks are able to move beyond a reliance on power over other people, and truly gain their own power to do things. Nadine gains incredible physical strength after her suicide attempt. Audrey focuses on learning how to run the company, instead of getting other people to do what she wants. Ben once told Cooper that men fall under Audrey's spell like ducks in a shooting gallery. But in a town where everyone has a secret, and everyone is looking out for their own interest, that sort of power can only take you so far.

As Audrey tells Bobby Briggs after she has begun to acquire power within her father's company, she's the one people have to suck up to now.

11
The Mother of All Bombs

LEIGH KOLB

Laura Palmer—the murdered Homecoming Queen who was taken more seriously in death than in life—is the central figure in *Twin Peaks*. She embodies the common reality that men see women as destructive forces to be destroyed or victims to be saved. Laura was seen as both.

The feminist literary icons Sandra Gilbert and Susan Gubar have explained (*The Madwoman in the Attic*) how, in the fury of the 1800s—war, industrialization, rapid social change—the Victorian-era ideal woman was submissive, confined to domesticity and physically thin, pale, and frail. The nineteenth-century poet Coventry Patmore wrote of the Angel in the House, a selfless wife whose virtue is in making a man "great" (p. 22). Angels are supernatural, celestial entities who are not alive and not of this Earth. It's no surprise, then, that these ideals culminated in what Edgar Allan Poe saw as a perfect literary subject: the death of a "beautiful woman," he says, "is unquestionably the most poetical topic in the world" (p. 25).

As Gilbert and Gubar point out, "the aesthetic cult of ladylike fragility and delicate beauty—no doubt associated with the moral cult of the angel-woman—obliged 'gentell' women to 'kill' themselves . . . into art objects: slim, pale, passive beings whose 'charms' eerily recalled the snow, porcelain immobility of the dead" (p. 25). Perfection, then, could easily be seen as a beautiful dead girl, preserved in plastic.

As the "progress" of the twentieth century pushed along, these ideals did not go away, but simply mutated in a world dominated by new forms of warfare and rampant capitalism and consumption.

As the starts and fits of social progress for women paralleled the invention of biological warfare, nuclear warfare, and advances in manufacturing, America did not quite know what to do with women, who had been—ideally—socially, civically, or even literally dead. So the dying girl still enraptures us in our fictions and our realities. Female power and sexuality terrify us. Women's voices are consistently mistrusted or killed in deference to toxic masculine violence.

In *Twin Peaks*, we see all of these ideals unfold and exist in the chaos of modernity. From *Twin Peaks* to *Fire Walk with Me*, and especially in *Twin Peaks: The Return*, these violently colliding themes of feminine ideals, masculine power, and the ways in which warfare and modernity distort both, exist in explosive and disturbing ways, highlighting what it really means to be an American Woman.

David Lynch's avant-garde, dreamlike artistic style, along with Mark Frost's storytelling, combine to expose philosophical ideas about violence, femininity versus masculinity, and how we conflate it all in modern American society. Even in an alternative life as Carrie Page, Laura says, "I tried to keep a clean house, keep everything organized. I was too young to know better." Is there no way out?

Mrs. Palmer, There Are Things Dark and Heinous in This World

In *The Return*, it's made clear that the Trinity nuclear test on July 16th 1945 birthed a kind of evil (BOB via the ancient Judy) that was unleashed upon the world and manifests itself by feeding off human pain, raping, killing, and destroying. While the creation and detonation of the bomb was ostensibly to bring about peace via destruction, Hannah Arendt points out that "The Second World War was not followed by peace but by a cold war and the establishment of the military-industrial-labor complex" ("On Violence," p. 111).

She goes on to say that aggressiveness is an instinct much like hunger or the sex drive. She notes that "lack of provocation" appears to lead to "instinct frustration," or "repressed aggressiveness," which psychologists say will cause a "damming up of 'energy' whose eventual explosion will be all the more dangerous" (pp. 157–58). *The Return* shows us what the original *Twin Peaks* iterations did not: that this insatiable hunger for garmonbozia that we see Black Lodge creatures devour (BOB and Judy especially) was born from the insatiable destruction of the evils of nuclear warfare. If not born, the evil was unleashed—and the dammed-up "energy" that explodes does so in the literal sense (a nuclear bomb), but also in the lives of individuals as they inhabit a world that is increasingly hostile to the values it pretends to revere (community, connection, love, and the concept of "home" that is woven throughout the *Twin Peaks* story).

We find out in *The Return* that Sarah Palmer herself is one of the "dark and heinous" things that Dale Cooper warns her about in the original series. The prevailing theory is that Sarah Palmer is Judy, or is at the very least inhabited by Judy, as she seeks to reclaim BOB and the garmonbozia that Laura provides. According to David Auerbach, "BOB was a garmonbozia glutton, and Laura was an everlasting gobstobber of garmonbozia, until she died (an outcome which BOB/Leland did not want). The Black Lodge consumes garmonbozia, but cannot generate it independently." Laura—as victim, prostitute, Queen—was valued most highly as a consumable good.

Laura's pain and suffering was misunderstood and fed upon by those around her (whether they wanted to feast on it or somehow save her from it). We're taken back to that Victorian ideal and to the literary manifestation of it—this idea that a dying or dead girl both embodies the fear and oppression of women and also positions the protagonist—often seen as Dale Cooper, but also revealed to be Judy—to have motive. In all of these themes, however, the young woman lacks the agency to define herself. *Twin Peaks* shows us that one of the most "dark and heinous" things in the world is how we dismiss and ultimately destroy girls and women.

According to feminist psychologist Carol Gilligan,

> As we have listened for centuries to the voices of men and the theories of development that their experience informs, so we have come more recently to notice not only the silence of women but the difficulty in hearing what they say when they speak . . . The failure to see the different reality of women's lives and to hear the differences in their voices stems in part from the assumption that there is a single mode of social experience and interpretation. (*In a Different Voice*, p. 173)

Naido's eyes are shut; her voice is garbled as she desperately tries to communicate with people. Andy understands that she's very important, and she is. So many women in *Twin Peaks* have the answers and provide essential information and wisdom, but their voices are often obscured until they cannot be anymore.

Consider the revelations and contributions of the following women's voices: Laura Palmer (via her diary), Audrey Horne, Margaret Lanterman ("The Log Lady"), Diane Evans, Norma Jennings, Tammy Preston (especially in *The Secret History of Twin Peaks*), Betty Briggs, Ruth Davenport, Maggie Brown, Constance Talbot, and Cynthia Knox.

Many of the wives of *Twin Peaks* are seen as being "embittered," as one critic writes. However, this criticism does not take into account the heavy burdens these women are carrying, and the remarkable mental and emotional loads they must bear. When Janey-E snaps at Dougie and says, "What a mess you've made of our lives," she is stating a fact. Without her, their lives would have fallen apart.

You'd Better Hurry. My Mother Is Coming

In *The Return,* "Part 3," Dale Cooper is released into a kind of White Lodge waiting area before he is incompletely returned to Earth as Dougie Jones. As he falls, he descends into a purple landscape, an ocean-like world of dark liquidity that brings to mind childbirth. He navigates a canal and a hallway—confused, like an infant experiencing a new world for the first time. Naido "sacrifices" herself for his safety, and American Girl (played by the actress who played Ronette Pulaski) tells him to hurry because "my mother is coming." Both Naido and American Girl share Diane's aesthetic—their haircuts and clothing—and we will later learn that Naido is Diane. These women lead the way, and help Cooper navigate himself into the next realm. The theme of women and mothers having knowledge that guides characters persists throughout the *Twin Peaks* universe.

The "mother" that American Girl warns Cooper of is The Mother, or Judy. This is clear in the revelations of "Part 8," as we see the same creature who emerged from the glass box (as she was chasing Cooper) vomit a primordial soup of evil—including BOB, in concert with the nuclear bomb.

Arendt says, "To beget and to give birth are no more creative than to die is annihilating; they are but different phases of the same, ever-recurring cycle in which all living things are held as though they were spellbound" (p. 179). Birth and death are intertwined in such a way that the possibility of creation is so often met with the reality of destruction. The realities of childbirth and motherhood and the nuclear bomb and its aftermath both illustrate the monstrous emptiness that modernity and patriarchy offer.

According to Bethany Webster, the concept of the "mother wound" is one that suggests that patriarchy leads to deep divisions between mothers and daughters: "The mother wound is a product of patriarchy . . . it is the mother's projection of her own unhealed wounds on the daughter and the dysfunctional coping mechanisms that have resulted from generations of female oppression. Patriarchy distorts dynamics between mothers and daughters that leave both disempowered." The Mother/Sarah Palmer and Laura illustrate this concept, as do the interactions in "Part 3" and "Part 8" that reflect the pain and destruction of birth, and an ultimate fear of a violent and vengeful mother.

On a less conceptual level, the realities of motherhood are shown via "Drugged-out Mother," Janey-E, Sarah Palmer, Sylvia Horne, Doris Truman, and Shelly Briggs. The desperation, addiction, violence, and emptiness that dominate most of the mothers' lives in *Twin Peaks* are indicative of a world, as Arendt says, that ensures "the general future of mankind has nothing to offer to individual life, whose only certain future is death" (p. 129).

The Past Dictates the Future

Arendt also notes that "The practice of violence, like all action, changes the world, but the most probable change is to a more violent world" (p. 177). The detonation of a nuclear bomb unleashed a kind of violent evil into the world that was capable of horrific violence and despair that especially victimized women, according to *The Return*.

The conflation of idolizing women as needing to be perfect, and that they are especially perfect as a dying or dead "angel-woman," with women's relative gaining of rights and autonomy in the twentieth century made way for a conflicting view of American womanhood. It was acceptable for women to work in industry, but not when the boys came home from war. Women (at least white middle- and upper-class women) were expected to be perfect mothers and housewives in a world where automation of household tasks and prepackaging of convenience foods whittled away at the necessity and valuing of household work. The backlash against women's rights, and the realization that women could indeed work and succeed in masculine fields, led to a contrast of ideals that answered the Victorian ideals in a grotesque way.

Women's liberation was to be feared, women were to be perfect, and women were to be sexualized without the benefits of being able to be sexual. This complicated fear and idolatry is illustrated by iconography of the world wars:

- **In World War I and World War II, pin-ups of scantily clad women became popular for American soldiers to collect and display.**

- The use of the word "bombshell" to describe a beautiful woman began in the 1930s and 1940s.

- World War II fighter planes had nose art of pin-ups, and sometimes had this artwork on the bombs themselves.

- The B-29 bomber that dropped the first atomic bomb (on Hiroshima) was named "Enola Gay" after the pilot's mother.

- In the early 2000s, America created the "Mother of All Bombs" (MOAB), which was dropped in Afghanistan in 2017.

Is Laura the antidote for the bomb, as is suggested by Señorita Dido giving her to the world? Note the imagery in "Part 8": the incredible bomb sequence at times looks like an ultrasound, or a frantic nebulous birth canal. As The Fireman floats up in the White Lodge, the gold sparkles that burst forth from his head resemble a uterus. Señorita Dido kisses the gold orb that contains Laura (a fertilized egg), and sends her through the fallopian tube-like golden arm that releases her into the world.

What do we make of women's capacity for violence, and their capacity for healing? American history suggests the two are monstrously intertwined based on a culture of treating women as perfect yet fallen others, best when oppressed (or even dead). It's no wonder that we have such twisted notions of women and warfare, and name our weapons after mothers. As Gilligan says, "In the life cycle, as in the Garden of Eden, the woman has been the deviant" (p. 6). We both worship and are terrified of female power, not knowing whether it is the bomb or the salve.

Write It in Your Diary

Gilligan brings up The Angel in the House within the context of how twentieth-century feminist thinkers framed the ideal:

Virginia Woolf's realization that she had to strangle this Angel if she were to begin writing illuminates women's need to silence false feminine voices in order to speak for themselves. (p. x)

In *Fire Walk with Me*, Donna asks Laura, "Do you think that if you were falling in space ... that you would slow down after a while, or go faster and faster?" Laura answers, "Faster and faster. And for a long time you wouldn't feel anything. And then you'd burst into fire. Forever ... And the angels wouldn't help you. Because they've all gone away." Woolf might have hoped the angels Laura references would have instead been women who give Laura a sense of independent self and power. Instead, Laura's angel only appears after she's been brutally murdered—a victim of both the mother wound and patriarchal violence.

Gilligan uses the Persephone myth to contextualize our persistent destruction of mother-daughter relationships through patriarchal violence and control, and our need for girls to "die" or be silenced for "the fertility of the Earth" and "the life cycle" to continue (p. 23). Gilligan says that "the imagery of the Persephone myth returns, charting the mysterious disappearance of the female self in adolescence by mapping an underground world kept secret because it is branded by others as selfish and wrong" (p. 51).

Laura keeps a diary, in which she feels more comfortable expressing her complex thoughts and desires than she does with anyone around her. Donna, Bobby, and James seek to understand her in flawed ways. Her parents are disconnected and abusive. She's the Homecoming Queen. She snorts coke and works as a prostitute. She is heard by no one, and understood by no one. Her diary is even violated by Leland/BOB. Laura is held hostage in life and in death. In the Red Room, the presence of three Venus statues— Venus de Medici, Venus de Milo, and Venus of Arles—illustrate the ideal woman, which Laura was supposed to be. The goddess of love, cast in stone, in various states of brokenness.

You Wanna Know Who Killed Laura?

We destroy girls and set up women to fail in a society that both idolizes and denigrates everything feminine, while not listening to their voices. In *Fire Walk with Me*, Dale Cooper tells Albert that he's seen visions of the next murder victim (whom we know would be Laura): "She's in high school. She's sexually active. She is using drugs. She's crying out for help." Albert replies, "Well damn, Cooper, that really narrows it down. You're talking about half the high school girls in America!"

In *Fire Walk with Me*, Laura looks up at her bedroom ceiling in despair—high, waiting for BOB to rape her. In *The Return*, we see that same overhead shot repeated as Becky looks up after snorting coke, in brief ecstasy before she's again beaten by Steven. Gersten looks up after Steven shoots himself. Diane/Linda looks up and cries as she's having sex with Dale/Richard, as she attempts to exorcise being raped by Mr. C.

In "Part 16," Audrey recreates her iconic, uninhibited dance at the Roadhouse. She's interrupted by masculine violence—a jealous man lunges across the room and begins beating another man.

Gilligan says that patriarchal societies are predicated on girls losing their voices and creating an "inner division or split, so that large parts of themselves are kept out of relationship . . . As girls become the carriers of unvoiced desires and unrealized possibilities, they are inevitably placed at considerable risk and even in danger" (p. xxiii). Society silences girls and women, and masculine violence—rape, assault, gunshots—crushes them.

The irony of Laura Palmer is that the show itself, and so many of the characters, want to "find" and "save" her: "Laura is the one." However, "the tragedy of Laura Palmer is that *no one* wanted her to die, yet *everyone* caused her to suffer." Even when Cooper attempts to rewrite her history in "Part 18," her wounds are opened and she suffers more. *Twin Peaks* shows clearly how society and so many men enact literal and figurative violence against women and girls.

You're a Very Bad Person, Chad

While even well-meaning men like Cooper end up trauma-tizing women, *Twin Peaks* shows that good men attempt to embody, as Gilligan would point out, an ethic of care and a more feminine, compassionate communication style.

The Return shows toxic masculinity through many char-acters, including the little boy who steals and shoots his fa-ther's gun in "Part 11." The child wears camouflage, like his father, and postures. Bobby—a rebellious son who has made good, just like Garland Briggs knew he would—looks almost confused at the display. In "Part 18," the cowboys at Judy's Diner accost the waitress and Dale/Richard shoots them and deep-fries their guns (what's more American than that?).

Mr. C, Richard, and Chad are perhaps the most revolting examples of toxic masculinity. Mr. C is a caricature of toxic American masculinity: he assaults and rapes women; he drives a sleek black car and a giant lifted truck. He intimi-dates through blackmail and violence, and kills a man after beating him in arm wrestling. If Dale Cooper is a (however flawed) model of modern masculinity, Mr. C is his foil. Richard, Mr. C's son (conceived when he raped Audrey), is a worthy protégé; we meet him for the first time when he's smoking in the Roadhouse and choking and assaulting a young woman, threatening to rape her. He violently steals from his grandmother. He kills a young boy and attempts to murder the witness. Chad lies and cheats, and is remarkably insensitive to everyone around him.

In "On Violence," Arendt quotes Jean-Paul Sartre's pref-ace to Franz Fanon's *The Wretched of the Earth*: "'irrepress-ible violence . . . is man recreating himself,' that it is through 'mad fury' that 'the wretched of the earth' can 'become men'." She goes on to quote Sartre: "a man feels himself more of a man when he is imposing himself and making others the in-struments of his will, which gives him incomparable pleas-ure" (p. 135). As Fanon and Sartre suggest, this is how men have become men throughout human history. This is not, as Arendt asserts, a sustainable model.

Twin Peaks shows that for men to be *good*, they must not revere or embody toxic masculinity and violence. The "good men" of *Twin Peaks* (Dale Cooper, Harry and Frank Truman, Ed Hurley, James Hurley, Garland Briggs, Hawk, grown-up Bobby Briggs, and Andy Brennan) value and display ethics of care and compassion.

Gilligan describes the following as traditionally feminine ethics and roles: "Sensitivity to the needs of others and the assumption of responsibility for taking care . . . an overriding concern with relationships and responsibilities . . . nurturer, caretaker, and helpmate." She notes that historically, men have—in "psychological theories and economic arrangements"—"tended to assume or devalue that care" (pp. 16–17). In *Twin Peaks*, the men who are considered to be good, to be "true" men (as the Log Lady describes Harry and Frank), value and embody that kind of care.

You Were Manufactured

While Arendt didn't write extensively about the nuclear bomb, what she did write was clear and in keeping with her prolific writing about the nature of violence. Here, she is responding to nuclear power, but could just as well be writing a synopsis of "Part 8":

> for it is not natural processes that are unleashed here. Instead, processes that do not occur naturally on earth are brought to earth to produce a world or destroy it. These processes themselves come from the universe surrounding the earth, and in bringing them under his control, man is here no longer acting as a natural organic being but rather as a being capable of finding its way about in the universe, despite the fact that it can live only under conditions provided by earth and its nature. (Quoted in Taylor, "On the Possibility of an Arendtian Nuclear Theory")

The "unnatural" creation of nuclear weaponry is related to the "unnatural" Blue Rose. In learning about the original case, Agent Tammy Preston understands that the Blue Rose

"is not a natural thing. The dying woman wasn't natural."
What is natural, supernatural, dreamt, or manufactured is
a question that runs throughout the *Twin Peaks* landscape.
In the book, *The Secret History of Twin Peaks*, we're given a
dossier that examines these questions over hundreds of
years of American history. The questions in *The Return* dwell
in the space between World War II and the present, and the
economic and social tumults that have come at the heels of
the first nuclear bomb.

   After the war, as Arendt points out, peace did not come. The
bomb simply made way for a cold war and a "military-industrial-labor complex." *The Return* shows the Convenience Store
as a hub of oil, capitalism, masculinity, darkness, and decay.
The Woodsmen—perhaps prophetic relics of an American
economy that relied upon coal mining—revive Mr. C, attempting to keep whole a destructive American masculinity based
on the burning of fossil fuels (note the older female patron at
Judy's Diner in the final episode—the front page of her news-
paper had a photo of windmills). We had to manufacture a
great deal after World War II—the 1950s saw American manufacturing at its peak, whether it be cars, microwaves, televi-
sions, or washing machines. America also had to attempt to
manufacture a social order that was pushing back against the
liberation that women had been fighting for generations.

   The rampant consumerism and capitalism that defines
the "greatness" of America in the post-World War II era was
great due to economic gains, not social gains, as it was an era
that celebrated the myth of gender roles—man as breadwin-
ner and woman as mother. Gilligan says that "these stereotypes reflect a conception of adulthood that is itself out of
balance, favoring the separateness of the individual self over
connection to others, and leaning more toward an autonomous life of work than toward the interdependence of
love and care" (p. 17). The "feminine" notions of love and care
have consistently been threatened by not only capitalism
and consumerism, but also the threats of nuclear warfare.
These social and economic frameworks are manufactured;
they are not natural.

Is It Future or Is It Past?

In "Part 8," we see a young girl—possibly Sarah Palmer—lulled to sleep by the voice of the Woodsman over the radio. It is 1956. She has just kissed a boy. She is a young teenager, basking in her youth and new love—and also lives in the shadow of a childhood that saw a nuclear bomb detonate. Arendt says of this generation: "It is only natural that the new generation should live with greater awareness of the possibility of doomsday . . . not because they are younger but because this was their first decisive experience in the world" (p. 119). When the girl opens her mouth while asleep, letting in the monstrous frog-moth, it's almost as if it's an organic process. If this is indeed what "awakens" Judy in Sarah Palmer, are we meant to see this as inevitable? The world does not truly have love and hope to offer—just destruction, while both silencing and using women in the destruction.

The gaping mother wound between Laura and Sarah seems inevitable in a culture that so dismisses, destroys, and punishes women and relationships between mothers and daughters. In *The Return*, both women remove their faces to reveal what hides behind the mask: Sarah reveals horror before she brutally rips apart an intimidating and offensive man at the bar, much like the night-vision wild lionesses that rips apart the bison on her television. Laura reveals pure light—perfection, or nuclear fallout. Neither can survive; both suffer.

What then, is it to be an American Woman? The slow, distorted song, "American Woman" by the Muddy Magnolias, plays when we meet Mr. C. Does violent masculinity define her? The song plays again when Diane's doppelganger goes to tell Gordon, Albert, and Tammy her story—that Mr. C raped her. Is that what it means to be an American Woman? To have been assaulted? When Mike tells Diane's doppelgänger that someone manufactured her, she says, "I know. Fuck you." Is that what it means to be an American Woman? To live with the knowledge that your ideal self—what you look like and how you behave—has been manufactured by a hostile society? Is it time for her to finally say "Fuck you"?

Manufactured, assaulted, ignored, killed, and wrapped in plastic. The Angel in the House has arrived on the shores of the twenty-first century. We'd better put down our weapons and listen to her.

12
It's Not about BOB—It Never Was

CHERISE HUNTINGFORD

Twin Peaks is, of course, a cautionary tale on the malevolence of the mundane.

But more than that, it's a love letter to insanity. "Normal" is the bad guy. *Crazy* is the hero rolling into town on a white steed—*or in an '81 Dodge Diplomat*—spooking head-twisters from the Douglas firs. Only an unraveler of "reason" can decipher the town's mysteries.

Lynch litters the Peaks with cryptograms—hints at the deception of the banal; abstruse clues to some barely submerged, bloated, and moldering horror, but *madness*, dissimilarly—in the endlessly strange place beside Snoqualmie Falls, at least—is not simply a teasing conceit; a lunatic zoetrope of symbolism.

Jiving dwarves, zigzagging alternate dimensions and arms that bend back . . . their manifestation portends a purgative for the small town's malaise; but they also bring with them something immense and transcendental. Something bigger than mere antidote—a jagged red pill to tear a hole in the universe itself.

I Have No Idea Where This Will Lead Us

I don't think that people accept the fact that life doesn't make sense. I think it makes people terribly uncomfortable.

—DAVID LYNCH

There's a specific movie genre dedicated to messing with its audience—coined by Andreas Holskov the "mind-fuck films"—and David Lynch is largely credited for its injection into mainstream cinema. Its primary typifier is dissonance; not much seems to add up, and nothing necessarily *has* to add up. The suspension of disbelief is wrought tenuously taut and the plot tightropes its way across with the attitude *I could give a shit*.

Twin Peaks, though made for TV, has always been described as "cinematic" in feel, barely contained within the rigid structure of primetime parameters, pushing the limits of episodic narrative; *and logic*. It's a mind screw movie eked out over months of viewers' cognitive distress.

The fact that people have such a hard time "getting" *Twin Peaks* has become an enduring intertextual gag. Even fans make the mistake of trying to theorize its contents—only to receive the proverbial finger Lynch so loves to dispense.

The director exploits this mythos of insanity to exponential degree in the first episodes of *Twin Peaks: The Return*, and if you didn't know better, you'd think it was satire; a dendritic, tumorous talking tree known as "The Arm"("The Return, Part 2"), inter-dimensional travel via plug points ("The Return, Part 3"), a couple slaughtered mid-coitus by a glass box entity ("The Return, Part 1"), and Shelly Johnson claiming James Hurley has "always been cool" ("The Return, Part 2")—but a few ludicrous inexplicabilities conspiring to cull early on the demographic which needs rational answers to understand the point of the show.

No matter how our brains may short-circuit and smoulder at the suggestion, we must accept that perhaps madness *is* the point—an exultation of madness to the extent that it holds intrinsic value in its purity; unencumbered by figurative didactic. *Madness for madness's sake.*

And yet—Lynch's television triumph is so *arresting* in its anti-rationalism, tearing in two that shivering scarlet swathe to reveal a glimpse of a freedom exquisite beyond conventional form; the implication that Lynch's distinct brand of madness—*his art*—has purpose beyond its own sake.

Despite (or *because of*) the show's unarticulated mysteries, we're made privy to a schism in our basic understanding of the world and its expression. And we're disturbed, mesmerized, disoriented; anything but unaffected, and moved to ponder the uniqueness of this surreal experience.

Have You Ever Seen Something Startling that Others Cannot See?

I believe I was visited by a Giant last night.

—DALE COOPER

Twin Peaks, for all its banal blue-collar burgh affectations, operates on a distinctly paranormal plane. The environs vibrate with an eerie electromagnetism; a Bermuda Triangle slap-bang in loggers' suburbia.

A "demonic" entity (named BOB—*the irony*) stalks the town in Seasons One through Three, as well as in *Fire Walk with Me* (a fulminant, holographic angel also appears at the apotheosis of the movie prequel), but the subtext is not that celestial creatures and denizens of the Biblical Pit walk among the simple folks; as we know, *subtext* is not really how Lynch rolls—his creative process, a transcendental meditative exercise, apparently (*Catching the Big Fish*)—is intuitive, not intellectual.

An explicitly *religious* theme might not tether the apparitions to something spiritual, but they, along with the rest of the Lynchian dementedness, remain artefacts of the *metaphysical*, at the very least suggestive of an alternate dimension on the flip-side of the TP reality.

Lynch does not romanticize madness—the frequent bizarrities are always discomfiting, and the "madmen/women's" sufferings are often extreme (pivotal character Laura Palmer, both psychically sensitive to the surrounding electromagnetic "force field", and privy to the greater horrors behind the picket fence, languishes between hard-to-watch states of grotesque mania and suicidal melancholy). Instead, madness is treated by Lynch with *reverence*—a posture often reserved for some deific aspect beyond our scope of comprehension, yet possessing the potential to hold sway over us. In *Twin Peaks*, madness indeed has metaphysical power (or is synonymous with it)—sometimes destructive, but always in opposition to the real antagonist, the innate insidiousness of humanity.

Socrates himself describes madness in telestic terms in *Phaedrus*:

> Madness, provided it comes as the gift of heaven, is the channel by which we receive the greatest blessings . . . the men of old who gave things their names saw no disgrace or reproach in madness; otherwise they would not have connected it with the name of the noblest of arts, the art of discerning the future, and called it the manic art . . . So, according to the evidence provided by our ancestors, madness is a nobler thing than sober sense . . . madness comes from God, whereas sober sense is merely human.

For Socrates, there are two types of insanity impinging on human affairs: "psychic disharmony" or mental illness, and possession by the gods—both of which Lynch explores, exploits, and juxtaposes to mind-bending excess in *Twin Peaks*—but it is only the latter species of madness that the philosopher believes to be the font of "the greatest blessings."

His words are plainly theistic; but Socrates's central point is that discernment—*or truth seeking*—is attained via communion with *something more than* our basic, limiting faculties of cognition: societally-shaped reason and rationale.

Oneiric shaman, Special Agent Dale Cooper, is arguably in touch with some obscure source of "divine madness"— if not also "divine" himself, as the *Twin Peaks* hero. Of course, Agent Cooper is not *mad* . . . at least not in the strictly diagnostic sense of the word. There's that Diane-dictaphone quirk, the inexplicable devotion to roadhouse gastronomy, and the Tibetan Method (*Twin Peaks*: "Zen, or the Skill to Catch a Killer"); but these are mere eccentricities. It is really in dreams—playground of the spirit dimension—that he departs from seeming sanity and opens himself to mystic suggestion—a nascent Oracle, in Socratic terms; *a divinely inspired madman.* And it is during this unconscious Delphic-esque delirium that the agent discovers various *Twin Peaks* truths, as well as a larger, less articulate, yet more profound Truth.

Unforgettable as he is, Agent Coop is not the first incarnation of his kind. Ancient Greeks frequented the Temple of Apollo to receive the augur priestess's visions—said to have been conjured during ecstatic "frenzies," and the Romantics went on to embrace this classical figure of a deranged psychic, reimagined as the *furor poeticus,* or the "mad poet"—possessed by an otherworldly Muse.

In response to the Enlightenment philosophy which denounced madness as the dangerous affliction of "non-reason," the Romantics invoked the Greek *furor poeticus* trope as "a revolutionary and liberating madness that could free the imagination from the 'restraint of conformity'."

The back-to-front world of *Twin Peaks,* in a mimesis loyal to Romantic creed, depicts "normal" as the true evil, and the rational, run-of-the-Packard-mill townsfolk play the bogeymen (*but what about BOB?*—more on him later). The upshot is that the town requires a hero who *defies* convention and conventional logic, inspired and driven by a kind of "madness"—in short: the mad poet incarnate.

Joseph Meringolo writes that the eighteenth-century spectacle of segregating madmen from the greater populace into those sanitarium-cum-torture-chamber prototypes, coincided with an "allegorical spectacle" of madness in the arts. Instigated by the Romantic thinkers as a rejection of pragmatic boundaries placed on creativity, works that celebrated the morbid, the monstrous, and the insane, contested the "institutional misappropriation" of madness. *Twin Peaks* is both notorious and esteemed for doing just the same; contesting the age-old restriction on creative thought, the taboo on non-empiric enigmas, and most acutely in that Cooper stands as the obvious proxy for Lynch—his creator having transposed himself not only into the character's permeable consciousness, but into the agent's ability to interpret the unseen glyphs of existence using secrets only revealed in reveries.

Lynch is a dark Romantic; Cooper, his mad poet. And, as it transpires—his monster, too.

You May Be Fearless in This World . . .

He is BOB!
Eager for fun!
He wears a smile.
Everybody run!

—MIKE

It's almost impossible to label Coop—the *real* one—as "deranged." His impeccable manners, fundamentally American values, and predilection for the prosaic pleasures of cherry pie and damn fine coffee offset his regular secondments beyond the red curtain (even as *The Return*'s reincarnate, fugue-addled Dougie, his co-characters perceive him as merely offbeat). The result is an idiosyncratic character imbued with charm and tinted by mystique—an easier pill to swallow than a full-blown lunatic. And so, we accept Coop's decorously proffered arm, led through shifting dimensions and insane dioramas, the likes of which would make us scream—did we not have our level-headed (albeit mildly eccentric) law enforcer as guide.

As federal agents go—even neo-noir styled ones who tend to eschew the finer points of jurisprudence—Dale Cooper is an unorthodox specimen. But he is not "mad" in his non-empirical methods of detection; he simply arrives at the answers via an alternate set of senses, during what can only be described as a spiritual encounter (MIKE, the possessing spirit of a one-armed travelling salesman who supplies the agent paranormal intel, makes himself known not just to Coop, but also to Laura and Leland Palmer (*Fire Walk with Me*); he is not a symptom of psychosis, a product of Cooper's imaginings—if not a supernatural being himself, he represents, at the very least, an interlinked sentience within *Twin Peaks*).

Upon waking from these encounters, Coop is burdened by hideous revelations; the Romantics would've called this "melancholia"—in the agent's case, not so much the real-world psychological moroseness (as generally understood by "melancholy"), but the abstract philosophical notion "mythologized since the time of Aristotle as a state of superior insight"—and "specifically considered by the Romantics to be a higher state of consciousness."

If we had to break the Lynchian golden rule and look for allegory, Cooper's apocalyptic discernments might stand for a profound world-weariness that, somewhat counterintuitively, can only come from almost pathological introspection; the kind of "madness" many believed afflicted the first Romantics—and the same madness that ultimately reveals itself in the Special Agent, allowing him to see through *Twin Peak's* masquerade and drag from the depths its rotting secrets.

Although it's not just *secrets* lurking below the plumb-line of the seen world—but of course, Coop as Oracle has already seen what waits for him.

But What about BOB?

When you see me again, it won't be me.

—The Man from Another Place

Stephen King's *Dark Tower* is a sprawling, dimension-traversing saga set somewhere that is occasionally reminiscent of the world we know; but only rarely. The place is fragmented, mercurial, and a force contrives to keep chaos its constant, but a hero—The Gunslinger—is called to resurrect the scales of balance.

The plot parallels *Twin Peaks* in its essential narrative, only shaded over in dusty strokes of western melodrama. More meaningfully, it mirrors the show's theme of inevitability; concentrated most acutely within its protagonist:

gunslinger Roland Deschain is compelled by *"ka"*—described by the author as signifying life-force, consciousness, and encompassing the uniquely human intellections of duty and destiny. In the vulgate, or "low speech" of the book's inhabitants, *ka* also means "a place to which an individual must go"—Deschain's fate is indelible and he marches grimly forward into the darkening desert to hunt "The Man in Black." The reader understands that The Gunslinger will see things through to the story's bitter conclusion—but will he survive it? *Ka* is a morality unto itself; it's unlikely to reward the hero just because he's the good guy.

Like *The Dark Tower* paladin, Agent Dale Cooper is driven by duty, his calling, and just as similarly—for all his noble intentions and all-American decency—he has no guarantee that he'll make it through to the other side. He is at once the *Romantic Hero*—another trope defying Enlightenment's empiricism, the figure characterised by a rejection of established norms—and, more starkly, the *Tragic Hero*.

The second season of *Twin Peaks* sees its central character succumb to the Black Lodge's influence; in the final scene, Cooper squirts toothpaste into the bathroom sink, contemplates his reflection in the mirror for a moment, and then promptly smashes his head into the glass (*Twin Peaks:* "Beyond Life and Death"). The cobwebbed mirror reveals a rictus-grinning Killer BOB: the credits roll in tandem with the sudden horror—*Coop ain't Coop no more.*

First possessed and then inflicted with retrograde amnesia—his memories and self-awareness locked inside the purgatorial Red Room, Cooper indeed cuts a crushingly tragic figure. Even when he is revived as the bona fide Special Agent twenty-seven years later—and only in *The Return*'s sixteenth episode—his miraculous (or metaphysical) recovery and resolute quest to right wrongs of the past do not change the inherent romanticism of his kismet. In the end, *ka* rolls on and Coop finally begins to comprehend a relentless truth—*or tragedy*—existing outside of what is "right" or "wrong", good, or evil.

We live in hope, however; in Lynch's inverted drama, the Tragic Hero might just supersede his unchangeable fate—

that metaphor for the desperate, disconsolate state of what it is to be human.

Cooper's evolution into the *Romantic Hero* achieves its full realization in *Twin Peaks*'s final series' instalment, *The Return*. In an ironic knife-twist akin to Shakespeare's greatest tragedies, Coop becomes the beast he has been chasing throughout Season One and Two—but; his calling, his *ka*, remains undeterred—this was always part of the plan.

Neel Burton, psychiatrist, philosopher, and author of *The Meaning of Madness*, writes:

> both the genes that predispose to schizophrenia and the genes that predispose to bipolar disorder may also predispose to creativity, especially given that both disorders may lie on a single spectrum of psychotic disorders. ("The Meaning of Madness")

Implicit in Burton's observations of these prominent psychological pathologies is that madness has the potential for some genus of the exceptional—Cooper's psychic vulnerability primes him to be both a vessel for demonic mischief, *and* sublime revelation; the two not necessarily independently existent.

"Madness"—in the context of Coop's extraordinary dire straits—should not be misconstrued as preternatural in origin; nor ultimately evil, necessarily. One uncharacteristically etiological moment of the *Twin Peaks* series—*The Return*, "Part 8"—makes this much clear. The episode is a glorious, fifty-eight-minute long aria to the out-of-this-world experimental filmmaking that made a young artist and his high-haired, schizophrenic-esque *Eraserhead* famous, but the setting—July 16th 1945 at 5:29 MWT in White Sands, New Mexico—is a flashback to our own objective history: the successful testing of the first atomic bomb.

The monochromatic blast is horrifying enough in its trigger of retrospect, but we also spy BOB's visage in the mushrooming cataclysm, straining against an embryonic sac—apparently birthed from within the nebulous, spreading radiation itself. This is the moment of BOB's genesis. And we are his creators.

Perhaps the silver-haired ghoul has been made manifest to wrest the town from its repressive coma; *Fire Walk with Me* certainly seeds this theory in its gear-shift from spectral sabotage to corporal culpability: the prequel movie to Seasons One and Two provides BOB more than just a couple of couch-creeping cameos—until Laura Palmer is discovered in her polyethylene shroud, he is in cahoots with her father in a vile game of incestuous tag, and it is never made explicit that Leland was an abuser only *after* BOB shows up.

Flash-forward to *The Return*, with BOB unequivocally unmasked as the leering countenance of human evil, and the Grand Guignol of *Twin Peaks*'s third season is the obvious corollary; ulcerated and drooling druggies, toxic relationships, severed heads and suicide . . . we'd like to separate from "normal" such abominations by calling them *madness*, but normal is just what they are.

In an uncanny echo of Cooper's skull-smashing mirror sequence, his possession—and later his possessed doppelgänger—reflects back the Twin Peaks visceral evil; Killer BOB was never a novel phenomenon in *Twin Peaks*; he only articulates the darkness already there.

The Dweller on the Threshold

These answers could not be reached except by an alternate path we've been traveling ever since.

—ALBERT ROSENFIELD

And will I tell you that these three lived happily ever after? I will not, for no one ever does. But there was happiness. And they did live.

—*The Dark Tower*

The year is 2017 and the Red Room bids us welcome.

What came before was but a taste of cherry pie laced with something deliciously defiant of adequate description. Now, we know the deal: *screw the pie*; this is David Lynch distillate, and we're mainlining only the good stuff—grade A, uncut, *WTF*.

With insanity an indiscriminate motif this time around, even our beloved Special Agent is officially certifiable—but he remains the hero. In fact, his newly acquired non-compos condition makes him the perfect hero: remember, logic and reason are the misdirection tools of the bad guys.

Literary theorist Northrop Frye notes that the Romantic Hero is "placed outside the structure of civilization and therefore represents the force of physical nature, amoral or ruthless, yet with a sense of power, and often leadership, that society has impoverished itself by rejecting." Coop has always been the Romantic Hero in his weird outsider ways, utility of higher consciousness, and his unwavering altruism. But it's inconceivable to comprehend this valiant and endearing figure in conjunction with Frye's portrait of an unfeeling, extreme force . . . until BOB, of course.

The theorist's description encompasses the qualities of the Sublime, too—another construct of the Romantic age, which refers to the superlative concept of "greatness," whether physical, moral, intellectual, spiritual, or artistic. Where the Sublime meets the Romantic Hero is in its greatness that surpasses calculation or measurement; much like Frye's exposition of the Hero as representative of a "force of physical nature," suffused "with a sense of power," the philosophical sublime describes a veneration of "fearful and irregular forms of external nature." Incidentally, this latter phrasing defines a type of "madness" too—the fearful irregularities that threaten our sense of equilibrium and normalcy.

When Lynch extols the virtues of madness—in the *Twin Peaks* hyperreality this translates into all things bizarre, seemingly nonsensical and esoteric, but most profoundly through his surrogate, Cooper—he elevates and expands conventional narrative "beauty" to that of Sublime proportions: terrifying, transcendent, unfettered by easy explanation. (Indeed, this is exactly how you would describe the *Twin Peaks* experience.)

The revelatory nature of the Sublime also stands for intrinsic Truth. The "Father of Romanticism" Jean-Jacques Rousseau (1712–1778) received critical acclaim for what he called "The Ethics of Truth"—a guide, simplistically speaking, to discovering authentic Truth. He was not so much concerned in answering specific questions pertaining to truth, but in the exercise itself of truth-seeking. His instructive ethics include an attunement to the metaphysical aspect of nature, using intuition (or Coop's dream forays) over cold logic, and remaining undeterred by societal obstacles of artifice along the path to obtaining real truth. For Rousseau, what qualifies as "real" truth is that which inspires happiness within its seeker—in this, the philosopher's notion reaches an impasse: as Cooper and BOB make evident, not all truth offers happy solace.

Rousseau's avoidance of Truth's specificity is fitting—truth in Twin Peaks is amorphous (straight answers are rare; conclusions even less so), but his utilitarian requirement—that valuable truth is only that which makes us happy—is paradoxically prescriptive. Aristotle opines, "He who has overcome his fears will truly be free"—and what greater joy is there than freedom?

Thus, confront the darkness we must.

Deputy Thomas Hawk relates to Coop a legend—it's played as a matter of Native American mythology ("Zen, or The Skill to Catch a Killer"); and it just happens to be the exact dichotomous mechanism that powers the town's subliminal force-field:

> There is also a legend of a place called the Black Lodge. The shadow-self of the White Lodge. The legend says that every spirit must pass through there on the way to perfection. There, you will meet your own shadow self. My people call it "The Dweller on the Threshold."

Hawk concludes with a caveat:

"But it is said, if you confront the Black Lodge with imperfect courage, it will utterly annihilate your soul."

Hawk's story is grimly forbidding, but its imperative stands, an echo of The Gunslinger's unchangeable *ka*: Cooper must descend into the black.

He must confront his shadow-self—and in turn, reveal ours. And thus, *truth*.

The idea of shadow selves is seeded in classic literature—Robert Louis Stevenson's gothic novella *The Strange Case of Dr. Jekyll and Mr. Hyde* perhaps the most loved: a mild-mannered doctor concocts a potion that unleashes his secret, secondary persona—the twisted Mr. Hyde . . . obviously, mayhem ensues. In Jekyll the boundary between "good" and "evil" erodes into a complex amalgam with a discomfiting, thrilling undertone: within us all is the untamed beast; restless in anticipation of escape.

In contrast, Lynch seemingly stokes the either-or dualism myth—in *Twin Peaks* there are the kooky, but essentially good folks, versus the profligates . . . these aren't *real* people, complicated and messy in their tell-tale hearts, beasts-and-men-in-one. And then that Dodge Diplomat rumbles into their digs, its rider destined to set ablaze the dualist delusion—even if he doesn't know it yet.

There might not be an explicit allegory in the Peaks, but the invitation to interpret at this point is too tempting; in any case, if we are all in fact afloat together in some cosmic sea of consciousness, we're bound to cross the creator's archipelago of motivations at some point. *Does* the town function as a metaphor for the layered landscape—or fathomless depths—of consciousness? Cooper's possession and "split" are suggestive of *something* bigger than devilish hijinks: even as "Bad Coop", the agent still proves a hero—the degenerates are drawn to him and swiftly meet their doom—the shadowed ambiguity is surely too close to the mind's anatomy to not have some connection to it.

And then there is *garmonbozia*.

In the denouement to *Fire Walk with Me*, Killer BOB delivers Leland—fresh from choking daughter Laura to death—to the Red Room. The Man from Another Place utters a slurring incomprehensibility that gets subtitled as *I want all my . . . garmonbozia (pain and sorrow)*. BOB is visibly compelled to extract some bloody essence from within Leland, and seconds later, we are affronted with a stomach-turning close-up, the crimson goblin's wet-lipped maw ingurgitating a spoonful of what looks like creamed corn.

The Atlantic columnist James Parker succinctly sum-
mates the scene's effect:

> Deep as we are in Lynchian wackiness here, the meaning is not
> obscure: The little red-suited man and his fellow denizens of the
> dream realm have a taste for human suffering, which they
> call garmonbozia and consume in the form of a viscous,
> pearlescent psychic distillate. ("How *Twin Peaks* Invented Mod-
> ern Television")

Contrary to our expectations, these forces for "good" do not
exact retribution upon Leland for his heinous crime. Worse;
we realise that BOB is beholden to the Room's resident
spirits. *Perhaps* he has even done their bidding beyond the
room's threshold, too. These "fearful", "irregular" entities,
like BOB, are neither good nor evil, but instruments of *the
Sublime*: a truth unexpected, and not necessarily to our
taste.

Immanuel Kant (1724–1804), considered one of the most
influential philosophers in the history of Western philosophy,
contends that those "fearful and irregular forms of external
nature" are not the real objects of the Sublime at all.

It was never BOB, or the creamed corn. It isn't the atomic
bomb; birthplace of cataclysm—or that whirling portal in the
sky where Major Brigg's head looms large. It's the *power behind* these conjured and curated artefacts of human narrative, stretching the reaches of the mind more forcefully than
reason can accommodate—*madness*, in a word. The madness
synonymous with the chaos and futility of the universe, and
the illogic force of *ka* that the Sublime reveals. Garmonbozia,
bombs, and doppelgängers . . . *Twin Peaks* in its absurdist to-
tality reveals the unerring Truth of humanness: we are he-
roes; we are monsters; there is both boundless joy and
inexhaustible pain (and sorrow) we are yet to encounter—
and there is no symmetry or algorithm to these conflicting
details of existence. To live without suppressing or repressing this knowledge is to embrace freedom.

To succumb to madness.

Coop, as the inevitable *tragic* hero, is an affirmation of madness as the consummate irony: mysteries are not always meant to be solved.

And hasn't Lynch always warned us as such?

IV

The owls are not what they seem

13
Reason and Catharsis

CHARLENE ELSBY AND ROB LUZECKY

As humans, we tend to categorize, rationalize, and describe away any variances within the world at large that we encounter in our day-to-day existence. Even when pushed, the limits of our rationality expand to make sense of whatever it is we want to make sense of, even when the world defies our every attempt to reason it away.

David Lynch's *Twin Peaks* reverses the traditional subjugation of humanity to logic in such a way as to release the contemporary viewer from the tyranny of rationality (the kind that Nietzsche describes in *Twilight of the Idols*). As we progress through the episodes, we attempt at every turn to make sense of it, in accordance with long-held beliefs relevant to physical causality, psychological causality, and every rational system that we believe restrains any describable possible world.

There's nothing wrong with the fact that red room doppelgängers create entities that revert to gold balls upon their return to the Black Lodge—they're tulpas, obviously. We make sense of it, and we use it to explain how it's possible for there to be a Dougie in addition to a Cooper and an evil Cooper. (He was manufactured.)

When, in our attempts to demand rationality of every possible world, we're thwarted by the appearance of the mystical, the absurd, or the contradictory, we are set at unease in such a way as to heighten the suspense of the program as it develops. When, finally, we're able to dismiss the rational entirely, the *Twin Peaks* viewer achieves a catharsis (defined according to an alternative interpretation of the word as used in Aristotle's *Poetics*) that frees the viewer from the tyranny of rationality. In the natural attitude, we expect everything to make sense and if it doesn't, we're a little upset by that. In the aesthetic attitude, on the other hand, we can experience irrationality freed from any of its negative consequences.

A World of Contradictions

Most of the time, the *Twin Peaks* universe makes no less sense than the one we have created. We conceive of the regular universe not as it is but as it is not—a way that makes sense to us. The extent to which we impose our concepts upon the world and not the other way around is a constant source of speculation for philosophy of mind, but its roots go all the way back to Plato.

In the *Republic*, Plato talks about the differences between the sensible world and the intelligible world. The sensible world is the one in which we live, while the intelligible world is that which is *abstract*; it is constituted of purely intelligible entities whose existence is not sullied by material. The material world is full of contradictions, and if we had to rely only on our senses to get an idea of what's really *out there*, then we'd all be fucked.

Plato considers an example. We have fingers, some of which are longer than others. If we look at a ring finger, we notice that it is shorter than a middle finger. (A smaller amount of flesh tone is perceived.) At the same time, it's longer than a pinky finger. (A larger amount of flesh tone is perceived.) Now the same finger is both long and short; at least, that's what our senses are telling us.

In order to make sense of that, we have to *abstract* from what we see. We invent a system of numbers to measure how long our fingers are, and we say that it's an *objective* measure of size. It's objective because it's not determined by the *rela-*

tive comparisons we make between perceptions. When we look at the sensible world, there's no *objective measure* of size that we can use according to which we can measure everything else. We have to gauge everything relatively to everything else.

What's happening here is that we have two observations that contradict each other, and in order to make sense of them, we create a concept under which to subsume these observations. We say that our perception of "short" and our perception of "long" are both variants of something called "magnitude," something that we cannot actually see. It is an intelligible entity. Nothing in the sensible universe is actually "one meter"—it is "one meter long" by some comparison to the abstract "meter" to which we compare it.

When we see a horse in a living room, it does not make sense—and then it does. The Log Lady explains—suffering is coming to those who behold the pale horse. Of course, we say, that makes sense. Sarah Palmer sees a pale horse before her daughter and her niece are murdered. This theory makes sense of the horse, and my unease with its appearance in the living room is quieted. The actual situation has not changed—the horse is in the living room. But our conception of it has, so that we are no longer unsettled by this contradiction—the contradiction between my usual idea of where horses go and the appearance of this horse in this non-standard place. *"Woe to the ones who behold the pale horse,"* becomes part of our conceptual framework for when we encounter pale horses. Sometimes when there is a horse in the living room, it means we need to get it out before it makes a mess of the place. Other times, if the horse is pale, it just means woe is coming. In either case, we can make sense of the situation.

When Diane gets texts from evil Dale Cooper, we don't know what to make of it. She seemed so put off by him when they went to see him in prison. Why would he send the texts? Is he harassing her? Maybe. Then it becomes evident that Gordon Cole knows about the texts. If Diane were secretly in cahoots with Evil Cooper, then she would have kept the texts secret. (That's what our general rule says about how people behave when they are in cahoots.) At the same time, she doesn't seem to be acting completely normally. Eventually, everything comes together—she's a tulpa. She's one of those manufactured people who turn into gold balls. (Now it all makes sense.)

Most of the time, the difference between the fictional world and the real world isn't about whether they make sense, but rather, how to make sense of them. We create general rules for how things within a certain world behave, and then we apply them. The interesting thing is, it doesn't seem to matter how strange those rules are that we create. In a fictional world, it's totally fine that Agent Dale Cooper scribbles on some insurance papers and in doing so uncovers insurance fraud. (He's probably just receptive to universal truths which others can't get at, because of the Black Lodge.) And when the rules don't apply, we're generally set at unease.

Either there's some rule that we don't know about, or the writers are hacks and it's a plot hole. In *Twin Peaks*, we generally assume the former—there's something we don't know. That's the mysterious thing about it. We assume that at some point we will know, and we set our observations aside until we can make sense of them.

Making Sense of the Surreal

We will latch on to any bit of rationality we can in order to make sense of what we're seeing. David Lynch knows this and usually gives us what we're looking for. We know that when Dale Cooper returns trapped in Dougie's life but also in his own body because Evil Dale Cooper staged a car accident, he is able to identify winning slot machines because of some mystical connection between those slot machines and the Black Lodge. And that's all fine. But why is everyone treating Dougie normally? Doesn't he seem a bit off to anyone else? We see Dougie in context and can't understand how his wife is acting as if he just needs a new suit. Eventually, she relates how Dougie had a car accident, and we infer that perhaps this is normal Dougie behavior and not a result of the fact that Dougie the tulpa has been replaced by Agent Dale Cooper returning from the Black Lodge. Now everyone else's behavior makes sense.

David Lynch also likes to leave us in suspense, waiting for *that thing* that's going to make sense of it all. And sometimes, he just doesn't seem to care about our attempts to make sense of things or not. It's as if he's doing it intentionally. He refuses to make things make sense, laughing at us as we struggle to put together puzzle pieces that just don't fit. He *abandons* us in suspense.

As viewers, we're willing to grant that there's a Black Lodge that we can access through a circle of sycamore trees that provides a safe space for doppelgängers and other entities not subject to continuous, linear time. That fact explains a lot of observations. We rework our construction of reality under a new framework in which that fact counts as primary. But what of the times when there's no such fact with which to make sense of what we see?

Sometimes, we get so used to an alternative reality that to see anything real doesn't make sense to us anymore. When Ben Horne and Beverly Paige are walking back and forth across the room trying to find a humming sound, we are set at unease just because this is precisely what would happen in real life. We have become habituated, on the other hand, to having our fictional reality presented to us in condensed form, cutting from one thing to the next and viewed from the standpoint that corresponds to nobody within the universe at all. So when two people are walking across the room, just as we would expect them to, it seems odd (and that is what's odd about it).

The Tyranny of Rationality

One person's abandonment is another person's freedom. Unbound by the usual laws of nature, human behavior, and logical necessity, the world becomes a place of infinite possibilities. The idea recalls that of the atheist existentialists—abandoned by a God whose nature it is to provide meaning to the universe, we are left in a meaningless universe. We're free to construct our own meaning, but often our attempts to do so are inauthentic. Our attempts to make sense of the universe are artificial, after the fact, and sometimes downright inaccurate. They make sense of the world only as long as we're willing to accept an untrue fact—that there is an inherent meaning to the universe, something according to which everything else makes sense. Gordon Cole's "Blue Rose" cases demand that another kind of rationality be applied to solve them because they don't make sense in the context of nature—we have to establish another context for them.

Recognizing that sometimes things just don't make sense can create a simultaneous sense of despair and freedom, the two main constituents of any existentialism. Existentialism, in turn, owes a lot to Friedrich Nietzsche, who belligerently refused to conceive of his own philosophy as systematic, and who conceived of systems as altogether limiting. In *Twilight of the Idols*, he describes how rationality came to be praised only after Socrates, whose own weakness demanded rationality as a treatment. The virtuous before Socrates did not have to abide by rationality, because they didn't need it.

Throwing away rationality, as David Lynch does, is something only the virtuous can do, those who are not subject to the same defects of character as Socrates was. That defect of character is a slavery to the passions, those things whose source we find in the sensible world. According to Nietzsche, retreating into the rational is an attempt to rid ourselves of the sensible world. Plato's notion of the intelligible world, that which is supposed to help us make sense of the sensible world, is really an attempt to get rid of the world—the only world we have.

Lynch doesn't let us explain away everything under an artificial rationality because that would be too easy. He taunts us and our attempts to rationalize by allowing us to become accustomed to a world unequal but analogous to ours, and then he films Episode 8 of *The Return* just to make sure we don't get too comfortable. He wants to point out to us the fact that we have been applying an alternative reasoning to his fictional world, and he wants us to know that it's not going to work. Even so, the fan base attempts to explain away episode 8, as if it were a part of the mythology and as if Lynch has some secret plan that will eventually be revealed to us. There's a giant insect crawling into the mouth of a little girl, and the internet tries to explain it away—the girl is Sarah Palmer and the insect is the physical manifestation of her psychic powers awakening. There is no end to the theories we will attempt to apply in order to make sense of the surreal, but none of them are satisfactory.

At this point we have to make a choice: *demand harder* that the irrational fit our rationality, or let it go—quit applying our standards of sense to what it is we're looking at and just go with it. Those who choose the former will either continue to suffer in the face of what does not make sense, or they will choose to believe something that isn't quite right—like the inauthentic existentialist. Those who choose the latter will be free of the tyranny of rationality; they will achieve a catharsis.

Freedom from Rationality

A catharsis achieved in the freedom from rationality consists in this: a recognition of the meaninglessness of the world, without the accompanying despair. When we recognize our own world as absurd, the accompanying despair is due to the fact that this is the only world in which we exist, the only one we have to make sense of. If there's no sense to be made of it, there's no world for us. The world in which we live defies our reasoning capacities. We exist as subjects constantly in search of some kind of universal meaning that will make sense of it. Agent Cooper has to leave the Black Lodge, and there's a billionaire who set up this room with a box on it and it's somehow possible to get to the glass box from the Black Lodge through a small tube.

The difference between the *Twin Peaks* world and ours is that we only live in one of them. Although we feel intertwined with the situations and characters represented on screen, we do not feel any capacity or need to interfere with its goings on. When our own world dissolves into chaos, we are despairing. When *Twin Peaks* dissolves into chaos, we are free—freed of our task to apply a rationality to that which does not make sense, and the consistent sense of unease that goes along with such a fruitless task. We can admit that David Lynch's world does not make sense, because we're not so attached to it as we are to this world.

The common interpretation of catharsis in Aristotle (Aristotle mentions catharsis *once* in the *Poetics*) is that it is a purging of negative emotions that we experience when we encounter a work of tragedy. We see bad things happen, feel pity and fear, and our negative emotions are purged. A more nuanced interpretation (that described by Timothy Trela in a 1974 dissertation, "Aesthetic Experience") is that catharsis is instead an experiencing of emotions of the sort one can only experience about an aesthetic object—in this case, *Twin Peaks*.

We can feel differently about a fictional world precisely because *it is not ours*. Thus the "purification" aspect of catharsis does not apply in the sense of our purging negative emotions, but the emotions are instead purged of their connection to the real world. They are only able to be felt in a world that is not one's own—in this case, the freedom from rationality we attain when we stop trying to make sense of where the creamed corn goes when Donna delivers Meals on Wheels to the old woman and her grandson.

We have a different way of apprehending fictional worlds, and that way of apprehending allows for us to experience these other worlds differently. From a rational standpoint, we allow other conceptual systems to apply to the fictional world (we allow them to make an alternative kind of sense), and from an emotional standpoint, we can feel emotions about things that appear to us as distinctly *unreal*. That is, our emotional relation to fictional entities is different *because* the things we are feeling *about* are not part of the world. Our emotions are *purged* of their relation to reality. Trela specifies: "For once, the emotions are allowed to be felt in themselves without any need to act upon them."

We feel no despair at the loss of the element of rationality within the *Twin Peaks* universe because it doesn't demand any action from us. The experience of irrationality is freed of its sense of futility because there's precisely nothing we can do about it. This moves us a step *beyond* the abstraction that allowed us to make sense of the world as it is. We experience contradiction in the sensible world and abstract from it to make sense of it. We experience contradiction in the abstract world and are beset by a profound despair at the futility of our attempts to make sense of what does not make sense. We experience contradiction in our attempts to make sense of a *fictional* world, and we are free to revel in its irrationality— as long as it has no consequence within the world we conceive of as real. We can experience the irrational without concurrently experiencing the loss of everything we think we know to be true.

What I am free of, ultimately, is my own demanding rationality—this strange idea I have that everything has to make sense. My attempts to abstract from it fail, and then I am free to focus on what's actually present (the birth of BOB from the Trinity nuclear test).

14
Diane, I Am Now Upside-Down

VERONICA MCMULLEN AND
KRISTOPHER G. PHILLIPS

There's something really compelling about Agent Dale Cooper. From the first moment we meet him, as he travels to the sleepy Northwestern town of Twin Peaks, we're drawn to him. There are any number of reasons for this. Rather than spend our time fawning over Agent Cooper, we would like to draw your attention to something strange about this familiar phenomenon.

It's not immediately obvious that we're drawn to the *actor* who portrays Cooper, Kyle MacLachlan, but rather we're drawn to Cooper himself (although you might by extension also really like Kyle MacLachlan). The opposite might be said for the character James Hurley; many viewers (ourselves included) have a visceral disdain for James Hurley, but most of us probably wouldn't harbor ill-will toward the actor who plays him, James Marshall, if we met him in the real world.

Finding ourselves emotionally invested in a character is so ubiquitous that it seems we're making hay out of nothing. So what exactly are we getting at? What's weird about this? After all, we find ourselves drawn to, repulsed by, or otherwise invested in fictional characters all the time. But herein lies the weirdness. We *know* that there's no such person as Dale Cooper, yet we are drawn to *him*. How can we be emotionally invested in the life of a person whom we know does not exist? How can something that we know does not exist, *cause* us to have emotional responses?

When faced with the seemingly straightforward question, "What exists?" we might come to any number of different answers, some more informative than others: for instance, we might say: "Everything." But that doesn't really help us very much. There are various things that common sense tells us exist: books, chairs, people, the United States, money, and so on. Common sense might also tell us that certain things don't exist. Santa Claus, for instance, is not real, neither is the Packard sawmill, and while we love Agent Dale Cooper, he's not real either.

When trying to work out what can help us determine what's real and what isn't, many philosophers offer the following candidate: a thing is real when it has causal powers. Put another way, a thing exists when it has or can have an effect on another thing and does not exist when it simply does not or cannot affect anything else. This view is pretty old; it dates back at least to Plato (428–348 B.C.E.), and it seems to be a useful test for existence. It seems to confirm our common-sense ideas about what exists. After all, books, chairs, people, the US, and money all affect us and others in various ways. Chairs stop us from hitting the ground when we try to sit; money allows us to get goods and services.

But we have a problem when it comes to fictional characters. It seems difficult to argue that Santa Claus does not *cause* excitement in children, or that James Hurley doesn't cause consternation in viewers of *Twin Peaks*. But don't we know that neither Santa nor James exist? The same goes for Agent Cooper. If Cooper can cause us to feel, then Cooper must exist in some way. But we know Cooper is fictional—that there is no Dale Cooper. How do we make sense of this? What is a fictional character, and how can they cause us to feel?

Reasons Can Even Explain the Absurd

In 1975, philosopher Colin Radford (1935–2001) posed a similar question, "So if we can be and if some of us are indeed moved to tears at Mercutio's untimely death, feel pity for Anna Karenina, and so on, how can this be explained?" ("How Can We Be Moved by the Fate of Anna Karenina?" p. 71).

This issue has come to be called the "paradox of fiction." Paradoxes are claims that seem to be at odds with themselves. We can see why Radford might think that our concern for Cooper's well-being after having been shot by Josie Packard is a little odd. After all, Cooper isn't real, and Kyle MacLachlan was never really shot. We know both of these things, yet we can't help but feel anxious about Cooper's well-being as we wait for Season Two to start.

The problem itself isn't a difficult one to understand. But it does seem so common that it's almost difficult to feel worried about it. Still, there's something really weird about the joy we felt when Cooper stops being the almost comatose Dougie Jones, and snaps back to his old self ("No knock, No Doorbell"). How can we explain our emotional investment?

At the end of the day, Radford thought that we can't. He thought we were just being straightforwardly irrational. He didn't come to this conclusion without reason, though. He floated several attempts at explaining why we might get so emotionally invested in Cooper's life, but didn't think any of them actually explain our feelings.

First, maybe we just forget that Cooper isn't real? But this doesn't seem promising. During the between-season hiatus we probably didn't rush up to the Pacific Northwest to see how Cooper was doing. At no point were we ever compelled to try to go find Leland ourselves, or let Cooper know that Leland was possessed by BOB. So it doesn't seem likely that we forgot that these were not real people. We didn't forget, we knew all along!

Perhaps it's not that we forget that Cooper isn't real, but that we "suspend our disbelief" about this alternate reality. To be sure, this is what good stories require us to do! They compel us to allow weird stuff to happen, stuff that would probably never happen in real life. It's pretty unlikely that speaking names to rocks before throwing them at a bottle is going to give us any real clues about who is connected to a crime, but in the world of *Twin Peaks*, we're along for the ride. Even if we do temporarily allow weird things to fly (and with David Lynch, they really *are* weird) when watching the show, it's not clear that this solves the problem. We might join in on Cooper's visions, or feel anxiety as Laura's doppelganger talks about her arms bending back, but that's not because we pretend any of this is real; we know better. So it must be something else.

What if the reason we feel genuine emotion is not a matter of the characters at all, but instead is because the characters remind us of *real* people? That would certainly explain why we feel the way we do. Is our distaste for James really rooted in our awful memories of our own angsty adolescence? Is James nothing more than a disgusting mirror Lynch is holding up to each of us? That's something of a depressing thought. But it's also not likely. The affinity we feel for Cooper is not for any of our quirky friends but for *him*. We really dislike *James* and we really like *Cooper*. We kind of want *Truman* to punch *Albert*. While it's of course possible that Andy reminds us of an old, somewhat naive friend of ours and that might help explain why we have a soft spot for him, it's *Andy* for whom we have that soft spot! So while appealing to people we know might serve as part of an explanation for why we love these characters, it doesn't tell the whole story.

So what's going on here? Is Radford right? Are we really just deeply confused about what's real and what's not? Are we irrational? We'd like to think not, but the problem is clear, it's insanely common, and our best attempts so far have done little to explain why we feel anything. There is one suggestion that Radford never really explored, though. What if Cooper, Cooper's doppelgänger, Laura, and all the rest of the folks in *Twin Peaks* are real? If those characters really exist, then it seems the explanation is easy. We love Cooper and want to see him snap out of the Dougie Jones stupor because Dale is real, Dale is not quite awake, and Dale has some unfinished business to attend to.

I Have a Definite Feeling It Will Be a Place Both Wonderful and Strange

If we go by the standard we mentioned at the start of this chapter (that things exist when they have causal powers) then it seems that these characters have to exist. If they didn't, the paradox could never get going in the first place! We hate James, love Cooper, we're probably weirded out by Gordon's shouting (except at Shelly), and so on. If the *characters* can cause us to feel things, then they must exist. But if Cooper and all the others exist, the question is, "How?"

Clearly, Dale Cooper is not a *real* person in the way we are. So what is he? What are they? Some philosophers have posed questions like these, and Amie Thomasson is one such philosopher. Thomasson spent her book *Fiction and Metaphysics*, discussing just these questions—she explains how it is that fictional characters can exist without claiming they exist in *real* life. She suggests that characters exist as abstract objects (or artifacts) and we can discuss them, and be caused to feel things both by and about them because they do, in fact, exist in that capacity.

What she means by "abstract artifacts" is interesting. It's clear that the *character* of Cooper is not the same as the human Kyle MacLachlan. MacLachlan is a "concrete" thing in the world. He has a physical body, he takes up space, and can directly interact with us if we were to meet him on the street. Cooper doesn't exist in this way. Some existing things are concrete (books, and chairs) but not all of them are. The United States, for example, is not a thing in that same way. The US is a country, which only exists because a number of people believe it to exist. The same might be said for the laws of the country. They exist because we agree that they do, and because they get enforced (and Cooper is an agent who acts on behalf of the law). But the law isn't something *physical*. It's an abstract thing. Despite being abstract, it still has an effect on people, though lamentably not as much on BOB. Thinking about the law as an existing thing is also helpful in explaining what Thomasson means when she says that fictional characters are *artifacts*.

There seem to be different sorts of laws that we might think or talk about. There are statutes at the local, state or federal level, laws of nature, and laws of mathematics and logic. Each of these seems to be quite different. Laws of nature are the rules that govern the world around us, the behavior of bodies and so on. Those are largely set and have little to do with what *we* think about them. They're there whether we know it or not. Yet, unlike the laws of logic and math, laws of nature seem somewhat flexible when it comes to our imagination.

As Radford suggested, when it comes to *Twin Peaks*, we can suspend our disbelief about events that violate the laws of nature. For instance, odd other realms housing evil doppelgängers don't merely appear and disappear in the middle of the woods, and Major Briggs's body can't continue to exist for twenty-five years without aging, especially without a head! But we're willing to let these things slide for the sake of a good story.

There's something very different, however, about governmental laws. While it's physically impossible for us (the authors) to dunk a basketball on a regulation hoop, there is nothing about the physical laws that stops us from committing a crime. That's exactly why there are agencies like the FBI. But the fact that we could violate governmental laws isn't the only difference between those and the laws of the physical world. Governmental laws only *exist* because there's a government, and the government only exists because people agreed that it exists! Put another way, the government and all the laws that came from it are *artifacts* of human thought.

This is exactly what Thomasson means about characters too! Just like other artifacts created by humans, characters exist, can cause things to happen, and could be lost to oblivion. Thomasson thinks that Cooper exists in this way— he's an artifact (a creation) of human minds, and exists so long as we have some record of *him*. But he's not a physical thing, the way a DVD of *Twin Peaks* is a physical thing, he's more like a governmental law—an abstract object.

While it might sound odd at first to think of characters in this way, Thomasson's approach can help us explain a lot of things that seemed inexplicable. We think it can help resolve all kinds of questions, not the least of which is why it is that we have such powerful reactions to fictional characters. If Thomasson is right, then we're not being *irrational* when we cry for the child Richard Horne runs over, despite the fact that we know "that no one has really died, that no young man has been cut off in the flower of his youth."

Of course we know Richard didn't *actually* kill a child; of course we know that there is no Richard either, at least not in the concrete way you and I exist. But what we do mourn is the *character*, which really exists. There's nothing all that odd about having an emotional response, in this case mourning, when faced with the loss of something important to us—even if it's not a physical thing.

But There Is Still the Question: Why?

In addition to solving Radford's paradox, Thomasson's account can help us make sense of some recent studies about how people interact with characters. Even better than that, though, is that when we combine the studies about human-fictional character interaction with Thomasson's account, we can offer a full explanation of why we love Dale Cooper so much! Recent studies have located two different kinds of interactions viewers have with characters: Parasocial Interactions and Wishful Identification.

Not only do we feel a connection to the character Agent Dale Cooper but the phenomena that appear in the show bring to light many odd goings on. Whether it's Leland's possession, Cooper's strange dreams, the backwards (or forwards?) talking doppelgängers, or old waiters who seem oblivious to Cooper's having been shot, these additions to the show brings a sort of absurdity to *Twin Peaks* that seems to push us closer to Cooper—he is the agent in charge of the investigation and he seems to be able to handle anything.

Because of his smooth demeanor, his comfort with the truly bizarre, and his charismatic persona he seems to be the safest person to hold on to for safety or comfort. That being the case it made it even more surprising that the ghostly entity was able to possess Cooper during his time in the Black Lodge at the end of Season Two. But that event *caused* us (the viewers) to *feel* more than just a dismissive "Awe, I really liked him." It caused in us a feeling of surprise, we felt sad, angry, or confused as to what happened and why, it made us think twice about *how* that even happened.

Some viewers remained a third-person viewer, passively watching the events unfold from the outside, helpless to intervene. These viewers might have been concerned, but moved on shortly after the show came to a close (only to return twenty-five years later!). Other viewers may have *empathized* with Cooper; feeling that special anxiety that comes along with genuine human interaction (this is odd, of course, for all the reasons we've discussed above). Still another group of viewers may have, figuratively, put their feet in his shoes.

The first group we described is probably how most of us felt. We felt the feels, but moved on when the show ended. The next group, those who *empathized* with Cooper are caught up in what is referred to as "Parasocial Interaction." Briefly put, this is a one-sided relationship where the person puts effort, emotional energy and time into a relationship where the other person doesn't know it's happening. Of course Cooper doesn't know how much some folks empathize . . . he's an abstract artifact! The final group, consists of folks who "wishfully identify" with Cooper. They want to become, or at least act like, Cooper (and let's be real here, who *wouldn't* want to have the kind of success Cooper/Dougie Jones has at the slot machines? "HELLLLOOO-OOOOO!").

According to Rebecca Rubin and Michael McHugh ("Development of Parasocial Interaction Relationships"), Parasocial Interactions are one-sided relationships viewers have with characters. These *relationships* cause people to have emotions toward these characters similar to those the viewer's have toward their actual friends. In other words, some people view Agent Cooper as their friend! According to Rubin and McHugh, Parasocial Interactions happen when the *friendship* between the viewer and character grows.

This happens because the viewer and the character bond over time through experiences the character has, but since the viewer is also witness to these experiences, he or she feels as if she was there with the character, and spent time *together*. With actual friends or family members, the more time we spend with another person, the more we start to get a feel of who they are as a person. We start to expect certain behavior from them—answers to certain questions, remarks or comments to certain conversations, and so on—but this also happens with some viewers and fictional characters!

After spending so much time watching a show like *Twin Peaks*, you start to notice little quirks characters have, especially main characters like Cooper. Once a viewer starts noticing these little quirks or starts understanding the character's humor they can start predicting the character's next move or what they'll say next. This creates a stronger bond between us and the character which leads us to see the character as a friend (even though the character is an abstract artifact rather than a flesh-and-blood human). Rubin and McHugh claim that this bond is intentional and that casting directors intentionally choose actors for specific roles in order to facilitate these emotional bonds between viewer and character (p. 279).

There is a sense in which we might think that people who form parasocial interactive relationships with fictional characters are a little nutty. But it's not all that far removed from the natural and altogether commonplace responses we all feel to fictional characters. If it's at all weird that we cry at the death of a fictional child at the hands of a fictional drug addict/dealer (who might be the child of Audrey and doppelganger Cooper), then why does it seem so odd that we'd think of Cooper as our friend? Of course, for any of this to happen at all, there must *be* a Cooper in the first place! And we've argued that there is! Thomasson rescues us again! But the question remains . . . "Why?" Why do we bond with Cooper?

Diane, I'm Holding in My Hand a Small Box of Chocolate Bunnies

When we're first introduced to Cooper, he's talking into a voice recorder as if he were talking with a woman named Diane. This raises several questions. Who is Diane? Why is he recording his thoughts onto these tapes? Is he going to send them through the post to the mysterious Diane so that she can listen to them? Is that really the most efficient way to handle FBI business?

It seems that Diane is something of an assistant—he notes how much his lunch cost, and let's her know that she should try the cherry pie if she ever finds herself in the middle-of-nowhere Pacific Northwest. But we don't know anything about Diane. And after a few episodes, we accept that we probably never will (. . . at least for twenty-six years or so). While we wonder what Cooper's reasons are for chatting into a voice recorder and addressing Diane, we learn not just about Cooper's activities and diet, but quite a bit about him as a *character* or *person*. This creates a sense of being involved in Cooper's life that goes beyond merely passively watching him interact with others. We get a sense of his personality, his quirks, and his inner monologue. It's a cool plot device, and there's little doubt that Lynch was aware of the effect it has on us as an audience. We don't come to care about Cooper the way we do just because of his one-sided relationship with Diane, however.

Among all the quirks Cooper has, perhaps the most endearing is his reaction to every cup of coffee he drinks. It's as if he feels about coffee the way we feel about our loved ones—coffee, no matter who is serving it, seems to be the thing that he loves most in the world (unless it was brewed with a fish) and we decidedly enjoy his enjoyment of his coffee. Because of this we think of him when we drink our own cup of coffee which in turn creates a type of inside-joke between us and Cooper. This strengthens our bond with him and serves as a solidifier of our friendship with him.

This is unsurprising in some ways. Coffee is a powerful thing and is an important part of many people's lives. Coffee can be a morning routine, and it can be the avenue by which we catch up with old friends. So when we see Dougie Jones get his first cup of coffee, and mumble to himself "Damn good coffee," it's like sharing a cup with a friend we haven't seen in years. If Thomasson is right, and we think she is, then there is a sense in which we *are* sharing a cup with an old friend.

The Heart—It Is a Physical Organ. But How Much More an Emotional Organ?

Believing that Cooper is our friend, empathizing with him, and sharing a cup of coffee with him is not the only way we might interact. Another way people interact with characters is when a viewer seems to think they *are* that character or they are experiencing the same thing as that character; this is called "wishful identification." So even though we may feel a type of friendship with Agent Cooper others may believe they are him, or at least *want* to be *like* him.

This type of identification with a character seems odd at first but it is real and when you think about it, it's not that unreasonable. When you're young and you see a person who seems larger than life, like a firefighter or a policeman, you want to be them when you grow up. We all had people we looked up to, and many of them were not people that we knew personally. Of course some were, but when presented with an (admittedly incomplete) picture of famous athletes, musicians, or even fictional characters, we found ourselves wanting to model our beliefs, behaviors and lives after them. What child in the 1990s didn't want to "be like Mike"? And who wouldn't look at Dale Cooper and think, "This guy gets it"?

According to Srividya Ramasubramanian and Sarah Kornfield ("Japanese Anime Heroines"), wishful identification occurs when we see a character who has personality traits we want to have, or the life we want to live, and we want to be that character. When watching *Twin Peaks*, we see the life FBI Agent Dale Cooper is living—truly enjoying his coffee every time he drinks it, meeting quirky figures like the Margaret "the Log Lady" or Deputy Andy Brennan, and somehow seamlessly blending Sherlock Holmes-esque Western reasoning with Eastern philosophy—that seems like a pretty appealing life.

If we wanted to have such a life, we might imagine ourselves in his shoes and imagine that we experience what Cooper is experiencing—both the bad and the good. According to Ramasubramanian and Kornfield the viewer is more likely to identify with a character if there are already similarities between them and the character (p. 193). An interesting twist to this type of identification is that the viewer could potentially flip between having a *parasocial interaction* and a *wishful identification* interaction. This means that the viewer, when watching *Twin Peaks*, could go from being Cooper's friend to putting themselves in his shoes and believing they are living Cooper's life, and then back again to being his friend. These are not the only ways people interact with characters. You might cycle between parasocial interactions, wishful identifications, and just plain old third-person viewing. One minute you're sipping on your coffee alongside Cooper and the next you're banging your head against the mirror in a manic haze of ghostly possession and then the very next minute you're back on your couch watching as a third-party viewer enjoying a strange yet addicting show.

There Are Clues Everywhere—All Around Us

As we can see, we're now faced not only with a single puzzle regarding Dale Cooper, but a series of interconnected puzzles. Why do we feel genuine emotion for characters when we "know" they are not real? Why do we empathize with, and form lasting friendships with, friendships that remain as strong as ever despite a twenty-five-year absence—and even *identify* with characters when we "know" they're not real?

There are clues everywhere. Thomasson offers us the best idea of what the picture on this puzzle is. When she said that characters are *real*, it provided us an important hint as to how everything fits together. We are moved by Agent Dale Cooper because he is *real* in an important sense. We can discuss *him* as a character, we can move forward with our discussion of how and why we experience emotions toward and as a result of him. We understand that he is not, in fact, a flesh-and-blood person, but he is nevertheless real. We see him on screen; he is a character we seem to get along with, a character we look up to, and a character we *identify* with. Cooper is like the owls, however, in that he is not what he seems.

15
The Evil in These Woods

PETER BRIAN ROSE-BARRY

Twin Peaks is a television show about lots of things: pie and coffee, love and hate, innocence and depravity, logical deduction and deep intuition, and still more. But if the show is about anything, it's about good and evil.

Sheriff Harry S. Truman speaks openly to Special Agent Dale Cooper about "the evil in these woods" and after Laura's killer is discovered, Truman wonders out loud about BOB and expresses his inability to understand what just transpired: "I've lived in these woods all my life. I've heard some strange things. Seen some too. But this is way off the map. I'm having a hard time believing." In reply, Cooper asks "Is it easier to believe a man would rape and murder his own daughter? Is that any more comforting?" and a horrified Truman seems to reluctantly agree that it isn't. Major Garland Briggs interjects: "An evil that great in this beautiful world. Finally, does it matter what the cause?" Cooper, in an obvious Cooper moment, insists that it matters because "it's our job to stop it" ("Arbitrary Law").

Cooper is right: it does matter. But there's something crucial going on in the above discussion that's worth making explicit. If it's our duty to stop evil, we're only going to be able to live up to that duty if we understand evil in the first place. To understand evil, we'll probably have to know a thing or two about its causes, as Briggs suggests; we will have to have some idea of where evil people come from, how they become evil, how they might be reformed and rehabilitated (or not), and a lot more. So, it will help to think a bit about how evil people are portrayed in *Twin Peaks* and what makes them *evil* and not merely bad or flawed or nasty or whatever.

One pretty obvious example of an evil person in the town of Twin Peaks is Killer BOB. Obviously, there is going to be a lot we don't understand about BOB, even after viewing what sure feels like a backstory in *Twin Peaks: The Return*—apparently, BOB's genesis has something to do with the Manhattan Project and the first test of the atomic bomb in the 1940s ("Part Eight"). But BOB isn't the only example of an evil person in *Twin Peaks*—actually, he might not even be the *best* example of an evil person in *Twin Peaks* especially if we're interested in understanding evil and evil people.

This is going to come as a surprise to some, but there is good reason to think that a character like Windom Earle, Cooper's nemesis and former partner, is a *better* illustration of what makes someone evil, *better even than BOB*. I'm going to try to explain why. The idea isn't that BOB is a supernatural demon, the sort of creature we can't really understand. The idea is that Earle is actually *a worse sort of person*, worse even than Killer BOB.

How Evil Is Understood in *Twin Peaks*

According to one influential understanding of what evil is, evil is essentially the absence of goodness—a *privation* of goodness. This way of understanding evil has its roots in the African philosopher and theologian, Saint Augustine. As a young man, Augustine was tempted by a religious sect known as the Manichees who posited the existence of two different kinds of substances or "principles" that comprised the entirety of the universe: one is identified with light and goodness, the other with darkness and evil. Crucially, these two principles have always existed and they are in perpetual conflict, neither able to eliminate the other entirely.

Augustine eventually came to regard Manicheism as a heresy; if even God cannot eliminate the principle associated with darkness and evil, then there is something that He cannot do. Augustine struggled to understand how evil could exist in a universe created by a supremely powerful and loving creator and he eventually settled on the conclusion that evil is nothing—or, even better, that evil is *nothingness*. After all, if God really did create everything and if everything that God creates is good, then there is just nothing that isn't good. Goodness and existence are tied up with one another. But that means that evil could only be tied up with non-existence, the absence of goodness or its "privation."

Twin Peaks often seems to understand evil in the way that the Manichees understand it, *not* as Augustine understands it. BOB isn't nothing; he's akin to a force of nature. BOB isn't the creation of God or anything like Him, but was seemingly vomited from the entity dubbed "The Experiment" in *Twin Peaks: The Return* ("Part Eight"). The White and Black Lodges seem to be in conflict, as are their residents, including malevolent entities like the Woodsmen on one hand and seemingly benevolent entities like The Fireman on the other. By the end of *Twin Peaks: The Return*, Regional Bureau Chief Gordon Cole describes an entity known to Major Briggs and Special Agent Philip Jeffries as 'Jiao Dai'—over the years the name was shortened to 'Judy'—that feels old and ancient ("Part Seventeen"). All this strongly suggests that the town of Twin Peaks resides in a Manichean universe, which doesn't bode well for those hoping to eliminate evil.

But that's not the only way that *Twin Peaks* represents evil. In *The Symbolism of Evil*, the philosopher-anthropologist Paul Ricoeur suggests that while evil is symbolized in various ways, it is notably symbolized as *defilement*, as the corruption of what was clean and pure by something external to it. The obvious symbols of evil in *Twin Peaks* are often dirty and exceptionally so; Sarah Palmer describes BOB as having "long, filthy gray on gray, long hair" ("The One-Armed Man") and the eyes of Woodsmen are shockingly white in contrast to their blackened, soot-covered skin. More importantly they clearly *defile*. They enter that which was pure (as is in the case of Cooper) or that which is corrupted but not entirely so (as is the case of Laura Palmer and the deeply flawed but ultimately repentant Leland Palmer).

We witness some sort of bug-frog creature hatch from an egg in the desert years after The Manhattan Project and crawl into the mouth of a young girl as she sleeps by crawling into her mouth, literally entering and contaminating her. This way of understanding evil too does not conceive of evil as nothingness, but rather attributes agency to it; so understood, evil defiles, corrupts, taints, and stains.

Evil is thus conceptualized in multiple ways in *Twin Peaks*, both as a kind of Manichean principle and as that-which-defiles. But there is still one more way that evil is understood, most notably in its portrayal of BOB.

The Vicious, the Incontinent, and the Bestial

Aristotle's *Nicomachean Ethics* is a classic work of moral philosophy and continues to be influential today. Aristotle doesn't quite use the term 'evil' but an important section of the *Nicomachean Ethics* helps to understand what makes someone evil, and not merely bad, or flawed, or nasty, or whatever. It will also help to explain why Earle is a better example of an evil person, better even than BOB.

Aristotle distinguishes between three conditions of character that should be avoided: vice, incontinence, and bestiality. Two of those sound odd to contemporary readers. Rest assured: he doesn't mean what you think he means. All three have contraries. The contrary of vice, for example, is virtue. A virtue is a morally praiseworthy and excellent character trait, exemplified by traits like courage and generosity and honesty and justice. Virtues are complicated mental states that ensure that the person who has them will tend to act and think and reason and feel in particular ways.

The virtue of generosity, for example, will ensure that the generous person tends to perform certain generous actions, like helping those in need. But it will also ensure that the generous person will help in the belief that she acts rightly, that she helps for the reason that someone is in need, and that she will feel good about what she does. Someone who helps others in need but believes that those she helps are losers or helps for the reason that other people will be impressed by her or feels only pain when helping just isn't a generous person even if she does help out. Similarly, moral vices, like cowardice and miserliness and dishonesty and injustice, will ensure that the person possessing them will tend to act wrongly but also to think and reason and feel in morally dubious ways.

Incontinence is rivaled by continence. Aristotle is clear that both the continent and incontinent person are capable of rational calculation, but the incontinent person abandons it while the continent person does not. The incontinent person understands that he isn't doing what he himself thinks is right to do, but he does it anyway, typically because he is led astray by his feelings or because he is too concerned with pleasure. The Greek term for incontinence is *akrasia* and literally means "lack of mastery," although the term is often translated into English as "weakness of will." That means that the incontinent person lacks mastery over himself, that he lacks something like self-control. By contrast, the continent person has mastery over himself and has the strength of will that the incontinent person lacks.

That leaves bestiality. The contrary of bestiality is a divine sort of virtue, a rare condition of character among human beings. Divine virtue is a state more honorable than virtue and distinct from it. Bestiality is similarly rare; it is also worse than vice and distinct from it. Aristotle explains that the term 'bestial' is "a term of reproach" reserved for people whose vice exceeds the human level. When Aristotle gives particular examples, he refers to those who tear pregnant women apart and devour their children and savage people near the Black Sea rumored to eat raw meat and engage in cannibalism. He also mentions bestial states that result from disease or madness that will sound familiar to contemporary readers, including sexual trauma and compulsive behavior—say, the compulsive eating of items that aren't food, like hair or nails or dirt. Common to all is that they lie outside the limits of vice, just like bestiality itself.

Twin Peaks: Population 51,201

The opening credits of *Twin Peaks* include an image of a sign that lists the population as 51,201. However, in *Welcome to Twin Peaks: A Complete Guide to Who's Who and What's What*, we're informed that this is a typo and that a 1990 census puts the population of the town at 5,210. Mark Frost has explained that ABC didn't believe that anyone would care about a dinky rural town and called for the original pilot sequence to be altered and the population revised.

Do we see vice, incontinence, and bestiality among this small population? Pretty clearly. Consider incontinence. Under the tutelage of John Justice Wheeler, Benjamin Horne explains that while he wants to be good, he finds that "Sometimes the urge to do bad is nearly overpowering" ("Variations on Relations"). That suggests that his will is weak, a vast improvement of course considering what Ben was like in earlier episodes.

Laura Palmer is pretty clearly ruled by her appetites but sometimes she seems to understand that she's taken the wrong path. Cooper, by contrast, has the self-mastery they lack. This is pretty obvious when he resists Audrey Horne's advances, noting that "What I want and what I need are two different things" ("Realization Time"). Virtue is on display: Cooper is endlessly brave and sympathetic; Sheriff Harry S. Truman and Deputy Hawk and Ed Hurley are courageous and just; Wheeler is honest; Pete Martell is kind, and so forth.

Other characters exhibit something like virtue but perhaps not the real thing: Deputy Andy Brennan kind of stumbles into courage despite himself; James Hurley is empathetic to an obnoxious degree; Special Agent Albert Rosenfield is admirably committed to rejecting violence, but he's often a misanthropic dick. Major Garland Briggs may well exhibit the sort of divine virtue postulated by Aristotle, especially given his transcendence in *Twin Peaks: The Return*.

Vice abounds in Twin Peaks; vices like greed, cruelty, dishonesty, malice, callousness, and injustice are on display in characters like Leland Palmer, Leo Johnson, Catherine Martell, Josie Packard, Andrew Packard, everyone in the Renault bloodline, and so on.

If anyone in *Twin Peaks* exhibits vice, it is Windom Earle. He is well possessed of intellectual virtues like intelligence, but he is plagued by moral vices including malice, callousness, cruelty, misanthropy, and still more. He mocks Major Briggs's fear that love is not enough—"Oh Garland, please! I shall weep!" ("The Path to the Black Lodge"). He relishes toying with Cooper's virtue and shows no remorse for killing Catherine. He doesn't just lack moral virtue. His moral compass doesn't just point away from goodness; it points towards something else, something darker. His disdain for goodness is evident when he talks about the White Lodge:

> Gentle fawns gamboled there amidst happy, laughing spirits. The sounds of innocence and joy filled the air, and when it rained, it rained sweet nectar that infused one's heart to live life in truth and beauty. Generally speaking, a ghastly place, reeking of virtue's sour smell. ("Variations on Relations")

Worse, Earle clearly embraces wickedness. He likes it and seems like he wants to throw his arms around it. He continues:

> But I'm happy to point out that our story does not end in this wretched place of saccharine excess. For there is another place, its opposite. A place of almost unimaginable power, chock full of dark forces and vicious secrets. No prayers dare enter this frightful maw, for spirits there care not for good deeds or priestly invocations. They are as likely to rip the flesh from your bones as to greet you with a happy "Good Day." And if harnessed, these spirits in this hidden land of unmuffled screams and broken hearts will offer up a power so vast that its bearer might reorder the Earth itself to his

liking. Oh . . . this place I speak of is known as the Black Lodge and I intend to find it. ("Variations on Relations")

If Anyone's Vicious, It's Windom Earle

Can BOB be described as vicious? That's too weak. He doesn't just want to use other people, like Earle does; he wants to consume them. Like a beast, he has a singular pursuit: garmonbozia, pain, and sorrow. He seems to lack a conscience altogether. In *The Secret Diary of Laura Palmer*, Laura records what may or may not be a dream in which she converses with BOB; when she threatens to make him sorry, he replies "CAN'T FEEL SORRY, LAURA PALMER" and "NO CONSCIENCE." He presents as being all appetite, all id. After Laura tells BOB that he should "Do whatever you need to do," BOB replies that "I DON'T NEED THINGS . . .I WANT THINGS." This sentiment is echoed in *Twin Peaks: The Return* when Mr. C—Cooper's doppelgänger occupied by BOB—explains over a bowl of creamed corn: "'If there is one thing that you should know about me, Ray, it's that I don't need anything. I want" ("Part Two"). (Note how Mr. C juxtaposes needs and wants in contrast to Cooper.) His bloodlust is certainly animalistic as are his movements; think of how he crawls across the floor and over the furniture in the Palmer living room towards Maddy Ferguson ("Coma"). Mark Frost has referenced vampire mythology when explaining BOB, noting Leland's fateful admission that "I invited him in, and he came inside me" ("Arbitrary Law") much in the way that inhuman vampires often can only enter if invited in much vampire lore. How *couldn't* the beastly BOB count as bestial?

If all this is right, why is Earle is a better example of an evil person than BOB? The answer is suggested by Aristotle.

Why Is Vice Worse than Bestiality?

While Aristotle thinks that there three conditions of character to be avoided, he doesn't regard them as being equally bad. Some are worse than others. Incontinence is pretty clearly the least bad if only because the incontinent person recognizes that she acts wrongly and is therefore prone to regret. That leaves vice and bestiality. Which is worse?

You could be forgiven for thinking that the answer is bestiality. After all, Aristotle himself suggests that divine virtue is better than mere virtue. Parity of reasoning suggests that their contraries should be similarly related and that bestiality is worse than vice. But Aristotle is clear on this point: he suggests that while bestiality is more frightening than vice, it is less grave. In other words, he thinks that vice is worse, that vice is the worst condition of character to be avoided.

Why is vice a worse condition of character than bestiality? The idea's pretty simple. In cases of bestiality, Aristotle thinks, the best part of a human being is not corrupted but absent. Exactly what the "best part" of a human being is might be up for debate, but for Aristotle, it has something to do with our capacity for reason. Because we human beings have the capacity for reason, we can understand our badness and our wickedness in a way that mere beasts cannot. For this reason, Aristotle concludes, perhaps surprisingly, that mere beasts who can't understand their wickedness are "less destructive" than human beings who can.

You might have thought that a shark in the middle of a feeding frenzy or a rampaging elephant, both of whom lack any sense that they are acting wrongly, are more destructive than any human being could be. But there's something to Aristotle's thought here. While a single human being typically lacks the physical ability to cause the damage that a shark or elephant can cause, our capacity for reason ensures that human beings can come up with endless and varied ways of inflicting harm. To see this, consider the various ways that Earle torments Cooper; he murders Cooper's beloved Catherine—as she sleeps next to him, no less—and he kidnaps Annie, Cooper's new flame; he plays a macabre game of chess that threatens to kill Cooper's friends as the game progresses. Killing Cooper is too easy and Cooper confirms that "if Windom wanted to kill me I'd already be dead"

("The Condemned Woman"). Simple murder isn't nearly evil enough for Earle. He needs something more dramatic, more horrible; he wants Cooper's soul. Sharks and elephants have only a few ways they can wreak havoc; we have innumerable ways at our disposal.

What's true of dumb beasts is true of bestial people: they too lack the capacity for reason or understanding typical human beings possess, the best part of creatures like us. If so, then we should expect that they too have a pretty limited means of wreaking havoc at their disposal. Like a shark or an elephant, BOB might be more frightening than Earle, but he lacks something that Earle has in spades: the capacity for coming up with new and worse ways of tormenting his victims. Earle also seems to understand his wickedness in a way that BOB doesn't. Not much in the *Twin Peaks* canon suggests that BOB is self-reflective in this way: he only reveals that he doesn't need; he wants.

That's why Earle is a better example of an evil person, better than even than Killer BOB. The term 'evil' is a superlative so it makes sense to suppose that the evil person just is *the morally worst sort of person there is* (I've argued for this in my two books on evil). Bestiality is a terrible condition of character and should be avoided, but vice is still worse. And someone with a worse condition of character is a worse sort of person. Since the vicious Earle suffers from a worse condition of character compared to the bestial BOB, Earle is a morally worse sort of person. And that means that Windom Earle is a better example of an evil person than Killer BOB.

If the human, all-too-human Earle is a better example of an evil person compared to even BOB, should we find comfort in that fact? It's not obvious why we should. In the real world, the world outside of *Twin Peaks*, it's just us human beings. Demons and monsters are hard to come by.

If only demons and monsters could be evil, we could probably sleep soundly doubting the very existence of evil people. But if we human beings are better examples of evil people, we can't have that sort of confidence. Just like in *Twin Peaks*, evil men may well walk among us. But all is not lost. If evil had to be understood in the way that the Manichees understand it, for example, there would be little we could do to stop it; evil would be a permanent and ineliminable feature of our world. But if evil really is human, all-too-human, then we can join Cooper in being committed to fighting to stop it. That is something to hope for.

16
Doppelgängers, Doubles, and Tulpas

ROBIN BUNCE

T*win Peaks* is a show like no other. Much like Special Agent Chester Desmond, it's got its own MO—*modus operandi*. The clue is in the name, the operative word would be "Twin."

Twin Peaks is all about duality, doubles, doppelgängers, and tulpas. By focusing on shadows and reflection, on divided and fractured selves, the show creates an ongoing sense of the uncanny, and the aesthetic effect, beloved by surrealists, of *mise en abyme* (in which the viewer is lost in an endless hall of mirrors).

Duality is at the show's heart. The death of Laura Palmer, *Twin Peaks*'s founding myth, was the climax of a double life. Laura was doubled in many ways. She was both the stereotype of the wholesome homecoming queen, and the sexually promiscuous junkie. She was also doubled by her cousin Maddy Ferguson, by her doppelgänger, and finally by Carrie Page. Laura is one of many fractured or doubled selves presented by *Twin Peaks*.

Almost every major character, across all three seasons, is doubled in some way. Leland is apparently possessed; Phillip Gerard is schizophrenic; MIKE, is literally split in two by the removal of his arm, which subsequently takes on a life of its own; the Fireman and "senior Droolcup" are "one and the same"; Catherine Martell assumes the persona of Mr. Tojamura; Ray Monroe is a double agent; Denise was once

Dennis; Leo Johnson, Windom Earle, and Ben Horne go through transformations, as the result of personal cataclysms; and since the end of Season Two, Special Agent Dale Cooper has been doubled by his doppelgänger Mr C.

It's not just the characters that are doubled. The town of Twin Peaks has a dual character. To be there is to experience, "the most beautiful dream . . . and the most terrible nightmare, all at once" ("Zen, or the Skill to Catch a Killer"). Moreover, events in the town are doubled, in fact tripled, by the plot of *Invitation to Love*, and by the strange happenings of the Black Lodge, both of which mirror the "real world" of Twin Peaks. The town also has an evil twin, Deer Meadow, a logging town like Twin Peaks, which was, nonetheless, "everything Twin Peaks was not" (*The Secret History of Twin Peaks*, p. 559). In short, Doubles are central to *Twin Peaks*.

Have You Ever Had That Feeling, Charlie?

Doubles, and doppelgängers fascinated philosophers, literary critics and psychoanalysts for well over a century, as they "lend imagery to a universal human problem—that of the relation of the self to the self" (Harry Tucker, p. xiv). Audrey Horne's predicament in Season Three is the epitome of the existential danger that haunts *Twin Peaks's* moral universe. Twenty-five years after the explosion at Twin Peaks Savings and Lone, she feels like she's "somewhere else . . . and like I'm somebody else" ("No Knock, No Doorbell"). Somewhere between Season Two and Season Three, Audrey has lost herself. Audrey's loss of self points to a double duality in her character.

First, as she no longer knows who she is, she can no longer trust herself. Therefore, she is constantly in two minds. Second, the Audrey we knew before the explosion, has been replaced by a radically different character. Before the explosion, Audrey was fiercely independent, vivacious, carefree, daring, idealistic, in control of herself, and possessed of a prodigious ability to manipulate others. In Season Three, however, she is altogether different. She's trapped, unable to leave a dreary house, unable to escape a man she despises. She's in a state of limbo, constantly waiting for the phone to ring.

Audrey's duality and loss of self are thrown into sharp relief at the end of her story arc. For the first time in Season Three, we catch a glimpse of the old Audrey, the Audrey we assume to be her true self. Once again, she is the center of attention, dancing to her own tune. Once again everyone moves to her rhythm. However, the re-emergence of Audrey's true self is fleeting, and by the end of the scene her confidence is shattered. Unable to help herself, she pleads for help from a man she loathes. Our final glimpse of her reaffirms just how lost she is. Although she has come face to face with herself in a mirror, her environment is wholly alien. She is more lost than ever.

Audrey's predicament, her apparent loss of self, has been a preoccupation of philosophy since the beginning of the modern period. In a sense, self-loss is a peculiarly modern danger, which is born out of the unique character of the modern world. Strangely, then, for all of its surreal and other worldly qualities, *Twin Peaks* revolves round a tangible threat, which is rooted in the reality of modern life. In fact, while Audrey's experience is uncanny, dreamlike and bizarre, it is also immediately recognizable. In one sense, Audrey is simply a person whose youthful dreams have been dashed, a middle-aged person who has changed because the world has moved on and left them behind, someone who lives with the disappointment of unfulfilled promise.

The *Twin Peaks* moral universe revolves around questions of the self. Agent Cooper and BOB are, perhaps, the two poles of *Twin Peaks*'s ethics. Cooper is moral because he has accepted his own duality, and integrated all aspects of himself into an authentic whole. Cooper is both a highly rational forensic investigator, a modern-day Sherlock Holmes, and a mystic who trusts his intuitions and seeks truth in dreams. Cooper's moral goodness flows from his ability to harmonize these two apparently contradictory aspects of himself. In that sense, Cooper is always able to act authentically, because he has achieved a kind of self-mastery.

BOB is altogether different. While Cooper's self is whole, BOB is an "inhabiting spirit" a "parasite which attaches itself to a life form" ("Demons"). BOB can never be a complete autonomous self, because he "requires a human host." What's more, while Cooper lives in a way that is true to himself, BOB must continually hide his true nature. Whilst inhabiting Leland, BOB must remain "the man behind the mask" (*Fire Walk with Me*); he can only show his "true face" momentarily. Even when inhabiting Mr C, BOB is still in disguise. Indeed, Mr C's comment "You're still with me" ("Case Files") indicates that Mr C has a considerable degree of autonomy, that BOB has perhaps less control over his new host than he had over Leland. Moreover, while Cooper is multifaceted, having effectively integrated his rationality and subconscious, BOB is essentially one-dimensional. BOB is a creature who feeds on "fear and the pleasures," in the form of "garmonbozia" (pain and suffering) (*Fire Walk with Me*).

Laura Palmer's life and death fits this moral typology. As Laura's story unfolds, we learn that her murder was not merely a heinous crime, it was the final act in her struggle between self-loss and self-mastery. Her diary reveals her constant struggle between something that insists she is "an evil, wrong, bad person" (*The Secret Diary of Laura Palmer*, p. 141) and her own desire to "make it out of the woods in time *to be Laura*, good and true and pure" (p. 17). *Fire Walk with Me* shows the victory of her true self. By the end of her life she knows that BOB's plan is "to be me or . . . kill me." Her final act is to embrace her own death, in order to avoid self-loss.

Self-interest and Self-loss

Self-loss, the fate that Laura Palmer escapes, but to which Audrey Horne succumbs, has troubled philosophers since at least the seventeenth century. The seventeenth-century writer François de La Rochefoucauld was one of the first thinkers to study the way in which the dynamics of the modern world affected the self.

La Rochefoucauld was concerned with the court of the French King, and the way in which it encouraged self-deception and self-loss. Paradoxically, for La Rochefoucauld self-loss began with self-love, or more precisely *"amour-propre,"* which La Rochefoucauld defined as a kind of self-interest which boarders on egotism and narcissism. Based on his observations of the French Court, La Rochefoucauld argued that *amour-propre* led to self-delusion. Praise and flattery were conspicuous features of the French court. However, while praise appears to be focused on celebrating the virtues of another it is, in reality, rooted in self-love.

La Rochefoucauld summarized this insight in the pithy maxim, "We usually bestow praise only to receive it." Moreover, praise, he argues, is mediated by our own inner *amour-propre,* "the greatest flatterer of all." In that sense, La Rochefoucauld believed that people were inclined to believe the praise that they received, because it resonated with their own arrogant self-perception. In this sense, praise merely reinforced existing self-delusion.

What's more, the desire for promotion within the French Court led to a further danger of self-loss. Courtiers, interested in gaining the King's favor, feigned virtues that they did not possess. However, over time, "We are so accustomed to disguise ourselves from other people, that in the end we disguise ourselves from ourselves."

The *Twin Peaks* narrative presents a host of characters whose self-interested behavior has clearly undermined their authentic selves. Josie Packard's desire for the Packard fortune, and the profits of a Ghostwood property deal provide ample opportunity for modern competition to lead to self-loss. Josie's plan required her to dissimulate. Her disguise, like the disguises worn by the courtiers of La Rochefoucauld's era, is rooted in feigned innocence and virtue. Yet, over time, Josie's perpetual need to wear a mask has eroded her true self.

Catherine Martell summed up Josie's loss of self in terms immediately recognizable from La Rochefoucauld's analysis of the French Court. "Well I think that early in her life, she must have learned the lesson that she could survive by being what other people wanted to see, by showing them that. And whatever was left of her private self, she may never have shown to anyone" ("Variations on Relations"). Her self-delusion was so intense, that her duplicity "may not have seemed untrue to her." Josie's establishing shot emphasized her narcissistic *amour-propre*, by showing her gazing into a mirror. Notably, this autoscopic shot was recreated early in her final episode—reminding the viewer of the character's predisposition to self-love.

Not all of the characters in *Twin Peaks* are as susceptible to the baleful consequences of self-interest coupled with modern competition. Norma Jennings is *almost* seduced by the need to feign virtue when food critic M.T. Wentz visits Twin Peaks. Her motivation, like that of La Rochefoucauld's courtiers, is to gain material advantage through feigning more virtue than she really has. However, in the final analysis Norma Jennings refuses to be drawn into the business of pretense. Rather than deceiving herself, she retains a true estimation of her virtues, and therefore never loses herself in deception.

The same essential dynamic re-emerges in Season Three. Entrepreneur Walter Lawford, encourages Norma to change the name of the Double R, and to maximize her profits by using cheaper ingredients. The dynamic between remaining true to herself, and seeking self-interest is underlined by the Lawford's proposal to change of name of the Double R. Renaming the Double R Norma's Double R, would have the perverse effect of branding the chain with Norma's identity, in a way that is wholly at odds with Norma's true self. Indeed, it would turn Norma into a brand, objectifying her, in order to make a profit. In so doing, this business move would undermine her humanity.

At the end of the season, Norma pulls out of her deal with Lawford. The contrast between Josie and Norma is stark. On the one hand, Josie choses self-interest over the love of others, and therefore loses herself. On the other, Norma chooses love of her community and Ed over narrow self-interest. The result is self-realization through the love of others rather than self-loss through the pursuit of self-interest.

Self-loss or Self-determination?

La Rochefoucauld was not the only thinker who believed that the dynamics of modern society threatened self-loss. Jean-Jacques Rousseau was also concerned about the modern need for esteem and praise. Rousseau argued that the roots of self-loss were to be found partly in human nature, and partly in the nature of the modern world. Again, Rousseau was concerned about the problems that arose due to human *amour-propre*, which he defined thus:

> *Amour-propre* is only a relative sentiment, factitious, and born in society, which inclines every individual to set greater store by himself than by anyone else, inspires men with all the evils they do one another . . . I say that in our primitive state, in the genuine state of nature [outside of society] *amour-propre* does not exist. For, since every individual human being views himself as the only Spectator to observe him, as the only being in the universe to take any interest in him, as the only judge of his own merit, it is not possible that a sentiment which originates in comparisons he is not capable of making, could spring up in his soul. ("Discourse on the Origin and Foundations of Inequality among Men," p. 218)

Rousseau's definition of *amour-propre*, is more complex than that of La Rochefoucauld. In essence, for Rousseau, *amour-propre*, is a form of self-love. However, it is not simply the natural and legitimate desire for self-preservation. Rather, *amour-propre* is the desire for honor or esteem in the eyes of others, the "universal desire for reputation," the "ardor to be talked about" (p. 184). *Amour-propre* is also a desire to be respected by others, and to be respected when compared to others. *Amour-propre* is a particular problem in a modern society.

For Rousseau, the decline of religion and aristocratic customs were two of the distinctive features of the contemporary world. As traditional value systems declined, Rousseau argued that people depended increasingly on the esteem of others to establish their self-worth. On this basis, Rousseau argues that *amour-propre* leads to self-loss, because we increasingly seek approval in the eyes of others. Consequently, we conform ourselves to the prevailing system of values, in pursuit of social esteem. Rousseau argues that "the social man always outside of himself, knows how to live only in the opinion of others; and it is, so to speak, from their judgment alone that he draws the sentiment of his own existence" (p. 187). This desire for esteem leads to pretense of virtue. The more people craved esteem, the more they sought to deceive. In this sense, Rousseau saw the desire for esteem as something that was true of modern society at large, not simply of the French Court.

Esteem and personal values also play a role in the moral world of *Twin Peaks*, particularly in the field of law enforcement. Deer Meadow's Sheriff Cable value system is clearly based on esteem. He saw no value in seeking justice for Teresa Banks as "Banks was a drifter and nobody knew her" (*Fire Walk with Me*). As she was a nobody in the eyes of the local community, Cable accorded her no value. Similarly, Chad Broxford's values are conventional. He could see no reason to respect Margaret Lanterman's information as she was a "10-96"—police code for a psychiatric patient.

Hawk, by contrast, saw past the stigma attached to Margaret Lanterman, "I know she seems like a strange one, but her information's always been spot on" (". . . Brings Back Some Memories"). Similarly, members of the Blue Rose task force all have their own MO, their values are independent of prevailing societal norms. Albert Rosenfield's disdain for a value system based on esteem could not be more obvious. During his confrontation with Ben Horne, Albert makes no bones about his disregard for the established social hierarchy:

> Mr. Horne, I realize that your position in this fair community pretty well guarantees venality, insincerity, and a rather irritating method of expressing yourself. Stupidity, however, is not necessarily a

inherent trait, therefore, please listen closely. You can have a funeral any old time. You dig a hole, you plant a coffin. I, however, cannot perform these tests next year, next month, next week or tomorrow—I must perform them now. ("The One-Armed Man")

Nor is Agent Cooper driven by esteem. Cooper's values come from within. This is clear when he describes the basis of his fundamental moral convictions and his approach to detection:

Following a dream I had three years ago, I have become deeply moved by the plight of the Tibetan people, and have been filled with a desire to help them. I also awoke from the same dream realizing that I had subconsciously gained knowledge of a deductive technique, involving mind-body co-ordination operating hand-in-hand with the deepest level of intuition. ("Zen, or the Skill to Catch a Killer")

Even Phillip Jeffries remains true to his own mission. Jeffries is missing, but he is never lost. On his arrival in the FBI offices in Philadelphia on February 16th 1989, even after traveling instantly thousands of miles in space and two years in time, he remains true to his mission, determined to report what he knows to his colleagues at the FBI.

Cooper and the other members of the Blue Rose Task Force have escaped the modern trap of self-loss, by remaining true to values they have determined themselves.

Doppelgängers and Absolute Selves

Doppelgängers have been an explicit part of the fabric of Twin Peaks since the end of Season Two. The problem with doppelgängers can be understood by comparing two cryptic statements, both addressed to Cooper after he left Twin Peaks in search of Earle. At the end of Season Two the Arm introduces the doppelgänger motif stating, "When you see me again, it won't be me" ("Beyond Life and Death"). Yet in Season Three Ronette Pulaski's double tells him, "When you get there you will already be there" ("Case Files").

The first statement highlights the idea that a doppelgänger is not *truly* the person it doubles, while the second points to the fact that in some important senses the doppelgänger and the host are one. Andrew J. Webber argues that the doppelgänger and the person they double should be understood in terms of "host and visitant". He argues that while the person who is double has a place in the world, somewhere they belong, the *"Doppelgänger* always appears as an interloper, an unwanted guest, out of place in the texts it visits" (*The Doppelgänger*, p. 9).

In some ways doppelgängers were a feature of *Twin Peaks* before Cooper ventured into the Black Lodge in pursuit of Earle. Cooper's doppelgänger seems to appear in *Fire Walk with Me*, a week before Laura Palmer's death. As Phillip Jeffries makes his mysterious reappearance, Cooper is briefly doubled on the surveillance camera. Jeffries, clearly aware of Cooper's double, attempts to warn Gordon Cole with the words "Who do you think this is there?" (*Fire Walk with Me*).

Laura also has a doppelgänger experience in the movie. She briefly sees herself standing in the picture that she is given by Mrs. Chalfont. This could be the doppelgänger whom Cooper meets at the end of Season Two. Even if it is not, Laura is still a doppelgänger in the original sense of the term, "people who see themselves." Indeed, even in Season One, Cooper appears to meet Laura's double in the Waiting Room. The identity of the "beautiful woman" who he meets "twenty-five years later" is never clearly established. The Arm introduces her as "my cousin," acknowledging "doesn't she look almost exactly like Laura Palmer?" Responding to Cooper's insistence that "It is Laura Palmer," the Arm's cousin responds "I feel like I know her" ("Zen, or the Skill to Catch a Killer"). In that sense the relationship between the beautiful woman of the Red Room and Laura is like that between Mr C and Cooper—they share experiences and outward appearance, but are not the quite the same person.

The theme of doppelgängers in *Twin Peaks* points to another danger to the self. Doppelgängers undermine the notion that there is an authentic self to be lost or saved. Doppel gängers undermine the distinction between the self and others, indicating that it is not as clear as is often assumed, for the doppelgänger is both another, and a second self.

The term "doppelgänger" entered literature and philosophy as part of a critique of Johann Gottlieb Fichte's philosophy of the self. Fichte, originally a follower of Immanuel Kant, attempted to refine Kant's theory of knowledge, by rethinking the self's relationship to the world. His *Foundations of the Science of Knowledge* describes a process of intersubjective recognition, which Fichte presents as the mechanism through which the self learns about the world at large.

Fichte's idealist epistemology begins with a free act of the ego. Through reflection, the self recognizes its own subjectivity. Put more technically, the self posits itself absolutely. At the same time, by positing itself, the self necessarily recognises its own negation. More simply, the I recognizes the logical necessity of the not-I. At this point, however, the self has merely recognized the I and the not-I as logically necessary categories. It's only through the process of mutual recognition, whereby selves interact with each other, that each self comes to recognize its limits, and discovers the phenomenal realm— the world of things outside the self. The driving force which leads to the perfection of each consciousness, by which each self gets a better understanding of itself, is the on-going process of recognition between one self, and others. So, for Fichte, the clear distinction between the subjective self, and the not-self is crucial to his account of human understanding.

Jean Paul, the writer who created the word doppelgänger, used the figure of the uncanny double as part of his satirical critique of Fichte's philosophical idealism. Inspired by the philosopher Friedrich Jacobi, no relation of *Twin Peaks*'s resident psychiatrist, in his novel *The Invisible Lodge*, which had nothing to do with the *Twin Peaks* Black Lodge, Jean Paul used doubles to explore Fichte's philosophy

Whereas Fichte presents a world where the boundaries between I and not-I are clear, Jean Paul presents self-identical characters, and stories in which the boundaries between the self and the world are blurred by mirrors, reflections, portraits, shadows, and magnetism. Rather than Fichte's clear distinction between the absolute I and the other, Jean Paul creates the doppelgänger "as an ambivalent amalgam of self and other." Rather than a series of egos recognizing each other, developing an ever-clearer picture of the world, Jean Paul's characters see themselves in dreams. And rather than presenting a world in which there is a clear distinction between subject and object, many of Jean Paul's characters are hybrid *subobjektiv*.

Jean Paul's novels were an early example of how doubling could make everyday experiences and situations uncanny. His novel *Hoppelpoppel*, the title itself an example of double-talk, subverts the safety and sense of belonging of the home, by replacing one of the family members with his doppelgänger. Immediately, homeliness is subverted, as an outsider, clothed in the appearance of a family member, invades the home.

This is exactly what happens in the Palmer household. The family home, which should be a place of safety, affection, and belonging is turned into an uncanny space, where relationships are poisoned. Leland, a father who owes his daughter unconditional love, becomes her abuser. As Andrew Webber notes in his analysis of the doppelgänger in German Romantic fiction, "The Doppelgänger is typically the product of a broken home. It represents dysfunction in the family romance of structured well-being, exposing the home as the original site of the "unheimlich" [uncanny]."

Doubles in Jean Paul's novels also serve to make narratives artificial. Rather than the characters behaving in an authentic or naturalistic way, Jean Paul's characters wear masks. Otherwise naturalistic situations are also made theatrical. The family home in *Hoppelpoppel*, for example, becomes a stage set. The double nature of *Twin Peaks* has similar consequences. Viewed from the White Lodge, the whole world of Twin Peaks looks like a movie, projected onto a screen above a theatrical stage. Equally, the repeated use of the spotlight in scenes related to doubled characters, emphasizes the extent to which doubles play a part. *Twin Peaks* also uses the vocabulary of theater when dealing with doubles. Immediately before Cooper and Diane become Richard and Linda, Cooper says "'See you at the curtain call."

The sexual or romantic possibilities of identical doubles were also explored in Jean Paul's novels. *Hoppelpoppel*, is sometimes described as a double romance, as Vult and his doppelgänger Walt compete for the affection of the same woman. Sex with, and attraction to doubles is an ongoing theme in *Twin Peaks*. Having fallen in love with Laura, James later falls for her double Maddy. Mr C, wearing the body of Cooper, gains the confidence of Diane, only to rape her. Put the other way around, Sheriff Truman falls in love with Josie Packard, only to find that he has fallen in love with a mask, rather than the authentic person underneath.

A final example uncanny attraction, is Ben Horne's attraction to Audrey. Having assumed the persona of Hester Prynne, Audrey becomes the object of her father's sexual desire. In this scenario, not only is Audrey playing a role, she is also literally wearing a mask. Yet at the same time, the attempted seduction is the first time Audrey has seen her father without a mask, for at home, he plays the role of the family man, whilst in reality he is a regular client at One-Eyed Jack's.

Twin Peaks, One Self

While many of the themes first explored by Jean Paul occur in *Twin Peaks*, there is a difference. Jean Paul's doppelgängers undermine the notion of a true and unique self. *Twin Peaks*, by contrast, does the opposite. Again, Cooper is central to the *Twin Peaks* moral universe. The arc of much of Season Three is Dougie's awakening. Before *Twin Peaks* can reach its climax, before Laura can be saved, and Judy can be defeated the *true* Cooper must re-emerge.

But there is moral aspect of the self which *Twin Peaks* explores, for the show equates moral goodness not simply with authenticity, but with wholeness. Published in 1846, well after the heyday of doppelgänger literature, Fyodor Dostoyevsky's first novel *The Double* tells the unhappy tale of

Yakov Petrovich Golyadkin and his double, or *dvoynik*, Mr Golyadkin Jr. Richard Ayoade's excellent movie *The Double* (2013), is a modern re-imagining of Dostoyevsky's novel, and uses all of the techniques of modern cinema to explore the doppelgänger motif.

Commentaries on the novel note the way in which Dostoyevsky's uses the doppelgänger to explore the psychology of splitting. The concept, developed by psychologist Pierre Janet in 1899, describes a psychological process whereby a person who is unable to deal with the negative aspects of their character attributes them to another. This could be a description of Leland Palmer—unable to face up to his guilt as an abuser, he creates an alter ego who is blamed for his appalling actions. Laura, is the polar opposite. Laura has never committed acts as heinous as her father's, yet she recognizes that she has the potential for great love and great wickedness; she recognizes that she is both good *and* evil.

Laura, then, is like Mitya from Dostoyevsky's final work *The Brothers Karamazov*. Like Dostoyevsky's earlier character Mitya Karamazov must wrestle with his demons, but rather than splitting them off into a double, Mitya owns the noble and the wicked aspects of his character. Laura does the same, and in order to stop her becoming like her father she sacrifices herself. In that sense it's the wholeness of Laura's self that makes her the show's shining example of moral goodness, and Leland's splitting which makes him the show's original sinner.

Twin Peaks borrows heavily from the uncanny world of Jean Paul, but its philosophy is closer to that of Rousseau, La Rochefoucauld, and Dostoyevsky. David Lynch and Mark Frost's show remains committed to the notion that their characters have authentic selves, that they should remain true to those selves, and that they should recognize that they have responsibility for their best and worst actions.

This may well be "Existentialism 101" ("No Knock, No Doorbell") but faced with the pressures of the modern world, it's a precious moral message.

17
Through Plastic Our Secrets Seen

ANDREW M. WINTERS

Everybody knew she was in trouble . . . but we didn't do anything.
All you good people! You want to know who killed Laura? You did!
We all did!

—BOBBY BRIGGS

"She's dead, wrapped in plastic." And with these ominous words spoken by Pete Martell in the *Twin Peaks* "Pilot," the town of Twin Peaks is set on course to no longer be the quaint mountain town the citizens once thought it to be.

It's shocking for anyone to find a body. It's even more shocking when a body appears on the shores of a river, wrapped like an unfinished meal, when you expect to find only fish. But this body was not just any body.

Mr. Martell had come across the corpse of the town's sweetheart, Laura Palmer—Homecoming Queen, Meals on Wheels volunteer, tutor, and beloved by her parents, Leland Palmer and Sarah Palmer. It was no wonder that Laura's death would alarm the citizens of Twin Peaks. Her body used, abused, filled, and drained against her will. How could someone thought to be so pure have been the victim of something so ugly? How had she come into contact with those who were capable of such abhorrent acts? The innocent are often preyed upon and there are times when we make it easier for bad things to happen. While the victims of such atrocities are not to be blamed, perhaps Laura was not as innocent as the townspeople would like to think.

As the investigation by FBI Special Agent Dale Cooper reveals, we begin to see that even Laura's jock boyfriend, Bobby Briggs, was not fully aware of the extent to which her deviant behaviors betrayed the image she displayed. While not her killer, Bobby is not as innocent as the rest of the town would believe. He also has his own secrets that become manifest as the investigation of Laura's death develops. After the powdery residue is discovered in Laura's diary, and its contents read, Bobby is soon identified as one of the dealers selling cocaine to high school students. Without Laura's death, it's likely that Bobby's activities would have remained secret.

Death appears to be this way; it reveals to us many things about the dead. It also has the ability to reveal to us many things about the living—things we wish would be kept secret. For example, as the American Hospice Foundation mentions, when we go through a deceased person's materials, we may become exposed to previous marriages, hidden children, and shameful acts that the deceased did not wish to share while alive ("Secrets Discovered after a Death"). In gaining access to these things we become aware of our own secrets and the possibilities of others discovering them. So, while death reveals to us the lives that are lost, it reveals to us the lives that we live.

While the first and second parts of *Twin Peaks*, in addition to the prequel *Fire Walk with Me*, all convey our abilities to live double lives, the eight episodes of Season One (1990) center on the capacity for a single death to unravel an entire community.

The Will to Not Be Seen

We often follow paths that are not of our own design. Our careers, relationships, aspirations, they appear to be bequeathed to us, rather than childhood fantasies manifest. Perhaps we should be telling children what they will become rather than asking what they'd like to be when they grow up. Surely, the citizens of Twin Peaks did not dream of becoming waiters, truck drivers, hotel clerks, and mill workers when they were children—yet, somehow they did.

Shelly Johnson's job at the Double R Diner leaves her tired. Having dropped out of high school to marry Leo Johnson, she appears depressed, fearful, and lonely. Leo's occupation as a truck driver has him in a regularly fevered state, which he deals with through angry bouts—often leaving Shelly bruised and heartbroken. Few children, if ever, express the desire to become overworked waitresses living in an abusive relationship. So, how did she end up this way, along with the other citizens of Twin Peaks?

Perhaps the German philosopher, Arthur Schopenhauer (1788–1860), can offer some insight to how we are unable to fulfill our childhood wishes. He writes, "All *willing* arises from need, therefore from deficiency, and therefore from suffering. The fulfillment of a wish ends it; yet for one wish that is fulfilled there remain at least ten which are denied" (*The World as Will and Idea*, p. 119).

Before wishing to be successful, rich, or secure in our career, we wish for security in the more basic aspects of human life. In Shelly's case, this is most likely to have been love. Why else would she have been willing to leave high school to marry Leo? If she was already experiencing the warmth and affection from other aspects of life she may have been more willing to fulfill more advanced wishes regarding her career or a chance to leave the small mountain town. But she didn't and she entered a life in which she was unlikely to pursue an independent career or find escape. So, while she attempted to have the wish of being loved and cared for granted, she was willing to deny the other wishes that children dare to make. Unfortunately, for Shelly, none of her wishes would come true.

Even the townspeople who have achieved success of the kind for which we might aspire are not well—even when they have had their more basic wishes fulfilled, they still have many other unfulfilled wishes. Ben Horne, owner of The Great Northern Hotel, Horne's Department Store, and One-

Eyed Jack's Casino, is deeply dissatisfied with his children,
Audrey and Johnny, often avoiding them. Josie Packard,
owner of Packard Sawmill, is deeply fearful of the townspeople. Catherine Martell, who operates the mill, frequently reveals her deep discontent with her own husband, Pete. Dr.
Lawrence Jacoby, harbors a deep sadness and the inability
to sympathize with his patients.

Before tending to the ways in which they each live a dou-
ble-life, as a result of their own discontents, we must first
ask: *Why do they continue to live the lives they live?* Fear,
loneliness, depression, anger, denial, these are all indicators
of a life not well lived. A friend or family member who would
be undergoing such strife would receive advice to make significant changes. Even when presented with such advice, the
characters are also hard pressed to make what we would believe are healthy changes.

We shouldn't fault them too much for doing the very
things that we do on a daily basis to ourselves. A smoker
knows to quit. A person in an abusive relationship knows to
leave. A person in a dead-end job knows to look elsewhere
for employment. Why do we settle for these sorts of lives?
The kind of lives our younger selves would kick our own
asses for living. Even if we should not be concerned with becoming the visions dreamt by a younger self, we continue to
pursue these lives when we are unhealthy, uncomfortable,
and unsuccessful.

As Schopenhauer observed, we believe ourselves to be
free to choose. We believe that we can at any moment choose
some different path. A smoker can choose to quit at any moment. A person can freely leave the abusive relationship. A
person can quit a horrible job at any moment. But they don't;
we don't. Just as we do not freely become different people,
Shelly does not leave Leo (nor does she stop smoking), Leo
does not quit being a truck driver, Ben does not leave his
family, Josie does not leave Twin Peaks, and Dr. Jacoby does
not quit his profession. No, somehow, as Schopenhauer seems
to have gotten correct (p. 46), no matter how much we reflect
or resolve to become different people, we are determined to

be the very people we condemn. So, even when we see the citizens of Twin Peaks despise the very people they've become, we must recognize that they are like us. We, too, continue to live the lives we despise.

Given we do not choose what we have become, there must be some other feature of us operating, resulting in us becoming the things we wish that we weren't. What we share in common with Shelly, Leo, Ben, Josie, Catherine, and as we'll see in a moment, Laura, is some basic core component, which is both the strongest and weakest element of our core. Schopenhauer called this the *will*, which he understands as the fundamental "kernel of every phenomenon" (p. 50). But this operates blindly within our bodies and is made manifest through the "vital and vegetative processes, digestion, circulation, secretion, growth, reproduction" (p. 47). The will we have in common with the townspeople of Twin Peaks is also what we have in common with all other elements of life. And like them, we keep those aspects of our lives that we detest hidden in hopes that they will never be brought to light.

The Twin Lives We Live

Given the lives that we live are not of our own design, we are left living a two-fold life, a life that we are content making manifest to the eyes of others, while much of our own life is kept hidden away. Shelly's discontent with her job and marriage lead her to hide away in the arms of Bobby Briggs. Leo's realization of his own poverty leads him to hideaway in the night, trafficking drugs and women across the US-Canadian border. Ben Horne's success leads him alienated from his family, hiding away underneath the gaze of One-Eyed Jack's with only the young female workers to keep him company. Jacoby's coconuts hide his secrets for him, Laura's secrets recorded in her sultry teen voice, revealing her own discontents in the episode "Traces to Nowhere."

Hey, what's up, Doc? It's Laura, in case you haven't guessed. It's Thursday the twenty-third and I'm so bored. Actually, I'm in kind of a weird mood. God, James is sweet, but he's so dumb, and right now I can only take so much of sweet. Hey, remember that mystery man I told you about? Well, if I tell you his name then you're gonna be in trouble. He wouldn't be such a mystery man anymore but you might be history, man. I think a couple of times he's tried to kill me. But guess what? As you know, I sure got off on it. Hmm, isn't sex weird? This guy can really light my F-I-R-E as in red corvette. Uh-oh, here comes mom with milk and cookies.

Not only does Laura reveal to Dr. Jacoby her discontent with Bobby, whom everyone believes she is dating, but she reveals her discontent with James, whom very few know she is seeing on the side. Instead, we gain insight into the life that she hides from others, the use of cocaine, prostitution, close calls with death by the hands of a strange man, the life that would destroy those who take themselves to be closest to her.

This "strife, conflict, and the fickleness of victory" drives the will (p. 73). In this case, they drive Laura to become the person that no one would want to see her as—the addict and prostitute. But it is her desire and suffering in her own boredom that pushes Laura to engage in a double life. Her body is the only individual that can live those lives. Everything else is an idea, a figment. It is by treating everything else merely as a causal antecedent to the expression of her will that she is capable of engaging in a life that would be harmful to those who would come to know it.

Passion Only Injures Itself

Why do we live the sort of lives we know would hurt those who are closest to us? We go so far to live the lives that would harm even ourselves. Surely, we might say that Laura's own capacity to harm James, Bobby, and her parents stems from her cocaine addiction, but something led her to use cocaine in the first place. Furthermore, she is not alone in her discontents. The townspeople each suffers in his or her own way. In the desire to be free of such suffering they each engage in acts that would likely harm those for whom they care most.

For example, "Big" Ed Hurley, Jr., owner of Big Ed's Gas Farm is someone whom we think should be content. Well-respected by the community as a member of the Bookhouse Boys, he was also a very successful mechanic. He also appeared to be kind and looked out for the well-being of the other townspeople, including his nephew James Hurley (the same James that Laura was seeing behind Bobby's back). But his desire to be with his high school sweetheart, Norma Jennings, led him to sneak behind his wife's back. His desire and guilt consumed him. His relationships suffer, especially the one with his wife, Nadine, who unsuccessfully attempts suicide after becoming suspicious of his affair.

Many of us have experienced similar difficulties in maintaining appearances of how we want to be seen by those we care about most, while not properly tending to our passions, emotions, and vices. Even with the best intentions we may harm those who are closest. Why do we do these things?

For Schopenhauer, we only know pain directly (p. 203). Gratification and pleasure are only experienced in hindsight—as the thing experienced when we see the suffering that we've overcome. So, it is through the desire, the yearning, of things that are not present that we are able to experience ourselves.

For someone like Ed, then, the desire to be with Norma intimately and the desire to be tentative to the needs of Nadine keeps him in a constant state of desire without end. While the viewer from the outside would think that such a life is one wrought with pain and suffering, Ed is intimately connected to himself in the inability to fully satisfy his life. He can't fully satisfy both desires. The satisfaction of such desires would render him transparent to himself.

Ed's plight is our own. Through our pains we come to know ourselves most intimately—our pains, desires, fears, and anxieties reveal to us our core values. While when pain is no longer present we have the capacity to become complacent. When pain is no longer present we have no need to overcome ourselves, but, instead, slip away into banality. From this state of boredom and mediocrity we are more inclined to seek new experiences, which lead us to create dramas. So, while we express the preference to have a comfortable existence, the way that we live is much like Ed's—we make things much more complicated than needed and in doing so we see ourselves in the light of the gaze of the other.

Laura's situation is different from Ed's, but is more telling about the sorts of lives we seek to live. Ed's situation is the result of having neglected and, in some ways, having rejected the life he desired to live. Laura's life, on the other hand, was just beginning to blossom. Her future appeared to have been filled with so much more potential than Ed's and many of the other townspeople. Why would Laura live the kind of life that would hurt those who were closest to her? Many of us would think that her life was close to ideal. We strive to be popular, adored by others, recognized for our talents, and given opportunities to flourish.

She appeared to have these with ease. Her talent, intelligence, and beauty provided her with the opportunity to receive accolades that many of us must work for (often to no avail). But these accolades are the very sort of things that others strive for because of their values. Like us, Laura did not have the opportunity to develop those values for herself—she was set on a path not of her own design. Even when her basic wishes were fulfilled, and she achieved success, these wishes and successes were not her own. By being successful in accordance with other people's values, she was neglecting her own opportunities to develop the value system she set out for herself. While the other townspeople's discontents were the result of neglecting and mismanaging their passions, emotions, and emotions, Laura's own discontents are the result of not having the opportunity to authentically develop such passions as her own. The town and high school boys simply lacked the potential to light her F-I-R-E.

By pursuing strange men, exploring addictions, and tasting what was outside of the town, Laura was able discover her passions, emotions, and vices, the very kind that the townspeople were unhealthily suppressing. In opening herself to those delights, she began discovering the limits of her body and mind. Even at the cost of harming others, Laura was able to discover who she truly was—to see herself differently from how others saw her. She began seeing herself through her own eyes.

This desire to be seen by ourselves explains why we are not content with the lives that appear so charming and pure. We can only take so much sweet in our lives. We need the mystery man to bring danger into our lives—even when he may be trying to kill us. It's when he doesn't kill us that we know that we're alive. Strangely, the mystery man does not need to be someone else. We do a good enough job on our own preventing ourselves from breathing. Each morning when we look in the mirror, our hands may as well be around our own throats. It's when we stop breathing that we are seen by others. What reflection will they see when they look at our corpses laid open upon the examiner's table?

The True Nature of Virtue

Death reveals our true characters. It shows us who we are. Even as the townspeople were reacting to the news of Laura's death, their concerns were drawn to other matters. Even though Ben Horne showed more affection towards Laura than his own children, he was more concerned with securing business deals with Norwegians, trying out new girls at One-Eyed Jack's (one of whom would turn out to be his own daughter, Audrey), and carrying on with an affair with Catherine Mandell to purchase the land of the sawmill. Although he was troubled by her death, Ben was more likely concerned with preventing his backdoor dealings from becoming known.

Even at Laura's funeral very few individuals were crying. Aside from her own father's spectacle of diving upon the casket, there was very little concern for the fact that she had even died. Even the next day, Shelly was mocking Leland's display, imitating his own cries as the lowering device bounced up and down, creaking and moaning with his own shouts.

James, Donna, and Agent Cooper appear to be the only people interested in understanding the truth behind Laura's death. James and Donna demonstrating the depth of their love and friendship for Laura with their willingness to put their own lives at risk. Agent Cooper's own efforts indicate his courage and professional demeanor.

Those who want to rush the burial indicate that they are not interested in the details of her murder. They want to move along, as if doing so will prevent discovery, or at minimum return their town to some sense of normalcy—regardless of how boring it may be. We act similarly in our attempts to rush the grieving process. In our inability to comprehend the death of a loved one, we often concern ourselves with funerary rites and how to quickly return to life. Such actions, however, are indicators of our cowardice to accept the inevitable. Those of us who are perhaps more wicked, appear to only be concerned with how well our secrets can keep, hoping they will be buried with the dead. It is with these actions that we demonstrate how awful we can truly be. While the dead are certainly dead, how we respond to death indicates how we have succeeded in becoming who we wish to be.

Blind Desire Leads Us to Sleep

We shun and fear death since we do not want others to know who we are. We do not want others to either see how cowardly or wicked we've become. It is not the death itself that is frightening, but it is the uncertainty of how we will be seen by even ourselves. Yet, death has the capacity to make manifest the phenomena of life. We begin to see how the world really is at its core, which is a reflection of our own will (p. 177). While the individual who has died becomes forgotten, the rest of the world becomes awake (p. 180).

This is what we have seen happen in the case of Laura's own death. We begin to see a town filled with people who are riddled with guilt about who they have become, how they treat others, and how they have neglected their own childhood dreams. We also see who Laura really was. While the rest of the townspeople suffer, Laura did not detest the vices she chose to pursue. Instead, she sought more devious ways to whet her appetite. She actively chose more devious ways to pursue the path of self-servitude regardless of whose life she destroyed. Bobby, Donna, James, her parents, and even herself, were destroyed by the wake of her actions. So, while we begin to see the suffering of the other citizens through Laura's death, when her corpse is laid out on Dr. Hayward's examination table we begin to see the monster she has become.

Some Lessons from Death

We are often taught that the unexamined life is one that is not worth living. But what happens when we do examine our lives and discover things that we wish were not seen? We may come to realize that perhaps not all lives should be lived. We may not always want to know who we are. We certainly do not always want to have others know those parts of ourselves that we keep hidden. When we die there is no guarantee that such secrets will be kept by the dead. As Laura's own death reveals, a corpse may be the single key needed to unravel an entire town.

Perhaps this is all too bleak. Let's end on a more cheerful note. Agent Cooper offers some friendly advice in "Realization Time" as we await the day when others discover who we really are: "Every day, once a day, give yourself a present. Don't plan it; don't wait for it; just let it happen. It could be a new shirt in a men's store, a catnap in your office chair, or two cups of good, hot, black, coffee."

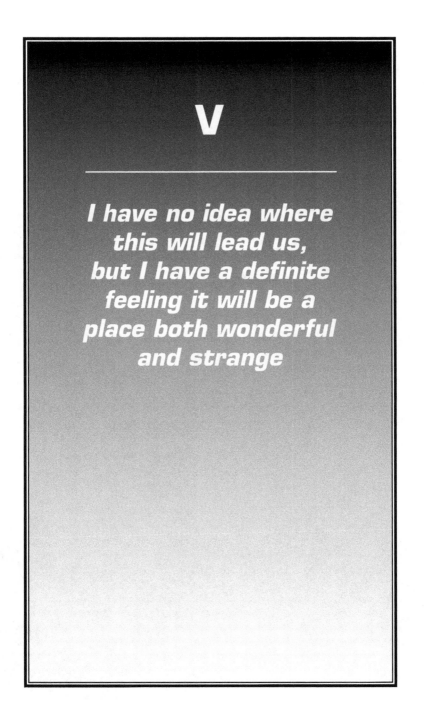

V

I have no idea where
this will lead us,
but I have a definite
feeling it will be a
place both wonderful
and strange

18
Repeating *Twin Peaks*

Mirt Komel

Repetition is one of the fundamental concepts in the history of philosophy, from Plato and Aristotle's discussions of *mimesis*, Nietzsche's eternal recurrence, Kierkegaard's experience of the impossibility of repetition, to discussions on the topic by thinkers such as Lacan, Žižek, and Deleuze.

Repetition is also a governing principle of pop culture in general. If something is a pop-cultural phenomenon, than it tends to repeat itself. The reverse is also true—if a pop-cultural product tends to repeat itself, then it becomes a phenomenon. Consider the *Star Wars* franchise—a series of stories that has repeated and continues to repeat a set of basic themes, not only in its nine scheduled Episodes, but also in its plentiful merchandise, from books and toys to cereal and video games.

The significance of repetition can be clearly discerned in the very notion of a TV series, starting with the very concept of *seriality* itself. A show is not a TV *series* without repetition. Every television show starts with a pilot, a singular event that, if it wants to become a TV series, needs to repeat itself in various episodic or serial repetitions. Tarantino describes the phenomenon in *Pulp Fiction* (1994).

Well, the way they make shows is, they make one show. That show's called a pilot. Then they show that show to the people who make shows, and on the strength of that one show they decide if they're going to make more shows. Some pilots get picked and become television programs. Some don't become nothing.

Every TV show is nothing more than the repetition of a pilot, of a singular, original event that is not only the springboard, but also the governing principle that defines everything else, guiding its own many repetitions. Repetition is, in a very distinct way, inscribed into the musical, textual and inter-textual reality of *Twin Peaks*. The series is an artistic cult phenomenon that disrupts and subverts the concept of the TV series and the very concept of repetition itself.

That Gum You Like

We can pin the excitement about the third repetitive iteration of *Twin Peaks* to a very precise date, hour, and location— that is, if Twitter can be properly understood as a location. But hey, if the metaphysically ambiguous Red Room counts as a location, maybe social media does as well.

We may frequently feel as if we're *firewalking* through social media, very much the way we might through a place with wavering red curtains where time is sometimes reversed and even abolished; we endlessly walk in circles; and we end up confused and uncertain about the true nature of reality.

On the 3rd of October 2014, at exactly 8:30, Lynch and Frost simultaneously tweeted a cryptic quote from *Twin Peaks* foretelling its return to television, realizing the fantasy of every true Peakfreak fan: "Dear Twitter friends: that gum you like is going to come back in style." I know this firsthand since I happened, by coincidence, to be on Twitter at the time.

Enacting a fantasy is always already a tricky business, for the pleasure obtained in its actualization is never the same as the one imagined beforehand. As Lacan points out in his *Four Fundamental Concepts of Psychoanalysis*, there's a difference between an *aim* and a *goal* of desire. The desiring subject can aim at the object of his desire, but by inevitably missing it, he achieves a completely different goal instead. Or as Cooper himself, wisely knowing the difference, points out: "What I want and what I need are two different things, Audrey" ("The Last Evening"). The heart of this phrase is repeated later on by his evil doppelgänger Mr. C, "Want, not need. I don't need anything."

The same can be said for our fantasies about *Twin Peaks: The Return*. Whatever our desires about the third season were, an unbridgeable gap opened between what we imagined and what Lynch and Frost actually did. For surely it is unlikely that any of us anticipated the story we were told in Season Three.

The quote from the tweet is, as we all know (or should know), taken from the famous Red Room sequence at the end of the second episode of Season One. Cooper is dreaming; the Dwarf appears and prognosticates, "I've got good news. That gum you like is going to come back in style" ("Zen, or the Skill to Catch a Killer"). Sure enough, twenty-five years later, the "gum" came back into style. The tweet was just another instance of the predilection Lynch and Frost have for repetition.

It Is Happening Again!

One of the best examples of the use of repetition in the series is the death of Maddy Ferguson, Laura's cousin. The Giant warns Cooper, "It is happening again!" ("Lonely Souls"). His warning refers to the fact that BOB is killing again, and it functions as a warning to Cooper, but also almost as a complaint about his inability to solve the case in time to prevent a second murder in Twin Peaks.

The sense of repetition is intensified by the fact that Sheryl Lee played both roles. To further echo the original crime, the vehicle BOB is using in both murders is also the same—Leland Palmer. BOB possesses his victims and plays with them. Lynch and Frost seem to enjoy putting the same actors in dramatically different circumstances throughout the series.

In this sense, the actors playing the roles are not so dissimilar from BOB; every actor or actress can be regarded as a demon that possesses its character, taking that character in a different direction in each iteration. This is also what happened when the audience was confronted with the older cast of *The Return*, where the actors inhabited their characters for "one last ride." Again, we have repetition combined with a certain sense of existential unease, highlighting the aspect of the human condition that is unavoidable aging.

In fact, the series is replete with repetition that is just *off* enough to leave us with a vague sense of unease. The murder of Maddy Ferguson looks, at least at first glance, like a perfect repetition of the murder of Laura Palmer. On closer examination, however, we can see a different conception of repetition at work here, since the original traumatic event, the actual murder of Laura Palmer, is entirely missing. We, the audience, did not witness Laura's murder until the movie *Fire Walk with Me*.

The famous opening scene of the pilot, a body wrapped in plastic, floating in the river and found on the beach, inaugurates the detective structure of the series: Laura Palmer is absent from the start, only her dead body remains for a short while until the funeral. However, her absence is nevertheless not a mere negativity, but rather an uncanny positivity, a presence of something absent. Think about Sherlock Holmes's classical deduction from the short story "Silver Blaze": the dog that did not bark functioned as the key clue in solving the case precisely because it was not a simple absence of *something*, but a defined *presence of absence*. Similarly, the presence of Laura's absence is embodied in the many partial objects she left behind—two diaries, pictures, videos, tapes, and clothing—that function as clues for the detective's investigation.

On a philosophical level there's a radical difference between mere absence as negativity, and positive absence, as best exemplified by Žižek's favorite example of "coffee without milk" that fits perfectly in the context of *Twin Peaks*, especially considering Cooper's own idiosyncratic obsession with coffee that stretches from season to season up until *The Return*: "Coffee" (*Twin Peaks: The Return,* "Part 4").

It's not unimportant how you order your coffee, and Cooper, to be sure, when asked by Pete Martell how he likes his coffee, answers: "Black as midnight on a moonless night." "Pretty black," Pete comments ("Northwest Passage"). And therefore, it's also quite a different thing if you order "just plain coffee" or "coffee without milk"—the former being absence as negative, expressed in the "just plain" implying indefinite absence of anything else, while the latter is absence as positive, expressed in the "without milk," a definite absence of something—and Laura Palmer is precisely this positive absence. The series could be described, in this sense, as "Twin Peaks without Laura Palmer."

Žižek humorously emphasizes this point with the following anecdote: A man walks into a cafe and asks for coffee without milk, to which the waiter replies: "Sorry, sir, we are all out of milk, but can I get you coffee without cream?" We can imagine a similar question posed to the creators of *Twin Peaks*: "Can I have more *Twin Peaks* without Laura Palmer?" "Sorry, we ran out of Laura Palmer, but can we offer you *Twin Peaks* without Maddy Ferguson?"

The second murder is not actually a repetition of the original, or, if it is, it is a repetition of an absent original, a repetition of a defined negativity that finds its existence not in the original, but in the copy. Furthermore, if we consider the function of the movie as prequel, enacting for us the murder of Laura Palmer in plain sight, then what's supposed to be first is actually the last in a series of repetitions.

Chronologically speaking, from the perspective of the viewer, we first experienced the positive absence of the original murder (Season One); then the repetition of this absence made present through the second murder (Season Two); and at the very end the retroactive enactment of the original that is actually a repetition of the second murder (the movie).

The murder of Laura Palmer in *Fire Walk with Me* could be viewed as the repetition of the murder of Maddy Ferguson, and not the other way around. It is the latter that produces the supposed original murder of Laura Palmer through a failed repetition of the former. If we add the second to last episode of *The Return* to this repetitive development, where the murder of Laura Palmer is undone through Cooper's traveling through time into the middle of the *Fire Walk with Me* timeline, than we can see how the whole structure of the murder of Laura Palmer corresponds to that of the trauma in the purely psychoanalytical sense of the word.

Meanwhile

In the final episode of the second season, during the Red Room sequence, Laura Palmer prophetically tells Cooper: "I'll see you again in twenty-five years." She then adds: "Meanwhile," while making a very strange hand gesture, one hand in an open palm, the other erected behind it, as in a reversed letter "T" ("Beyond Life and Death").

What happens "meanwhile"? Well, a hell of a lot of things, of course. Cooper starts to wander around the Red Room, which is now split into the White and Black Lodge, one superimposed on the other, meeting various characters that are also split into their good and evil selves. One of the doppelgängers is a white-eyed Laura Palmer who repeats the same gesture of the reversed letter "T," this time without the "I'll see you again in twenty-five years," only the "Meanwhile" accompanied with her signature scream.

There are at least two repetitions at work here: the re-meeting of Cooper and Laura that actually happened twenty-five years later in Season Three, and the gesture itself that repeats in the meanwhile when Cooper already re-meets Laura in the form of her doppelgänger. The missing "I'll see you again twenty-five years later," that is, mind you, *not* spoken by Laura's doppelgänger, could be interpreted as if twenty-five years have already passed, and the meeting is happening just "now" in their re-encounter a few viewer-wise minutes later.

Perhaps the use of the word "now" makes no sense at all, since the Red Room is, with its distorted temporal logic, presenting the future as something already past, both imploding in a perpetually floating present. All of this is much in tune with the magician's wording from the *Fire-walk-with-me* poem, where "one chants out between two worlds" longing to see the "darkness of futures passed," an irrational logic governing not only Red Room's temporality, but also *Twin Peaks* in its entirety. Think only about the specific way the movie *Fire Walk with Me* works as a prequel and sequel at the same time, thus forming a perfect "golden circle of appetite and satisfaction" for the cult viewers who enjoy repeating not the whole experience of *Twin Peaks*, but precisely its opposite, its un-wholeness or non-completeness.

The missing part is the key of unlocking the secret connection between *Twin Peaks* and repetition: the whole Lacanian point of enjoyment (*jouissance*), as distinguished from mere pleasure (*plaisir*), is that at the end we enjoy the nothingness, and don't want the pleasure of the whole story; we don't want to drink with pleasure coffee with milk, but to enjoy coffee without milk. Or, to make an even more pertinent Peaksian example, the difference between pleasure and enjoyment is the same as the difference between the two Venuses in the Red Room: one, in the waiting room, is the so-called *Venere vulgare*, a "vulgar Venus" showing all of her naked parts, the whole of her beauty, and the other is *Venere pudica*, a "pudic Venus" covering some of her parts, thus elevating beauty by not showing it all. This is a technique used by the authors of *Twin Peaks* as they cryptically unfold the mystery that is not—and indeed should not be—revealed in its entirety.

And that is also what makes the ending of *The Return* so brilliant and disturbing—it opened more questions than it gave answers. The very last episode completely disrupts the established temporal rules of the Red Room as described by the *Fire Walk with Me* poem, together with the logic of repetition, since now we are confronted not only with time-traveling, but also with different time-lines. The third season in general, but especially the ending is subject to a variety of interesting interpretations that keep popping up like popcorn in the hot pan that is *Twin Peaks*.

As foretold by the Giant in the opening of *The Return*, where he is re-named "Fireman," Cooper and Diane will became Richard and Linda in the ending: "Remember 430. Richard and Linda. Two birds, one stone" (*Twin Peaks: The Return*, "Part 18"). After Cooper defeats BOB, who was driving Dale's dopplegänger as the infamous Mr. C, he travels with Diane into another dimension through a portal under an electric tower exactly at the 430 miles milestone (from where? What was the starting point?). The shift is elegantly shown in the scene where Dale and Diane park their car in front of the motel: Cooper goes into the reception, while Diane sees her double, supposedly Linda. My interpretation is that the Cooper that comes out of the reception is already Richard, and that it is he who takes Diane in the room (this is where his stone-cold face during the sex-scene could come from).

Dale goes into a parallel room with Linda (and this is why the note found by the bed is signed by her), Dale and Diane settle in Richard and Linda through this diagonal experience. The next morning Dale, now Richard, wakes up in a different motel, now embodying both "good" Dale's and "evil" Mr. C's moral characteristic (discernable from his behavior in Judy's dinner), thus becoming more "human" than both have ever been, since both his previous incarnations were too extreme to be real, and that is why they functioned so beautifully in Lynch's surreal imagination in the first place.

Dale goes as Richard in search of Laura Palmer who herself is changed into Carrie Page, who remembers nothing of her previous, alternative line. My guess is as good as any, but I agree with those who say that Cooper actually managed to "save" Laura Palmer from dying by intervening in the *Fire Walk with Me* timeline earlier on, but that her sudden disappearance meant her transposition into this other timeline, where she remembers nothing, mirrored by the parallel universe itself, where we're confronted with a reality where everything looks like *Twin Peaks* never happened. A thesis strongly supported by the fact that when Richard and Carrie travel "back" (forward? In reverse?) to Twin Peaks, they find the RR Dinner closed, and the (former? future?) Palmer's house occupied by a Mrs. (and Mr.?) Tremond, who bought the house from a Mrs. Chalfont (both Mrs. being reminiscent of certain Black Lodge residents from the original TV-series and the movie respectively). After crossing the street, discouraged by the discovery that something is wrong, Richard turns around, as if Dale is realizing something, and asks: "What year is it?" In the house, just before going pitch black, we hear Sarah Palmer's voice calling for Laura. Carrie, as if realizing something, namely, that she is (to become?) Laura, screams in terror.

Laura's scream at the very end of Season Three is a repetition of the scream of her doppelgänger from the end of Season Two, itself already repeated in the movie, and can figure as a minimalistic key in order to understand the endings' work in relation to one another in terms of repetition. It is of no small importance in this regard that her first scream at the end of the original series replaces the omitted phrase "I'll see you in twenty-five years." Instead of an articulate, defined, timely wording, we get a scream that disrupts everything, as a scream does in general since it is like a "gunshot in the middle of a concert" (Stendhal).

The scream in its second repetition in the movie is, in this sense, not a scream at all, but rather a continuation of the same tune, since it reinforces what we were already habituated to through the series. We learned that Laura died, and unsurprisingly she did die at the end of *Fire Walk with Me*. In contrast, the third repetition of the scream, the one at the very end of *The Return*, is neither disruptive like the first one, nor is it conservative like the second one, but rather truly subversive: the last scream completely changes the original parameters, as if transforming the vocal chords that produced it in the first place.

The very last scene as a whole could be read in similar terms and thus explains the title of *The Return*: it's a return to a completely re-imagined *Twin Peaks* universe. This was as shocking for those viewers who expected a familiar experience as it was for Dale and Laura. who returned to the town of Twin Peaks only to discover that it is no longer there.

And it is precisely in this sense that *Twin Peaks: The Return* can be re-baptized as *Twin Peaks: The Repetition*, since the relation between the original TV series and its latest repetition is not a simple relation between an original and its copy, but the relation between the original and a copy that has managed to undo the original by reworking it completely anew.

19
A Pataphysical Cherry Pie

FERNANDO GABRIEL PAGNONI BERNS,
EMILIANO AGUILAR, AND EDUARDO VETERI

After opening in the early 1990s, *Twin Peaks* has become *that* series in which anything can happen. In its third season, the series is still weird, absurd, and experimental. Entire episodes are dedicated to a non-linear approach ("Gotta Light?") close to experimental film. Progressively, the show has become the epitome of weirdness.

The series, like everything that comes from David Lynch's mind, mostly rejects realism. Lynch "often provides a space that echoes or doubles the narrative" (Rachel Joseph), a device that challenges the fabric of reality. Behind the surface of the visible world as we know it through our senses, there are others stages of existence, invisible to us. The core of the series is metaphysics; alternative worlds, dimensions, and dreams pile up. Lynch's metaphysics is about living beyond the material realm experienced by the senses, about a duality between the physical sphere and another one, mostly unknowable.

Despite the fascinating metaphysics, the philosophy at the heart of the show is absurdist aesthetics. Lynch's aesthetics of the absurd and his surrealism (see Lynch's *Eraserhead*—1978—if you do not believe us!) take the show even closer to something slightly different: pataphysics—the philosophical science of imaginary solutions, the science that studies not general rules, but exceptions.

Pataphysics developed, like other artistic and philosophical movements, in the period from the 1890s through the mid-twentieth century, together with symbolism, Dadaism, futurism, and surrealism, all of these disciplines successfully blending together pragmatism, art, and philosophy.

Although pataphysics is a literary phenomenon, it has informed aspects of music, the visual arts and, more recently, new media. It was created not by a philosopher, but a playwright: Alfred Jarry who explained pataphysics as superimposed upon metaphysics the same way that the latter extends beyond physics. In brief, pataphysics—following metaphysics—describes a universe supplementary to this one, allowing imaginary, absurd solutions to concrete problems.

A Very Ordinary Small Town

What exactly is the "natural world"? The answer seems easy enough. It is the world in the ordinary sense of the word, as we receive it through our senses. The streets, our family, our house and school, the sky and the trees and the cats stuck up in them. All the things that encompass our world exactly as we see, hear, and touch them. The natural world is the material world around us.

Lynch takes pains to make us feel as if Twin Peaks is a commonplace, easily recognizable town (his love for peaceful little towns with a dark underside can also being observed in his movie *Blue Velvet*). All three seasons of *Twin Peaks* open with pastoral, almost dull scenes of life within a small town. Each episode title's credits are backed with the image of a little bird that fades away to open the path to a parade of ordinary images: daily life in factories, an empty road leading to town, a beautiful waterfall, a placid lake. The languid musical score highlights the image of peaceful life, without disturbances, whether it be murder or pesky philosophers insisting that the world is complicated.

In the first episodes, agent Cooper becomes increasingly enamored of the town's coffee and, most of all, of the cherry pie made in the Double R Diner. In the pilot, Cooper manifests his awe inspired by the town's trees. These details seem to set the series firmly in the physical realm. The natural world isn't just a world of physical objects, it's also constructed out of our own conceptions of it. It's not completely physical, but imagined as well. Enter metaphysics.

Two things will shatter this tranquility: the murder of Laura Palmer and the realization that beyond the surface of reality as we know it, other realms exist.

Reality Is Overrated

Those who ponder the questions of metaphysics wonder about the nature of reality—what kinds of things exist and what are those things like? Often, philosophers who do metaphysics attempt to provide an inventory of the things that exist. Are there concrete things such as birds, factories, cascades, and placid lakes?

Metaphysical questions include enquiries about the nature of existence, space and time, and cause and effect. One crucial question that is relevant to our analysis of *Twin Peaks* is: do our experiences of the universe give us insight into what it's really like? Do our experiences "track" reality? Or are our experiences of reality simply illusions that we mistakenly take to be objective? Does the real nature of reality lie somewhere our senses can't possibly reach?

It may well be that our perception of the universe (and by extension, the normal-seeming town of Twin Peaks) is just a pale reflection of a greater truth. Natural beings are limited by the sensible (what we hear, see, and touch). It's possible that there is another plane, cognizable only through alternative methods such as logical inference (philosophy), or the soul (religion, occultism). The latter plane mostly doubts the former. We wonder: does the sensible world exists?

The concept of duality is certainly not foreign to the history of philosophy. French philosopher René Descartes introduced a form of dualism that divided reality into two spheres, one purely material (the physical), and the other non-physical (he concluded that his mind belonged to this latter category). The challenge, then, is to determine whether what we consider to be reality is anything more than a figment of our mind or spirit.

There's some cause for concern that there could be a vast difference between appearance and reality. There could be a universe that transcends our perception of it. The work of some philosophers, such as that of Gustav Fechner is a useful tool to examine the metaphysics of *Twin Peaks*: Fechner's conception of the world was decidedly animistic, finding manifestations of the omnipresent animation of the world in many aspects around us.

Fechner also argued that the world was dual in aspect: the modern physical worldview showed only one side of the universe, the mechanistic side, while there was another one, the non-physical side composed by "mental" atoms. Mind and matter, for him, were just two cohabiting aspects of the same whole. And so, we must be prepared to find more than one meaning in life, as the latter is dual (*Life after Death*).

Twin Peaks, in turn, revolves around the idea of duality. The killer of Laura Palmer is (spoiler alert!) her father, Leland Palmer. But, it wasn't *really* her father. Leland was possessed by BOB, a creature from an immaterial world, and the killer himself operates according to the imaginative approach that Lynch takes to his beloved show: material worlds containing other, less straightforward worlds.

This approach is brought to a crescendo in Season Three, when Agent Cooper is seemingly divided into two and occupies two worlds at the same time. He lives in our reality (possessed by BOB), but he is also Dougie, an insurance agent. A great chunk of Season Three deals with Cooper living in the Black Lodge (after the end of Season Two). The Black Lodge exists, presumably, in another realm that overlaps with our reality. Cooper is even able to gets brief glimpses of our world from that parallel reality. Is there a *real* realm? If so, which one is it?

We didn't have to wait for *The Return* to be introduced to the notion of duality in *Twin Peaks*. The theme ran through the entirety of the first two seasons. For instance, one of the clues that could unlock Laura Palmer's past is a little heart-shaped necklace locket that was split into two parts. The other half could connect Laura with her murderer. The device of the half heart is so important that it occupies the poster of the movie *Fire Walk with Me* (1992), an extension of the mythos of *Twin Peaks*.

The locket also represents Laura's sense that she was not completely whole. She was a restless spirit eagerly looking for her identity, for her other side. That's why the device of the diary is of vital importance; it allows the detective and friends (and, by extension, viewers) to get brief glimpses into Laura's inner thoughts. Laura herself had a dual nature. As the episodes progress, it becomes clear that the murdered girl led a double life. On the surface, she was a good young woman with a nice boyfriend. The entries she wrote in her diary revealed Laura to be a much more complicated creature.

It's clear to viewers that some of the show's characters who knew her well have no doubt that there were two Laura Palmers. In fact, Laura is more than merely double. She maintains *many* identities. She is a popular high school student, a victim and a victimizer, a cocaine addict, a femme fatale, a victim of child sexual abuse, a fetish model, and a prostitute. We are first introduced to the idea that things are not entirely as they seem in *Twin Peaks* in this fairly linear way through the character development of Laura Palmer.

This theme deepens as the show progresses. There is a second diary belonging to Laura, one carefully hidden within a flower shop. Laura's cousin, Maddy, comes to the town to visit the Palmers. She's the spitting image of the murdered girl (Maddy is performed by the same actress). The likeness shared by the cousins seems a device for soap-opera theatricals (and it is), but it also highlights the concept of duality. Maddie seems to simply be Laura from another realm. As Cooper says, "When two separate events appear simultaneously . . . we must always pay strict attention."

The concept of duality flows continually through the series. There's a strong emphasis on the use of mirrors. There is almost no better metaphor for duality than a mirror. Not only are characters continually looking at themselves in mirrors (that could happen in any other series), but, in certain cases, the mirror reflects not the character's own image, but the image of BOB, a creature from another reality—a reality to which the more mystical characters in the series frequently allude.

The one-armed man chants, "through the darkness of future's past, the magician longs to see. One sings out between two worlds . . . fire . . . walk with me." In "Masked Ball," Hawk says: "Cooper you may be fearless in this world, but there are other worlds." Here we see duality, not simply with respect to characters, but with respect to reality itself. It may seem as if there is only one universe and that the universe is as we perceive it to be. In *Twin Peaks*, however, appearances are deceiving.

One character who seems to know that there is more to reality than what we perceive is Dr. Lawrence Jacoby. The eccentric psychiatrist wears tridimensional glasses—suggesting that reality is multidimensional. Most of the good people of Twin Peaks only see in two dimensions—the flat surface. Jacoby prefers instead to witness the overlapping realities. Not by chance, Jacoby is a psychiatrist, a man who toils in the dark corners of the human mind and the subconscious. Fechner, in turn, is considered a founder of scientific psychiatry since his psychology was intimately tied to his ontological theorizing.

The state of dreaming and the subconscious, both so dear to the aesthetics of *Twin Peaks*, were also useful tools for avant-garde experimentation. Surrealists such as André Breton and Alfred Jarry would love the possibilities that metaphysics and dreams could give to art. In fact, Jarry would take metaphysics and turn it into pataphysics.

The Pataphysical Plane—Imagining the Solutions

Fechner understood metaphysics in terms of "day view" and a "night view"—a duality. His experiments on the topic of vision damaged his eyes in 1839 and also led to what appears to have been a hysterical illness. In 1843, Fechner regained his ability to see while walking in his garden, and claimed to have seen the souls of the plants there. The idea that he could actually see the souls of plants superimposed upon matter is an idea laced with surrealism, and shares compelling features in common with Lynch's imaginative perspective in *Twin Peaks*, which is populated with glimpses of other worlds superimposed on ours.

Fechner's metaphysical beliefs in a double reality appealed to Jarry. Alfred Jarry, the very embodiment of the avant-garde (signifying experimentation in the forms and narrative in the arts), was a French playwright and artist best known for his surrealist farces. Jarry was very much interested in metaphysics and philosophy in general (including Fechner), to the point that he created his own commentary on metaphysics: pataphysics.

Pataphysics is a concept explained by Jarry in his fictional book *Exploits and Opinions of Dr. Faustroll, Pataphysician*, in which the author toys with metaphysics. The novel relates the adventures of Dr. Faustroll on his travels in a copper skiff on a sea that is superimposed over the city of Paris. The image of superimposition is discussed by Fechner and is employed extensively in *Twin Peaks*. Jarry's pataphysics explores the universe supplementary to this one.

Pataphysics is about recuperating the joy of life and dethroning the tyranny of the truth in science and metaphysics. Pataphysics is humorous, but it cannot be reduced to a joke. Contradictory? Of course! Pataphysics lies in the intersection between philosophy and literature. It has inspired recent philosophers such as Jean Baudrillard. As a surrealist, Jarry sought to embrace contradiction and unreasonableness, while privileging the nocturnal, dreamlike quality of life.

Lynch has never defined himself as a surrealist, but his work sustains a surrealist narrative that favors the disintegration of a clear narrative while making visible the dark side of human life. Lynch seems to be making use of a unique form of metaphysics, but it is a specific type of metaphysics deeply inspired by pataphysics as developed by Jarry.

Twin Peaks is an often-absurd universe where events are governed by obscure and completely unknowable chains of cause and effect, chance and predestination. Mr. Jennings toys with a domino piece between his fingers while a jury defines his future (if he may join society again), as if fate were nothing more than a game, an intricate network of pieces of chance ("The One-Armed Man").

The episodes are filled with clues and resolutions that came neither from any skill in detection nor from any action of the rational mind, but from chance. It seems that Agent Cooper is able to resolve things because he is open to seeing and hearing what the world or worlds lying beyond perceived reality have to say. The solution to enigmas and the gathering of clues come from the absurd and the connection with another world superimposed upon ours.

In the pilot, a series of blinking lights guides Cooper to find a little piece of paper underneath Laura's fingernails. There is no deduction, but chance. In fact, Cooper's investigation will be guided not by induction or deduction, but by the absurd, the interconnection with other planes of existence. One of Cooper's methods to find fugitives is the smelling of trees ("Pilot"), a system that seems to have much in common with pataphysics (it is simply absurd).

The phenomenon of multiplicity provides a metaphysical basis for making sense of intuition. From a dream he had, Cooper explains how he has generated a deductive thinking composed of sleep and the body with a deep level of intuition. To adjudicate the degree of guilt of each suspect, the agent uses this method: while naming each one, Cooper throws a stone at a glass bottle located a meter away, on a cut trunk. If the name connects with a guilty one, the bottle will shatter ("Zen, or the Skill to Catch a Killer"). This is a perfect example of pataphysics, the science of imaginary solutions to real problems.

Dreams are an important element in surrealism. "My dream is a code waiting to be broken," says Cooper, trusting the truth of dreams. The dreams will provide him with the solution for the crime against Laura: "break the code, solve the crime" ("Rest in Pain"). Cooper discovers that Laura also ran company ads in men's magazines thanks to the fact that some red curtains in the background of a photo set are similar to those he had dreamt about ("Cooper's Dreams"). The dream world, here, again is a source of solutions. In the episode "Realization Time" a bird is the source of knowledge and at the beginning of Season Two, a giant who recurrently appears to Cooper in dreams (hallucinations, maybe?) provides the agent with clues about the murder of Laura and alerts him that Maddy is in grave danger.

Animism, which refers to the idea of inanimate things imbued with souls, is also important in the *Twin Peaks*. This same concept is present in Fechner's plants and in the sea on the streets of Paris for Jarry. The main character embodying animism is, of course, the log lady, the woman who always carries a small log in her arms. She seems to share a psychic connection with the log and she often offers to others the advice that it imparts. She delivers cryptic statements to Cooper: "one day my log will have something to say about this"; "my log saw something that night" ("Traces to Nowhere").

It's easy to see that David Lynch created a fictional world in which multiple realities appear to exist alongside one another: dreams, hallucinations, animism. All of them connect with another plane of existence (never fully disclosed) superimposed on ours and replaces rational deduction with absurd solutions.

Twin Peaks takes the unknowable state of our reality and offers absurd surrealism—pataphysics—as solution. In sum, *Twin Peaks* is metaphysics with humor.

Bibliography

Altman, Mark A. 1991. *Twin Peaks: Behind-the-Scenes*. Pioneer.

Arendt, Hannah. 1972. On Violence. In Arendt, *Crises of the Republic*. Harcourt Brace.

Aristotle. 1997. *Poetics*. Penguin.

———. 1999. *Nicomachean Ethics*. Hackett.

Auerbach, David. 2017. Twin Peaks Finale: A Theory of Cooper, Laura, Diane, and Judy. *Waggish* (September 7th).

Augustine. 1961. *Confessions*. Penguin.

Barry, Peter Brian. 2013. *Evil and Moral Psychology*. Routledge.

———. 2013. *The Fiction of Evil*. Routledge.

Beiser, Frederick C. 1998. Bildung in Early German Romanticism. In Amélie Rorty, ed., *Philosophers on Education: Historical Perspectives*. Routledge.

Berlin, Isaiah. 1999. *The Roots of Romanticism*. Princeton University Press.

Boulège, Franck. 2017. *Twin Peaks: Unwrapping the Plastic*. Intellect.

Bowden, Lindsey. 2016. *Damn Fine Cherry Pie: And Other Recipes from TV's Twin Peaks*. Harper Design.

Bradley, Marshell Carl. 2012 *Who Is Phaedrus? Keys to Plato's Dyad Masterpiece*. Wipf and Stock.

Brotchie, Alastair. 2015. *Alfred Jarry: A Pataphysical Life*. MIT Press.

Burnham, Douglas. 2000. *An Introduction to Kant's Critique of Judgment*. Edinburgh University Press.

Burton, Neel. 2012. The Meaning of Madness. *Psychology Today* (September 24th).

———. 2015 [2008]. *The Meaning of Madness*. Second edition. Acheron.

Burwick, Frederick. 2004. *Poetic Madness and the Romantic Imagination*. Penn State University Press.

Bushman, David, and Arthur Smith. 2016. *Twin Peaks FAQ: All That's Left to Know about a Place Both Wonderful and Strange*. Applause.

Champlin, Charles. 1987. The "Brass Ring" that Eluded Orson Welles. *Los Angeles Times* (November 28th).

Coleman, Graham, and Thupten Jinpa, eds. 2006. *The Tibetan book of the Dead: First Complete Translation*. Penguin.

Dennis, John. 1939–1943. Miscellanies in Verse and Prose. In *The Critical Works of John Dennis*, Volume II. The Johns Hopkins Press.

Dukes, Brad. 2014. *Reflections: An Oral History of Twin Peaks*. Short/Tall.

Elster, Jon. 1998. *Alchemies of the Mind: Rationality and the Emotions*. Cambridge University Press.

Fechner, Gustav. 1943. *Life after Death*. Pantheon.

Fitzgerald, Helen. 2004. Secrets Discovered After a Death. *American Hospice Foundation* <https://americanhospice.org/working-through-grief/secrets-discovered-after-a-death>.

Freud, Sigmund S. 1957. On the Universal Tendency of Debasement in the Sphere of Love. In *The Standard Edition of the Complete Psychological Works of Sigmund Freud, Volume XI*. Hogarth.

Frost, Mark. 2016. *The Secret History of Twin Peaks*. Macmillan.

———. 2017. *Twin Peaks: The Final Dossier*. Flatiron.

Furst, Lilian R. 1976. The Romantic Hero, or Is He an Anti-Hero? *Studies in the Literary Imagination* 9:1.

Gilbert, Sandra M., and Susan Gubar. 2000 [1979]. *The Madwoman in the Attic*. Yale University Press.

Gilligan, Carol. 1993 [1982]. *In a Different Voice*. Harvard University Press.

Hayes, Marisa C., and Franck Boulègue. *Fan Phenomena: Twin Peaks*. Intellect.

Hoffman, Eric, and Dominick Grace, eds. 2017. *Approaching Twin Peaks: Critical Essays on the Original Series*. MacFarland.

Holskov, Andreas. 2015. *TV Peaks: Twin Peaks and Modern Television Drama*. Tenth edition. University Press of Southern Denmark.

Bibliography

Horton, H. Perry. 2016. *Between Two Worlds: Perspectives on Twin Peaks*. CreateSpace.

Hugill, Andrew. 2015. *'Pataphysics: A Useless Guide*. MIT Press.

Hume, David. 1978 [1738]. *A Treatise of Human Nature*. Oxford University Press.

Jarry, Alfred. 1996. *Exploits and Opinions of Dr. Faustroll, Pataphysician*. Exact Change.

Joseph, Rachel. "I'll See You in the Trees": Trauma, Intermediality, and the Pacific Northwest Weird. In Hoffman and Grace 2017.

Kant, Immanuel. 2012. *Groundwork of the Metaphysics of Morals*. Cambridge University Press.

Kaufman, Charlie. 2008. *Synecdoche, New York: The Shooting Script*. Newmarket.

Knicklebine, Scott. 1990. *Welcome to Twin Peaks: A Complete Guide to Who's Who and What's What*. Consumer Guide.

Lacan, Jacques. 1981. *The Seminar of Jacques Lacan: The Four Fundamental Concepts of Psychoanalysis*. Norton.

Lautréamont, Le Comte de. 1988. *Maldoror and Poems*. Penguin.

Lavery, David. 1994. *Full of Secrets: Critical Approaches to Twin Peaks*. Wayne State University Press.

Lynch, David. 1991. *Twin Peaks: An Access Guide to the Town*. Pocket Books.

———. 2016 [2006]. *Catching the Big Fish: Meditation, Consciousness, and Creativity: 10th Anniversary Edition*. TarcherPerigee.

Lynch, David, and Kristine McKenna. 2018. *Room to Dream*. Random House.

Lynch, Jennifer. 2011. *The Secret Diary of Laura Palmer*. Simon and Schuster.

Meringolo, Joseph. 2014. The Sanity of *Furor Poeticus*: Romanticism's Demystification of Madness and Creativity. Honors Thesis, Department of English, University at Albany, State University of New York.

Minguet, Anna. 2017. *Twin Peaks: Glorious and Bizarre*. Monsa.

Neidleman, Jason. 2016. *Rousseau's Ethics of Truth: A Sublime Science of Simple Souls*. Routledge.

Nietzsche, Friedrich. 1968. *The Will to Power*. Vintage.

———. 1974. *The Gay Science*. Vintage.

Parker, James. 2017. How Twin Peaks Invented Modern Television. *The Atlantic* (16th May).

Paul, Jean [Johann Paul Friedrich Richter]. 2017. *The Invisible Lodge*. Forgotten Books.

PCAST. 2016. President's Council of Advisors on Science and Technology. Report to the President on Forensic Science in Criminal Courts: Ensuring Scientific Validity of Feature-Comparison Methods. <http://blog.federaldefendersny.org/wp-content/uploads/2016/09/pcast_forensic_science_report_final.pdf>.

Plato. 1995. *Phaedrus*. Hackett.

Radford, Colin, and Michael Weston. 1975. How Can We Be Moved by the Fate of Anna Karenina? *Proceedings of the Aristotelian Society, Supplementary Volumes* 49.

Ramasubramanian, Srividya, and Sarah Kornfield. 2012. Japanese Anime heroines as Pro-social Role Models: Implications for Cross-cultural Entertainment Effects. *Journal of International and Intercultural Communication* 5:3.

Reed, Edward. 1994. The Separation of Psychology from Philosophy: Studies on the Sciences of the Mind, 1815–1879. In C.L. Ten, *The Nineteenth Century* (*Routledge History of Philosophy*, Volume VII). Routledge.

Rousseau, Jean-Jacques. 1997. *The Discourses and Other Early Political Writings*. Cambridge University Press.

Rochefoucauld, François de La. 2007. Moral Reflections or Maxims. In E.H. and A.M. Blackmore and Francine Giguère, eds., *François de La Rochefoucauld Collected Maxims and Other Reflections*. Oxford University Press.

Rodley, Chris, ed. 2005. *Lynch on Lynch*. Farrar, Straus, and Giroux.

Rubin, Rebecca B., and Michael P. McHugh. 1987. Development of Parasocial Interaction Relationships. *Journal of Broadcasting and Electronic Media* 31.

Russell, Bertrand. 1986. *Bertrand Russell on God and Religion*. Prometheus.

Schopenhauer, Arthur. 1995. *The World as Will and Idea*. Everyman.

Starobinski, Jean. 1993. *Blessings in Disguise, or, The Morality of Evil*. Harvard University Press.

Taylor, N.A.J. 2016. On the Possibility of an Arendtian Nuclear Theory. The Hannah Arendt Center.

Thomasson, Amie L. 2008 [1999]. *Fiction and Metaphysics*. Cambridge University Press.

Thorne, John. 2016. *The Essential Wrapped in Plastic: Pathways to Twin Peaks*. Thorne.

Tucker, Harry. 1989 [1971]. Introduction. In Otto Rank, *Double: A Psychoanalytical Study*. University of North Carolina Press.

Bibliography

Vardoulakis, Dimitris. 2010. *The Doppelgänger: Literature's Philosophy*. Fordham University Press.

Andrew J. Webber. 1996.*The Doppelgänger: Double Visions in German Literature*. Oxford University Press.

Webster, Bethany. 2017. The Most Insidious Forms of Patriarchy Pass through the Mother. *Womb of Light*.

Weinstock, Jeffrey Andrew, and Catherine Spooner. 2016. *Return to Twin Peaks: New Approaches to Materiality, Theory, and Genre on Television*. Palgrave Macmillan.

Wikipedia. 2018. Uncanny Valley. *Wikipedia: The Free Encyclopedia*.

Williams, Rowan. 2008. *Dostoevsky: Language, Faith, and Fiction*. Baylor University Press.

Wilson, James D. 1972. Tirso, Hat, and Byron: The Emergence of Don Juan as Romantic Hero. *The South Central Bulletin* 32.

The Bookhouse Gang

EMILIANO AGUILAR has an MA from the Universidad de Buenos Aires (UBA)—Facultad de Filosofía y Letras (Argentina). He usually disappears at the end of each month due to the number of chapters he has to deliver. Some neighbors swear that, when he leaves his home after several days of imprisonment, he likes to exclaim, with exhaustion, "I'm a human being!" He has published about science fiction in journals such as *Lindes* and *Letraceluloide* as well as contributing chapters to *Orphan Black and Philosophy*, *The Man in the High Castle and Philosophy*, and *Giant Creatures in our World: Essays on Kaiju and American Popular Culture*.

FERNANDO GABRIEL PAGNONI BERNS is a PhD candidate at Universidad de Buenos Aires (UBA) where he teaches seminars on international horror movies. He has published chapters in the books *Divine Horror*, *To See the Saw Movies: Essays on Torture Porn and Post 9/11 Horror*, and *Critical Insights: Alfred Hitchcock*. He is currently writing a book about Spanish horror TV, *Historias para no Dormir*. He writes his essays only early in the morning, because it is the best time to remember every detail of his dreams. Every night he dreams he writes essays.

ROBIN BUNCE is a historian based at Homerton College, University of Cambridge, specializing in the history of ideas. He has published articles on the history of philosophy from the seventeenth century to the present day. He also writes on politics and contemporary culture for the *Huffington Post* and the *New Statesman*. He is often mistaken for his doppelgänger, who leads an altogether more sinister life.

FELIPE NOGUEIRA DE CARVALHO is an ex-academic philosopher who now lives in the mountains of Brazil. He received a PhD in Philosophy and Cognitive Science from the École des Hautes Études en Sciences Sociales in Paris in 2013, and is the author of *The Perceptual Basis of Demonstrative Reference* (2010) and *Demonstrative Thought: A Pragmatic View* (2016). Since then he's chosen to quit Academia to search for the perfect cherry pie, but philosophy will never leave his heart. His next topic will be on the metaphysics of identity, as he wonders how on earth can David Bowie and a steam machine be the same as the individual named Phillip Jeffries.

CAM COBB is an Associate Professor at the University of Windsor. His research interests include social justice and special education, parental engagement, and narrativity and the arts. His work has been published in such journals and books as *Per la Filosofia*, *Cinema: Philosophy and the Moving Image*, and *Hemingway and Italy: Twenty-First Century Perspectives*. He has written his first music biography, entitled *What's Purple and Lives in the Ocean? The Moby Grape Story*.

CHARLENE ELSBY is the Philosophy Program Director and Assistant Professor of Philosophy at Purdue University Fort Wayne. She is the co-editor (along with Rob Luzecky) of *Amy Schumer and Philosophy* and has contributed twenty-one chapters to Popular Culture and Philosophy volumes, most of which appear to be random scribbles.

CHERISE HUNTINGFORD has, ever since those three Badalamenti bass notes first vibrated from inside her TV set, been cultivating a mildly insane love affair with *Twin Peaks* . . . in between doubling for Sherilyn (sometimes Sheryl) and perfecting cherry knots, in real life, Cherise has whiled away the time with a BA degree in psychology, writing for a London movie magazine, contributing chapters to *American Horror Story and Philosophy*, and dreaming that Special Agent Cooper makes her eggs in the morning. And some damn fine coffee.

TIM JONES is an elected city councillor for the Green Party in his home city of Norwich and also teaches Literature and Foundation Year Humanities subjects at the University of East Anglia. He certainly drank a lot of damn good coffee while writing his chapter, but alas prefers apple crumble to cherry pie.

LEIGH KOLB teaches English at East Central College in Missouri. She has contributed to *Sons of Anarchy and Philosophy*, *Philosophy and Breaking Bad*, and *Amy Schumer and Philosophy*, and written for *Vulture* and *Bitch Magazine*. Always drawn to the "wonderful and strange," she would be most content with a cup of black coffee and a slice of cherry pie while watching "Part 8," with a nightcap of a live performance by Edward Louis Severson. She dreams in Lynch, for better and worse.

MIRT KOMEL completed his Ph.D. in Philosophy at the University of Ljubljana, where he is currently employed as teacher and researcher at the Department of Cultural Studies of the Faculty of Social Sciences. Author of too many books on the subject of touch and language, while in a parallel timeline he wrote, besides many other unnamable things, also a monograph entitled *Twin Peaks and Postmodernism*. He fancies himself as one of Cooper's doppelgängers, due to his insatiable desire for black coffee, cherry pie, and naked truth.

S. EVAN KREIDER is an associate professor of philosophy at the University of Wisconsin—Fox Valley, and holds a PhD from the University of Kansas. His research interests include aesthetics and ethics, including their applications to pop culture. He'd say more, but right now, he needs to put a fish in Pete's percolator . . .

ROB LUZECKY is a lecturer at Purdue Fort Wayne. Having spent an indefinite amount of time in another dimension, he is now desperately trying to track down his doppelgänger. He's contributed numerous chapters to various Popular Culture and Philosophy volumes and co-edited (with Charlene Elsby) a volume on *Amy Schumer and Philosophy*.

VERONICA MCMULLEN is an undergraduate student at Southern Utah University. She is studying Philosophy, Strategic Communications, and German. When she's not writing philosophy papers, she listens to her log. Do you want to hear what her log has to say?

JEFFREY G. PHILLIPS is a Professor of Language Arts and Director of the Honors Program at Northwood University and will retire after forty-two years in the Spring of 2018, shouting "When you see me again, it won't be me," while driving off campus. A published professional cartoonist with a copyrighted character, he frequently can be found drawing portraits of long-haired, grinning maniacs with the caption, "Have You Seen This Man?" on student papers in lieu of comments. He is often recognized by his students, usually when they show up for classes. He is married with two sons who are addicted to brie and butter baguette sandwiches washed down with percolated fish coffee.

KRISTOPHER G. PHILLIPS is an Assistant Professor of Philosophy at Southern Utah University. He co-edited *Arrested Development & Philosophy* and has published learned articles on coffee, the philosophy of mind, the importance of a liberal arts education, and early modern philosophy. As a former barista, he agrees with Coop that we should "never drink coffee that has been anywhere near a fish."

MICHAEL POTTER is a philosopher and educational developer employed as a Teaching and Learning Specialist at the University of Windsor. His research interests include applications of pragmatist, anarchist, and nihilist philosophy to higher education, and humanities-based scholarship of teaching and learning. The author of *Bertrand Russell's Ethics* (2006), he has published in *The International Journal for the Scholarship of Teaching and Learning*, and guest-edited a special issue of the *Canadian Journal for the Scholarship of Teaching and Learning* on the role of the arts and humanities.

ELIZABETH RARD is currently working on her PhD in Philosophy at UC Davis, and is a Philosophy Instructor at Reedley College. She is completely human and has been so since she was born. She is definitely from this dimension. She likes her coffee hot and black, and her donuts stacked symmetrically. She currently resides in the Black Lodge, after she wandered off the path while hiking somewhere in the Pacific Northwest. She finds the chairs here to be quite comfy, although she is annoyed that her coffee keeps turning into a solid when she tries to drink it.

ELIZABETH RARD'S DOPPELGÄNGER is currently taking up residence in the life that once belonged to Elizabeth Rard. She enjoys wreaking havoc, grinning maniacally, and dancing to music that only she can hear. sdrawkcab gniklat yb flesreh sesuma ehS.

MONA ROCHA AND JAMES ROCHA spend the majority of their time solving murders, whether in mystical towns, rooms with glass boxes, strangely decorated lodges, or anywhere really, provided that it is only through the medium of their TV. They travel roughly as much as Harold Smith, but they are perfectly willing to read diaries, talk to wood, or interpret dreams—all in the pursuit of truth, justice, and solving TV mysteries before the main characters do. In their spare time, Mona teaches Classics and History while James teaches Philosophy, both at Fresno State. Finally, Mona and James are scared of owls, arm wrestling, and anyone named Robert.

PETER BRIAN ROSE-BARRY is the Finkbeiner Endowed Professor of Ethics at Saginaw Valley State University. He is the author of *Evil and Moral Psychology* (2013) and *The Fiction of Evil* (2016), in addition to multiple articles in ethics and social and legal philosophy. Where he's from, the birds sing a pretty song . . . and there's always music in the air. No relation to the dwarf.

RICHARD ROSENBAUM is a PhD student in Communication and Culture at York University in Toronto, and the author of four books: the short story collection *Things Don't Break* (2017); the novel *Pretend to Feel* (2017); the novella *Revenge of the Grand Narrative* (2014); and *Raise Some Shell* (2014), a cultural history of the Teenage Mutant Ninja Turtles. He contributed a chapter to *Neil Gaiman and Philosophy*. He takes his coffee black as midnight on a moonless night.

EDUARDO VETERI has an MA in Philosophy from the Universidad de Buenos Aires (UBA)—Facultad de Filosofía y Letras (Argentina). He is a lecturer in popular culture and contributed to *Iron Man versus Captain America and Philosophy* (2018). He develops all aspects of his life based on a method similar to the Tibetan system: instinct, luck and . . . a pile of mistakes.

ANDREW M. WINTERS teaches philosophy at Slippery Rock University of Pennsylvania and is an avid David Lynch fan. Lynch has taught him that dreams are more important than the thoughts we have while awake.

Index

Printed in the USA
CPSIA information can be obtained
at www.ICGtesting.com
JSHW012022140824
68134JS00033B/2827